1. The Lion Capital at Sārnāth.

THE EARLY HISTORY OF BENGAL

THE EARLY HISTORY OF BENGAL

F.J. MONAHAN

MANOHAR
2025

First published 1925
Reprinted 2020, 2023, 2025

ISBN 978-93-90035-44-1

Published by
Ajay Kumar Jain *for*
Manohar Publishers & Distributors
4753/23 Ansari Road, Daryaganj
New Delhi 110 002

Printed at
Replika Press Pvt. Ltd.

CONTENTS

LIST OF ILLUSTRATIONS

FOREWORD

As the author, my friend Mr. Francis John Monahan, died before the completion of the work of which the present volume is a part, I have been asked to say a word of explanation, by way of introduction. In 1885, the author, a distinguished member of the Indian Civil Service, went to Calcutta as Assistant Magistrate, and was sent from thence to Cuttack. Two years later he was transferred to Rajmehal, as Sub-Divisional Officer, and worked there under the late Mr. Robert Carstairs, whose long connexion with the Sonthal Parganas began about the same time. After short periods in the Dacca and Burdwan districts, in which he gained his earliest experience of the work of a Magistrate-collector, Mr. Monahan was in 1892 transferred to Sibsagar in Assam, and then commenced the long connexion with the Eastern Province which terminated with his transfer to Jalpaïguri as Commissioner seventeen years later. In Assam he held the post of Deputy Commissioner of Sibsagar for nearly three years, when he succeeded Sir Edward Gait as Director of Land Records. Early in 1898 Sir Henry Cotton, then Chief Commissioner of Assam, chose him as his Chief Secretary—a post which, with short periods spent on furlough, he held until the creation of the new province of Eastern Bengal and Assam. On the completion of the new administrative arrangements, he was appointed Commissioner of the Assam Valley—a post which he held for three years. After a short rest in Europe he returned to India as Commissioner of the Rajshahi division in Northern Bengal, and early in 1914 he was transferred to Calcutta as Presidency Commissioner. In 1917, and again in 1918, he represented the Bengal Government on the Imperial Council, and during the last few months of his service he held the appointment of Member of the Board of Revenue.

It was probably at Rajmehal that the author first acquired

an interest in the early history of the Province of Bengal which lasted throughout his career. He had the great advantage which comes of a scholarly knowledge of the Bengali language and an alert desire to know and understand the life of the people amongst whom his administrative work lay. For this and other good qualities he was esteemed by them. So far, however, as I am aware, he did not publish in any way the results of his studies until towards the close of his service, when he gave some public lectures in Calcutta. These were later published in the historical Review, *Bengal, Past and Present.* In these lectures the history of Bengal was carried up to the fourteenth century or so. After retirement from service he continued at work on his History of Bengal with a view to publication in book form, but only the portion here published was finished at the time of his sad and unexpected death on the 20th day of November, 1923. R. I. P.

It will be seen, then, that the present volume, which deals with the Maurya Period only, is but a preliminary part of an enterprise which had in view a History of Bengal from this early age until modern times. As to the matter covered by this description, the reader is referred to the Author's preface, which so far as I can ascertain is final and complete. Though what is here published is but a fragment of the projected work, it is yet complete in itself and of a value which makes it worthy of the study of all those who are interested in the History of India.

JOHN WOODROFFE.

OXFORD,
November 27, 1924.

AUTHOR'S PREFACE

It has seemed to the author of the following pages desirable that works on the history of India as a whole should be supplemented by others dealing with smaller and more homogeneous units, and he has set himself the task of presenting what is known of the history of Bengal from the establishment of the Maurya empire down to the first Muhammadan invasion. The term Bengal, as is well known, has borne different meanings at different times. Until very recently, the British official expression, 'Presidency of Bengal', covered most of Northern India, including what are now the United Provinces of Agra and Oudh, the Panjab, and the North-West Frontier Province, while the 'Lower Provinces of Bengal' included the present Bengal province, with Bihar and Orissa, under one provincial government. The existing province of Bengal comprises what, under British rule, has been known as 'Bengal Proper', and corresponds roughly (excluding the districts of Sylhet and Cachar now included in Assam, and some smaller areas) with the country in which the Bengali language is spoken. It is with the early history of this province that the author proposes to deal.

The subject of the present volume is the Maurya Period, the establishment of the Maurya dynasty on the throne of Magadha having been chosen as the starting-point, because, in the present state of our knowledge, it is the earliest event in the history of Bengal to which an approximate date can be assigned. That event followed closely on Alexander the

Great's invasion of India, the date of which (327 B.C.) is definitely known. As to what constitutes historical evidence there may be different opinions, but it seems to the author that history proper does not begin until a date can be assigned, that is, a definite time fixed for some event with reference to the present time. Without dates, we have only legends and stories beginning with ' once upon a time '.

This volume will be found open to the criticism that, while the subject is the history of Bengal, much of the evidence adduced relates directly, not to Bengal, but to the adjacent province of Bihar. It was necessary to discuss this evidence in view of the paucity of materials for early history in India, the known fact that, during the Maurya period, as often in later times, Bengal and Bihar were in close political association, and the strong probability that similar political and social conditions obtained in both countries. Of the Maurya period some few monuments survive in Bihar, but none in Bengal. We have, for the same period, the detailed account of social and political conditions in India furnished by the Greek Megasthenes, of whom we know that he stayed for some time at Pāṭaliputra but did not visit Bengal. Obviously, in dealing with the history of Bengal, though little direct evidence with regard to social and political conditions in that country during the Maurya period is forthcoming, we must notice the evidence for the period relating to Bihar, since it may fairly be conjectured that conditions in Bengal at that time approximated to those in Bihar, and the absence of Maurya monuments from Bengal can easily be accounted for. In later ages, as materials become more abundant, we shall find that Bengal, though often, if not always, associated politically with some part of Bihar, has a distinct political and social history of her own. We shall find, moreover, that from a time preceding by some centuries the Muhammadan invasion, the political centre in the lower Ganges Valley had shifted from Bihar to Bengal. There is, therefore, ample justification for treating Bengal as a separate unit for the purposes of history. It is, perhaps, hardly necessary to add that special interest may be claimed for the history of Bengal, because it is the establishment there of British political power, in the latter part of the eighteenth century, which may be said truly to have laid the foundation of the fabric which has grown into the present British Empire of India.

F. J. M.

LIST OF ABBREVIATIONS

A. R. A. S. I.—*Annual Reports, Archaeological Survey of India.*
De Anim.—*De Animalium Natura.*
E. I.—*Epigraphia Indica.*
Ind. Alt.—*Indische Alterthumskunde.*
Ind. Ant.—*Indian Antiquary.*
J. A. S. B.—*Journal of the Asiatic Society of Bengal.*
Jāt.—Jātaka.
J. B. O. R. S.—*Journal of the Bihar and Orissa Research Society.*
J. R. A. S.—*Journal of the Royal Asiatic Society of Great Britain and Ireland.*
K. A.—*Kautilya's Arthaśāstra,* translated by R. Shamasastry, Bangalore, 1915.
Mémoires.—Académie des Inscriptions, *Mémoires présentées par divers savants,* Série I.
P. E.—Pillar Edict.
R. E.—Major Rock Edict.
Smith, *Aśoka.*—*Aśoka, the Buddhist Emperor of India,* by Vincent A. Smith, 3rd edition, Oxford, Clarendon Press, 1920.
Takakusu.—*Record of the Buddhist Religion, as practised in India and the Malay Archipelago,* by I. Tsing, translated into English by J. Takakusu. Oxford, Clarendon Press, 1896.
Vin.—Vinaya.
Z. D. M. G.—*Zeitschrift der Deutschen Morgenländischen Gesellschaft.*
Schiefner, *Tārānātha.*—*Taranathae de Doctrinae Buddhicae in India Propagatione Narratio,* Edidit Antonino Schiefner, Petropoli, 1868.
Elliot, *Hist. India,* iii. 350–3.—*The History of India as told by her own Historians,* edited from the posthumous papers of Sir H. M. Elliot, K.C.B., London, 1867–77.

I

GANGARIDES AND PRASII

It is related by biographers of Alexander the Great that, after he had carried his victorious arms across the Panjab, and reached the Hyphasis (Bias) River, he was deterred from advancing further by accounts which reached him of the military strength of two nations by whom his passage of the Ganges would be opposed. The Greek and Latin authors whose accounts of Alexander and his conquests have come down to us wrote some centuries after his death, but professed to base their narratives on the evidence, now lost, of his contemporaries and followers.

Alexander's invasion.

September, 326 B.C.

Diodorus, who was born at Agyrium, in Sicily, and called Siculus, lived in the times of Julius Caesar and Augustus, and wrote in Greek a universal History, to which he gave the name of Bibliotheke, claiming that it was a library in itself. Describing the events which followed Alexander's arrival at the Hyphasis, he says:

Diodorus.

49 B.C.–A.D. 14.

'He (Alexander) had obtained from Phegeus[1] a description of the country beyond the Indus. First came a desert, which it would take twelve days to traverse; beyond this was the river called the Ganges, which had a width of thirty-two stadia, and a greater depth than any other Indian river; beyond this again were situated the dominions of the nation of the Braisioi[2] and the Gandaridai, whose King, Xandrames, had an army of 20,000 horse, 200,000 infantry, 2,000 chariots, and 4,000 elephants trained and equipped for war. Poros[3] assured him of the correctness of the information, but added that the King of the Gandaridai was a man of quite worthless character, and held in no respect, as he was thought to be the son of a barber. This man, the King's father, was of

[1] A local Indian chief.

[2] vv. ll. Βρήσιοι, Βρείσιοι.

[3] The Panjab chief, whom Alexander had defeated at the Hydaspes (Jihlam) in the preceding July, and who had become his ally.

a comely person, and of him the Queen had become deeply enamoured. The old King, having been treacherously murdered by his wife, the succession had devolved on him who now reigned.' [1]

Elsewhere, in a general description of India, Diodorus says:

'Among the southern countries, the first under Kaukasos is India, a kingdom remarkable for its vast extent and the largeness of its population, for it is inhabited by very many nations, among which the greatest of all is that of the Gandaridai, against whom Alexander did not undertake an expedition, being deterred by the multitude of their elephants. This region is separated from farther India by the greatest river in those parts (for it has a breadth of thirty stadia).' [2]

Quintus Curtius.

At what date Quintus Curtius Rufus wrote his *Life of Alexander* is uncertain, but most critics place him in and about the reign of the Roman Emperor Vespasian (A.D. 70–9). Quintus Curtius narrates that, after Alexander had reached the Hyphasis, he asked an Indian Chief named Phegeus [3] for information about the country beyond, and was told that beyond the river lay extensive deserts which it would take eleven days to cross. Next came the Ganges, the largest river in all India, the farther bank of which was inhabited by two nations, the Gangaridae and the Pharrasii, whose King, Agrammes, kept in the field for guarding the approaches to his country 20,000 cavalry and 200,000 infantry, besides 2,000 four-horsed chariots, and, what was the most formidable force of all, a troop of 3,000 elephants.

Plutarch.

Plutarch (born at Chaironaia in Boiotia about the middle of the first century A.D.) thus describes the attitude of Alexander's army towards the proposed advance beyond the Hyphasis:

'For, as it was with the utmost difficulty they had beaten him (Poros), when the army he led amounted only to 20,000 infantry and 2,000 cavalry, they now most resolutely opposed Alexander when he insisted that they should cross the Ganges. This river, they heard, had a breadth of two-and-thirty stadia, and a depth of one hundred fathoms, while its farther banks were covered all over with armed men, horses

[1] Diodorus, xvii. 93. McCrindle's translations are followed in these quotations.

[2] xviii. 6.

[3] Or, according to one text, Phegelas, possibly representing Bhagala.

and elephants. For the Kings of the Gandaritai and the Praisioi were reported to be waiting for him with an army of 80,000 horse, 200,000 foot, 8,000 war chariots, and 6,000 fighting elephants. Nor is this number at all magnified: for Androcottus, who reigned not long after, made Seleucus a present of five hundred elephants at one time, and, with an army of one hundred thousand men, traversed India, and conquered the whole.' [1]

Strabo, the great geographer, a native of Amasia in Pontos, who lived in the reigns of the emperors Augustus and Tiberius (27 B.C.–A.D. 37), writes: Strabo.

'The whole of India is watered by rivers, some of which unite with the two greatest, the Indus and the Ganges, while others enter the sea through mouths of their own. They all have their sources in the Kaukasos. At first they flow southward, but, while some continue their course in this direction—those especially which fall into the Indus—others are diverted, like the Ganges, towards the east. This river, which is the largest in India, descends from the mountainous country and turns eastward upon its reaching the plains. Then, flowing past Palibothra, a very large city, it pursues its way to the sea in that quarter and discharges into it by a single mouth.' [2]

'A letter written by Krateros [3] to his mother, Aristopatra, has been published which contains many other singular statements, and differs from every other writer, especially in saying that Alexander advanced as far as the Ganges. He says that he himself saw the river and the whales it produces, and gives such an account of its size, breadth and depth as far exceeds, rather than approaches, credibility; for that the Ganges is the greatest of known rivers in the three continents is a fact generally allowed; next to it is the Indus, while the Danube ranks third, and the Nile fourth. But different writers report of it differently, some assigning thirty and others three stadia as its mean breadth. According to Megasthenes the mean breadth of the Ganges is one hundred stadia, and the least depth twenty fathoms. At the meeting of this river and another the Erannoboas is situated Palibothra, a city eighty stadia in length and fifteen in breadth. It is of the shape of a parallelogram, and is girded with a wooden wall pierced with loopholes for the discharge of arrows. It has a ditch in front for defence, and for receiving the sewage of the city. The people in whose

[1] Alex. 62. [2] xv. i. 13. [3] One of Alexander's generals.

country this city is situated is the most distinguished in all India, and is called the Prasi (Πράσιοι). The King, in addition to his family name, must adopt the surname of Palibothros, as Sandrokottos, for instance, did, to whom Megasthenes was sent on an embassy.' [1]

Pliny. Caius Plinius Secundus (' Pliny the Elder '), who was born A.D. 23, and lost his life in the eruption of Vesuvius which destroyed Pompeii (A.D. 79), was the author of an encyclopaedic Latin work entitled *Historia Naturalis*. In a chapter dealing with the geography of India he thus refers to his authorities :

'For it has been explored not only by the arms of Alexander the Great, and of the Kings who succeeded him, by Seleucus and Antiochus, who sailed round even to the Caspian and Hyrcanian sea, and by Patrokles, the admiral of their fleet, but has been treated of by several other Greek writers, who resided at the Courts of Indian Kings, such as Megasthenes, and by Dionysius, who was sent thither by Philadelphus, expressly for the purpose. . . . Seneca, one of our fellow-countrymen, who has written a treatise upon the subject of India, has given its rivers as sixty-five in number, and its nations as one hundred and eighteen.' [2]

Discussing the Ganges, he says :

' The tribes called Calingae are nearest the sea, and higher up are the Mandaei and the Malli, in whose country is Mount Mallus, the boundary of all that district being the Ganges.

'This river, according to some, rises from uncertain sources, like the Nile, and inundates similarly the countries along its course; others say that it rises on the Skythian mountains, and has nineteen tributaries, of which, besides those already mentioned,[3] the Condochates,[4] Erannoboas,[5] Cosagus,[6] and Sonus [5] are navigable. Others again assert that it issues forth at once with loud roar from its fountain, and, after tumbling down a steep and rocky channel, is received, immediately on reaching the level plains, into a lake, whence it flows out with a gentle current, being at the narrowest eight

[1] xv. i. 35–6.

[2] Bk. VI, ch. 21.

[3] The Iomanes (Jumna), Prinas (perhaps Parnasa, another name of the Tamasa or Tons), and the Cainas (perhaps Cane, a tributary of the Jumna).

[4] Probably Gandak.

[5] There seems to be no doubt that the Erannoboas or Erinnoboas (Hiranyavaha or Hiranyabahu) is the Son, and that Pliny's distinction between Erannoboas and Sonus is erroneous (cf. Cunningham, *A. R. A. S. I.* xi, p. 154).

[6] Perhaps Kosi.

miles and, on the average, a hundred stadia in breadth, and never of less depth than twenty paces (one hundred feet) in the final part of its course, which is through the country of the Gangarides. The royal city (*regia*) of the Calinga is called Parthalis. Over their King 60,000 foot-soldiers, 1,000 horsemen, and 700 elephants keep watch and ward.'[1]

The above translation follows the reading—' Gangaridum. Calingarum Regia '.

An alternative reading, ' Gangaridum Calingarum. Regia ', seems to make the ' Gangarides Calingae ' a people having a king, capital city, and military force of their own.

Pliny adds :[2]

But the Prasii surpass in power and glory every other people, not only in this quarter, but one may say in all India, their capital being Palibothra, a very large and wealthy city, after which some call the people itself Palibothri, nay, even the whole tract along the Ganges. Their King has in his pay a standing army of 600,000 foot-soldiers, 30,000 cavalry, and 9,000 elephants, whence may be formed some conjecture as to the vastness of his resources.

In his description of the island of Taprobane (Ceylon), he remarks :[3]

' The island in the former days, when the voyage to it was made with vessels constructed of papyrus and rigged after the manner of the vessels of the Nile, was thought to be twenty days' sail from the country of the Prasii, but the distance came afterwards to be reckoned as a seven days' sail, according to the rate of speed of our ships.'

Arrian ('Αρριανός, Arrianus), distinguished as philosopher, statesman, soldier, and historian, was born at the town of Nikomedia, in Bithynia, a province in the north of Asia Minor, towards the end of the first century of our era, and died at an advanced age in the reign of the Emperor Marcus Aurelius. Like Strabo, he wrote in Greek. In his work entitled *Indika* occurs the following passage : Arrian.

' The greatest city in India is that which is called Palimbothra, in the dominions of the Prasii (Πράσιοι) which the streams of the Erannoboas and the Ganges unite.'

[1] Pliny, *Hist. Nat.*, Bk. IV, ch. 22.
[2] Bk. VI, ch. 22. [3] Ibid. 24.

It is clear that the people called by Diodorus Braisioi, Bresioi, or Breisioi, by Quintus Curtius Pharrasii, and by Plutarch Praisioi, are the same to whom Strabo, Pliny, and Arrian give the name of Prasii, by which we shall in future refer to them.[1] Their habitat is determined by the identification of their capital, called by the Greeks Palibothra or Palimbothra, with the ancient city, famous in Indian literature as the capital of Magadha (South Bihar) which stood on the site of the modern Patna, and the Sanskrit name of which was Pāṭaliputra.[2]

Pāṭaliputra.

According to a tradition, it was founded by King Udaya of the Saisunāga dynasty of Magadha, whose grandfather, Ajātasatru, had erected a fortress at the village of Pāṭali, on the right bank of the river Ganges, near the confluence of the Son, for the purpose of curbing the powerful Licchavi clan, who had their capital at Vaisāli[3] in the country of Videha, corresponding to the modern Tirhut, on the opposite side of the Ganges. Other ancient names of Pāṭaliputra were Kusumapura and Puspapura, both meaning 'flower-town'. Pāṭali, in Sanskrit, is the name of a flower, the 'trumpet-flower' (*Bignonia suaveolens*). Besides its strategic advantage, the position of the place at the confluence of the Son and the Ganges, no doubt, fitted it to be a centre of commerce. The present mouth of the Son is about sixteen miles upstream, or west, of Patna, but there is evidence that the course of the Son has changed, and that the ancient city stood near the junction of the rivers. An abandoned river-channel, still traceable, just below Patna, bears locally the name of Mara Son, or 'Dead Son'. Not far from Patna,

[1] Aelian has Praxii, Justin, Praesides, Nikolaos Damaskenos, Prausioi.

[2] Waddell, *Discovery of the Exact Site of Asoka's Classic Capital of Pāṭaliputra, the Palibothra of the Greeks, and Description of the Superficial Remains.* Calcutta, 1892.

Waddell, *Report on the Excavations of Pāṭaliputra (Patna), the Palibothra of the Greeks.* Calcutta, 1903.

Spooner, D. B., Annual Reports, *Archaeological Survey of India, Eastern Circle,* 1912–13 and 1913–14. Also *J. R. A. S.* 1915, pp. 63–89, 405–55. 'The Zoroastrian Period of Indian History.'

[3] The site of Vaisāli has been traced in Muzaffarpur district of Bihar. It is occupied by the present villages of Basar and Bākhira (*A. R. A. S. I.* 1903–4, pp. 81–122).

other great rivers, the Ghogra and Gandak, flowing from the Himalayas, discharge themselves into the Ganges on its northern bank. There have been, no doubt, many changes in these rivers in the course of centuries, but it is highly probable that, from the date of its foundation, Pāṭaliputra was a convenient centre for river traffic. It was also, in ancient times, a seaport, for there is evidence in Buddhist literature that the small craft in which trade was carried by sea in those days were able to ascend the Ganges to Patna, and even farther, to Benares. Thus it is related in one legend [1] that Mahendra, younger brother of the Emperor Asoka, travelled by ship from Pāṭaliputra to Tāmalitti [2] and thence to Ceylon, and a Jātaka story describes a company of woodworkers as sailing from Benares to an island in the ocean.[3]

Strabo, discussing the dimensions of India, says :

'As regards the length (of India) from West to East, we can state it with greater confidence as far as Palibothra, since it has been measured in schoinoi, and is a royal road of 10,000 stadia. The extent of the parts beyond can only be conjectured from the ascent of vessels from the sea by the Ganges to Palibothra. [4]

Even so late as the seventeenth century of our era, the Portuguese frigates were able to ascend the Ganges as far as Patna.[5]

In the course of its long history Pāṭaliputra has passed through many vicissitudes. It was, as we have seen, the chief city of northern India at the date of Alexander's invasion, and, on the establishment of the Maurya Empire, which followed closely Alexander's retirement from India, it became capital of the Empire—a position which it retained for at least a century. With the rise of the Gupta dynasty in the fourth century of our era, we find Pāṭaliputra again capital of an empire. In the seventh century the Chinese pilgrim, Yuan Chwang, found the buildings of Pāṭaliputra a mass of ruins and 'long deserted', the city having, it

[1] Vin. iii. 338 (Samantapasidika).

[2] Tamluk.

[3] Jāt. iv. 159.

[4] xv. i. 11.

[5] *History of the Portuguese in Bengal*, by J. J. A. Campos, Calcutta, 1919, pp. 116–17.

seems, yielded place to Kanauj. In the ninth century we find a copperplate grant [1] of Dharmapāla, the second King of the 'Pāla' dynasty, of Gauḍa, dated from Pāṭaliputra, but whether it was the capital, or merely a halting-place of that sovereign, is not certain. Later, the place evidently declined much in importance, as it is not mentioned in any other record of the Pāla or of the Sena kings, nor in the chronicles of the Muhammadan invaders and rulers down to the sixteenth century. About thirty-five miles south-east from Patna there is a small town, which stands on the site of the ancient and important Buddhist monastery of Uddandapura, said to have been founded by the first king of the Pāla dynasty, Copālal, and has been called, on that account, Vihāra or Bihar. This place, after its capture by Muhammad-i-Bakhtiar, in 1197, became a Muhammadan head-quarters, and gave its name to a province. In 1541 Sher Shah, the able Afghan adventurer, who made himself ruler of Bihar and Bengal, and thereafter of all North India, removed the seat of local government from the town of Bihar to that which stood on the ancient site of Pāṭaliputra, but was then known by the name of 'Paṭṭana', meaning 'the mart'—a name which seems to show that the place had retained some commercial importance. Thus Patna became a provincial capital, and has so remained to the present day.

Plan and scope of Ptolemy's Geography.

We shall now refer to evidence afforded by the 'Outline of Geography' (*Geographike Hyphegesis*) of Claudius Ptolemaeus (Ptolemy), but, before doing so, it is necessary to give some account of the plan and scope of that work, and of the data on which the portions of it relating to India, and especially to Eastern India, are probably based.

Compiled, in its original form, at Alexandria, about the middle of the second century of our era, it did not, like Strabo's Geography, aim at furnishing a complete descriptive account of the inhabited world. As McCrindle says: [2]

'Ptolemy's object in composing it was not, like that of the ordinary geographer, to describe places, but to correct and

[1] *E. I.* iv. 243.

[2] *Ancient India as described by Ptolemy*, p. 2.

reform the map of the world, in accordance with the increased knowledge, which had been acquired, of distant countries, and with the improved state of science. He therefore limits his argument to an exposition of the geometrical principles on which Geography should be based, and to a determination of the position of places on the surface of the earth by their latitudes and longitudes. What he considered to be the proper method of determining geographical positions he states very clearly in the following passage: "The proper course," he says, "in drawing up a map of the world is to lay down as the basis of it those points that were determined by the most correct (astronomical) observations, and to fit into it those derived from other sources, so that their positions may suit as well as possible with the principal points thus laid down in the first instance".'[1]

The method of indicating geographical position by latitude and longitude had been adopted before Ptolemy's time. He improved on his predecessors' work, (1) by introducing a new method of projecting meridians and parallels of latitude on the map so as to take account of the earth's spherical form; (2) by taking advantage of additional knowledge of the countries acquired from various sources.

Ptolemy exhibits the geography of India in two maps, one of 'India within, or on this side of, the Ganges', from the Greek point of view (ἡ ἐντὸς Γάγγου Ἰνδική, *India intrà Gangem*), the other for 'India beyond the Ganges', including Indo-China (ἡ ἐκτὸς Γάγγου Ἰνδική, *India extrà Gàngem*), and corresponding chapters containing lists of places, countries, mountains, rivers, &c., with longitudes and latitudes, and some very brief descriptive notes. The chapter on 'India within the Ganges' is arranged as follows. First, we have a general description of the boundaries of India; then an account of the coast-line, from the mouths of the Indus round to those of the Ganges, noting bays, gulfs, river estuaries, ports, and coast towns. Next, there is a list of the principal mountain ranges, seven in number, with the rivers rising in each of them, which are mentioned in the order in which their several estuaries occur, beginning with the Indus on the west, and working round the coast

[1] Bunbury's translation, quoted by McCrindle.

of the peninsula, as before, to the Ganges. Then follows a list of inland countries, nations, and towns, arranged by river-basins, in the same order. Lastly are given particulars of the islands near India. The chapter on India beyond the Ganges is similarly arranged.

Data relating to India. In compiling these chapters Ptolemy, no doubt, made much use of itineraries and reports of Greek and other European travellers, traders, and seafarers, who had visited India from the time of Alexander's invasion. Intercourse with India by sea had developed considerably, even in the time of Strabo, who records that, when he visited Syene with Aelius Gallus, Prefect of Egypt, he found that about 120 ships sailed from Myos Hormos[1] to India, 'although in the time of the Ptolemies, scarcely any one would venture on this voyage and the commerce with the Indies'. But such navigation must have received a great stimulus from the discovery of a Greek seaman, Hippalus, about the middle of the first century A.D., that is, after Strabo, and about a century before Ptolemy, the geographer, that the monsoons could be used to carry ships from the Red Sea across the Indian Ocean and back. In another place, it is true, Strabo speaks somewhat contemptuously of commercial sources of information about India. 'The merchants of the present day,' he says, 'who sail from Egypt to India by the Nile and the Arabian Gulf, have seldom made a voyage as far as the Ganges. They are ignorant men and unqualified for writing an account of the places they have visited.'[2] It may be noted, in passing, that Strabo, when he says that European merchants 'have seldom made a voyage as far as the Ganges', implies that some had done so, even in his time. It is likely that, before Ptolemy compiled his *Outline of Geography*, many Greek traders or sailors had sailed round the coast of India to the mouth of the Ganges, and up the Ganges to Tāmralipti, and even to Pāṭaliputra. Such men would be 'ignorant', in the sense that they would be neither qualified nor disposed to write accounts of their travels, nor

[1] Myos Hormos, on the Egyptian coast of the Red Sea (lat. N. 27° 12′), was founded by Ptolemy Philadelphus in 274 B.C.

[2] xv. i. 4.

capable of collecting all the information about history, manners, and customs, climates, natural products, &c., required for a work of the scope of Strabo's *Geography*, but they would be likely to record particulars of distances, or, at least, times occupied in journeys, and directions, which would be the information chiefly needed by Ptolemy. The accounts of India left by writers who accompanied Alexander on his expedition, and by Megasthenes, do not appear to have been utilized by Ptolemy, as may be inferred from his not quoting them, and also from apparent discrepancies between his statements and theirs. Thus he mentions only three affluents of the Ganges, whereas Pliny, on the authority of Megasthenes, gives the names of nineteen, one of which only, the Jumna, called by Pliny Jomanes, is mentioned also by Ptolemy, in the form Diamouna; Strabo, as we have seen, states that the Ganges has one mouth only, whereas Ptolemy gives the names of five mouths of the river, with their respective longitudes and latitudes. As regards the enumeration of rivers, it should be noted that, for all those mentioned by him, Ptolemy gives the longitudes and latitudes of their sources and mouths, or confluences with other rivers, no doubt conceiving these data to be ascertainable from the sources of information available to him. Probably he did not include in his lists other rivers of India mentioned by Megasthenes or other Greek authorities because he had not information enabling him to give the positions of their sources and mouths or confluences with sufficient precision. Probably, too, he contemplated that, with the increase of knowledge regarding India, his *Outline of Geography* would, in time, be gradually filled up, and his work improved in completeness and accuracy of detail.

As to the mouths of the Ganges, if conditions in the delta of that river were similar to those which obtain at present, we may suppose that doubt might arise as to how many mouths the river should be considered to have. The tract known as the Sundarbans is traversed by many creeks and channels large and small, all fed from the Ganges, and discharging into the sea by many mouths, all of which may be regarded as mouths of the Ganges. At the present time there are seven principal estuaries,[1] but there are many smaller mouths not named on the maps in ordinary use or in gazetteers. At the same time there is one estuary, that of the Hooghly, which is regarded as the principal mouth, and is the only one ordinarily used by sea-going ships. It is likely enough that, in Megasthenes' time also, there was one mouth of the Ganges used by, and well known to, navigators. The traditional mouth of the river, at which the annual bathing festival is held, is not the Hooghly mouth, but that of an insignificant channel, which traverses Saugar Island a few miles to the east, and is known as the Dublāt Khāl. In view of the frequent changes in these channels, attempts to identify the five mouths, of which Ptolemy gives latitudes and longitudes, with any of the existing seven principal estuaries, are probably vain.

Defects. Ptolemy's maps of India, as we have them, are not only incomplete, but also seriously distorted and confused, owing to inaccuracy in the astronomical observations and other information on which they are based, and, in consequence of these errors, the localities which can be identified are, for the most part, widely misplaced in his tables of longitudes and latitudes. That many of his names cannot be identified is not surprising, when we consider how Indian names are liable to be transformed and disguised in European mouths, and also the probable accumulation of mistakes in the successive copies of Ptolemy's work, which have been made in the course of centuries. The oldest existing manuscripts of his Geography, preserved in the Vatopedi Monastery of Mount Athos, is believed to date from the end of the twelfth or beginning of the thirteenth century.[2] Vivien de Saint-Martin has drawn attention to analogies between Ptolemy's account of India and geographical indications contained in some of the Purāṇas, and suggested that the archives at

[1] *Imperial Gazetteer of India*, vol. xxiii, p. 140.

[2] Victor Langlois, *Géographie de Ptolemée*, Paris, 1867. Preface, pp. v, vi. In the photographic reproduction of the Vatopedi manuscript published by M. Langlois, the two chapters relating to India are missing, but the two maps of India, with marginal explanations, are given (see Plates 6 A, 6 D).

Alexandria may have contained a summary description of India extracted by a Brahman from them.[1] The portions of Purāṇas and other works of Indian literature which are concerned with geography, furnish lists of names, which may have been utilized by Ptolemy, but do not indicate localities with sufficient precision for his purpose.

He is not much concerned with political divisions, but indicates the general position of different countries by brief notes and by the longitudes and latitudes of a few points in them, such as towns, and river mouths and confluences. Many towns are noted without indication of the country or nation to which they belong. In some editions of Ptolemy's maps there are lines showing approximately the boundaries of different countries.[2] Whether there were such lines in the original maps is not known. In the photographic reproduction of the Vatopedi manuscript published at Paris in 1867 they are not shown. Where a town is a seat of government, Ptolemy indicates this by 'basileion' (*regia*) or 'metropolis'.

Eastern India. Prasiake.

Examining his maps and tables which relate to Eastern India, we find that he shows a country, Prasiake, containing seven towns, distributed on both sides of the Ganges, about its confluences with the Sarabos (probably Sarayu = Ghogra) and the Soa (probably Son). The Sarabos confluence is placed in long. 136° 30′, lat. 32° 30′, and that of the Soa in long. 136° 10′, lat. 31° 30′. Palimbothra is not mentioned among the towns of Prasiake, and is shown, as a 'royal city' (βασίλειον, *regia*), not near the Soa confluence, but in long. 143°, lat. 27°. After Palimbothra, the next town on the Ganges mentioned is Tamalites, long. 144° 30′, lat. 26° 30′. Farther on, there is a note: 'All the country about the mouths of the Ganges is occupied by the Gangaridai, with this city—Gange, a royal city (βασίλειον, *regia*)—long. 146°, lat. 19° 15′.' The city last named is shown near the junction of the branches of the Ganges leading to the Mega ('great') and Kamberikhon mouths respectively (long. 145° 30′, lat. 19° 30′).

[1] *Mémoires*, vol. v, pt. 1, p. 3; vol. vi, pt. 1, p. 160.
[2] Cf. Plates 6 B, 6 C.

Ptolemy's Prasiake is, evidently, the country of the Prasii. From his placing Palimbothra, not in Prasiake, nor near the confluence of the Son and Ganges, but far to the south-east and lower down the Ganges, we must suppose that his attention was not drawn to the fact that Palimbothra stood at the Son confluence, and that he had before him indications of distance and direction for that confluence which led him to place it in long. 136° 10′ and lat. 32° 30′, and other indications of distance and direction which led him to place Palimbothra in long. 143°, lat. 27°. It is not clear, however, that Ptolemy places Palimbothra in the country of the Mandalai, as Vivien de Saint-Martin [1] and McCrindle [2] have assumed.

The passage in question runs :

'Farther east than the Adeisathroi, up to the Ganges (μέχρι τοῦ Γάγγου, *usque Gangem*), are the Mandalai, among whom (ἐν οἷς, *in quibus*), this city :

Asthagoura	142°	25°
And on the river itself (πρὸς αὐτῷ τῷ ποταμῷ, *apud ipsum fluvium*) these cities :—		
Sambalaka	141°	29° 30′
Sigalla	142°	28°
Palimbothra, royal city	143°	27°
Tamalites	144° 30′	26° 30′
Oreophanta	146° 30′	24° 30′'

The only town definitely assigned to the Mandalai is Asthagoura, which is placed in longitude a degree west, and in latitude two degrees south of Palimbothra.

The names Sambalaka, Sigalla, and Oreophanta have not been identified. Tamalites, no doubt, represents the Sanskrit Tāmralipti and Pāli Tāmalitti. We have seen that a Buddhist legend represents Prince Mahendra as sailing from Pāṭaliputra to Tāmalitti, and thence to Ceylon, and later references, Chinese as well as Indian, show that for many centuries, Tāmralipti, situated near, but not necessarily at, a mouth of the Ganges, was a well-known seaport for the trade of Northern India with Ceylon as well as with Indo-China and China.

Tamalites.

[1] *Mémoires*, vol. v, pt. 1.
[2] *Ancient India as described by Ptolemy*, p. 168.

Tāmluk, the name of a small town, the head-quarters of a subdivision of the Midnapore district, is probably the modern vernacular form of Tāmralipti. The present town of Tāmluk is on the right bank of the Rupnarayan River, about twelve miles from its junction with the western branch of the Ganges, or Hooghly, but the courses of these rivers have been subject to frequent change, and it is likely that the ancient port of Tāmralipti may have been situated on a western branch of the Ganges. Vessels proceeding to and from Pāṭaliputra by sea would touch at Tāmralipti, and it is not surprising to find the two places mentioned together in Ptolemy's list, but, no doubt, owing to defective information, he has placed them much too close one to the other.

Gangarides Gange

As to the situation of the Gangarides, the only information afforded by Ptolemy is that they held all the country about the mouths of the Ganges, which might include the whole delta, and that their territory contained the royal city of Gange in long. 146°, lat. 19° 15′. Neither Gangarides nor Gange can be identified with any name occurring in Indian literature.

The anonymous *Periplus Maris Erythraei*, believed to be the work of a Greek merchant of Berenice in Southern Egypt, who carried on business with India in the latter part of the first century A.D., mentions Gange, at the mouth of the Ganges, as a port from which fine muslins and other goods were exported. It is quite likely that there may have been on one of the Ganges branches, near its mouth, besides Tāmralipti, a second port, which was also the capital of the people whom Ptolemy and other Greeks and Romans called Gangarides. Possibly it is not mentioned in Indian literature because it was not on the main route to Pāṭaliputra.

From the extracts of Diodorus, Quintus Curtius, and Plutarch, given at the beginning of this chapter, it will appear that, at the time of Alexander's invasion, the most important power in Northern India was that of the two nations, Prasii and Gangarides, who inhabited the country along the lower Ganges, now comprised in the provinces of Bihar and Bengal.

Clearly, the people called by Diodorus Gandaridai, and by Plutarch Gandaritai, are the same as the Gangarides (ae, ai) of Pliny, Quintus Curtius, and Ptolemy. It is not certain whether the two peoples at that time formed one state or a confederation, but the evidence seems, on the whole, to point to two states, with separate kings and forces, but united in a close confederation—so close that the population of both was sometimes included under one name, as Prasii, or as Gangarides. Evidently, at the time of Megasthenes' deputation to the court of Sandrokottos, the Prasii were the predominant partners in the confederation, and their chief city, Pāṭaliputra, was regarded as the capital of the whole region.

The name Prasii probably represents the Sanskrit *prāci* or *prācya*, meaning 'eastern', a term which was applied, in an extended sense, to the countries of *āryavarta* lying east of Prayāga (Allahabad), the eastern limit of Madhyadesa —that is, to the peoples of all the region lying between the Himalayas and the Vindhya mountains, from Prāyaga to the Eastern Ocean—and, more particularly, to the people of Magadha. The Greek and Latin authors whom we have quoted make no mention of Magadha, but their evidence as to the political importance and power of the state, confederation, or empire, which had its capital at Pāṭaliputra in Magadha at the time of Alexander's expedition and subsequently finds ample confirmation in Indian literature.

Magadha. The term Magadha itself was one of varying extension. Strictly, it meant a limited area, east of the Son and south of the Ganges, but, with the growth of the Magadha state, its name came to be applied to a wider region. These various geographical meanings of the names Prācī or Prācya and Magadha explain why Ptolemy gives the name of Prasiake to a comparatively small tract of country around the confluences of the Son and Chogra with the Ganges.

The reason for his interrupting his enumeration of towns along the Ganges, after the seven in 'Prasiake', and resuming it after mention of the Mandalai, whose country extends

[1] Lassen, *Ind. Alt.* i, pp. 93 sqq.

up to the Ganges (*usque Gangem*), may, perhaps, be found in the physical features of the region. For a little to the east of Magadha proper a tract of hilly country extends close up to the southern bank of the Ganges. This hill tract may have been the country of the Mandalai, probably inhabited then, as it is now, by races differing from those of the plains. Farther down its course, the Ganges again leaves the hills and divides into the various branches, by which it finds its way, through level country, to the sea. Pliny seems to regard Tamalites as being in the country of the Prasii, for when he says that it is seven days' sail from Ceylon to the country of the Prasii, he must mean to Tāmralipti, not Pāṭaliputra.

We have next to consider Pliny's reference to the Calingae, Calingae. the people 'nearest the sea', and 'Parthalis', their 'royal city', or that of the Gangarides-Calingae. In other passages he refers to a tribe whom he names, without locating them, Maccocalingae, and to the Modogalingae, who, he says, inhabited a large island in the Ganges. Vivien de Saint-Martin takes the Gangarides-Calingae, the Maccocalingae, and the Modogalingae to be branches of the Calingae, and Parthalis to be Burdwan. The Sanskrit name, Kaliṅga, was applied, it appears, in ancient times, to the greater part of the eastern coast region of the Indian peninsula, from the Ganges southward. Later, it took a more restricted sense, covering, roughly, Orissa, a term which has also varied in meaning. Even in modern times the limits of Orissa to the north-east have sometimes extended as far as the western branch of the Ganges in its lower course.

Ptolemy does not mention the Calingae or Parthalis, but gives the name of a town, Kalliga, in the country of the Maisoloi, long. 138°, lat. 17°, which may be connected with Kaliṅga.

With regard to the Modogalingae, inhabitants, according to Pliny, of a large island in the Ganges, it may be observed that, in the Ganges delta, tracts of country surrounded on all sides by river channels are commonly called islands (*dvīpa*, *dia*),[1] and, in English records of the eighteenth century, the area now comprising parts of the Murshidabad and Nadia districts which is enclosed by the main stream of the Ganges, its western branch, the Bhāgirathi, and the Jalanghi, is referred to as 'the island of Cossimbazar'. From the evidence of Pliny and Ptolemy we may suppose that, in and about the time of Megasthenes, the inhabitants of the Gangetic delta, generally, were known to Greek travellers and writers by the name of Gangarides, but that some of them were akin in race, customs, and language to the neighbouring people of Kaliṅga, and were for that reason called Calingae or Gangarides-Calingae. At a time when the Prasii enjoyed a political supremacy or hegemony over this region, it would be regarded by the Greeks as the country of the Prasii. The identification of Parthalis as Burdwan must be regarded as doubtful.

Vaṅga.

In Indian literature we find mention of five nations inhabiting the countries to the east of Magadha in ancient times, namely, those of Anga, Puṅdra, Vaṅga, Suhma, and Kaliṅga. There will be occasion hereafter for discussing the location of the countries indicated by the first four names: here it may suffice to notice that from the third, Vanga, the present name of Bengal is derived.

Historical importance of Lower Ganges valley.

There is no hint in Indian legend or history of an important political rôle having been played by a nation of the Ganges delta about the time of Alexander's invasion, with regard to which, indeed, that literature is wholly silent. There is no reason, however, for rejecting the Greek evidence, from which we may infer that, at that time, the Gangarides, if they were not the most powerful nation of the Ganges valley, were at least associated with the Prasii on equal terms. Later, as it would seem, in the time of Megasthenes's deputation to the court of Sandrokottos, the Prasii had become the paramount power, and the importance of the Gangarides had waned, but that they still enjoyed some

[1] The word *dvīpa* means also land lying between two rivers (= Persian *duāb*): cf. Rapson, *The Successors of Alexander the Great*. *Cambridge History of India*, vol. i, chap. xxii. *Dia* is the local Prakrit equivalent.

measure of independence is indicated by the title of ' royal ', which Ptolemy gives to their chief town. It may be supposed that the people called by the Greeks Gangarides then formed a subordinate state under the suzerainty of Magadha.

We seem to have here the first example of a phenomenon which has occurred more than once in the history of India, namely, that the power which has commanded the resources of the lower valley of the Ganges has been able to attain thereby the political hegemony of northern, and sometimes of all, India.

It has sometimes been assumed that the trend of conquest in India has always been from north to south, and in Upper India from north-west to south-west, and that the eastern Gangetic plain, being inhabited by peoples of comparatively weak physique and unwarlike character, has been fated to be overrun and conquered by the hardier and more vigorous races of the north-west. But apart from evidence that unwarlike qualities have not been invariably and universally characteristic of the people of Bihar, or even of Bengal, it is fully established that, from very ancient times, wars in India have usually been carried on by professional mercenary soldiers, and, consequently, an Indian state possessed of extensive, fertile, and populous territory, with a well-ordered government, and regular and abundant revenues, has been able to maintain a relatively powerful army, recruited, it might be, in part, from beyond its own frontiers, and, by that means, to extend and consolidate its dominions. So it has happened more than once that the power which has obtained control of the revenues of Bengal and Bihar has been able to bring under its sway the greater part of India. The latest and most conspicuous example of this may be found in the growth of the present British Indian Empire.

II

CANDRAGUPTA

Origin. It is practically certain that the Sandrokottos of Greek and Latin accounts is the same person as Candragupta, who, according to Indian tradition, handed down in the Purāṇas as well as in Buddhist and Jaina literature, founded the Maurya dynasty. Of his origin and early career there are various legendary accounts, the details of which need not detain us, but the tradition that he came to the throne of Magadha by a revolution, supplanting the Nandas, seems to find support in Diodorus's reference to the low estimation in which the ruler of the Prasii and Gangarides at the time of Alexander's invasion was held. Dr. Spooner has, in two important articles,[1] advanced the opinion that the Maurya family, to which Candragupta belonged, was of Persian origin, but, while the evidence of Persian influence on Maurya architecture, and some of the customs of Candragupta's Court is strong, Dr. Spooner's conclusions, some of which have been contested by other scholars,[2] can hardly be regarded at present as established by historical evidence.

Accession. Candragupta is believed to have come to the throne about the year 321 B.C., and, according to Purāṇas as well as Buddhist books, he reigned for twenty-four years. The name of his son and successor is given in the *Viṣṇupurāna* and in Jaina and Buddhist books as Bindusāra, in certain other Purāṇas as Nandasāra or Bhadrasāra. In the *Deipnosophistae*—a miscellaneous collection of anecdotes and extracts by an author named Athenaeus, of whom little is known except that he was a native of Naucratis, a town on the left bank of the Canopic branch of the Nile, and wrote, probably,

[1] *J. R. A. S.* 1915, pp. 63–89, 405–55, 'The Zoroastrian Period of Indian History'.

[2] V. A. Smith, *J. R. A. S.* 1915, pp. 800–2; Keith, *J. R. A. S.* 1916, pp. 138–43; Thomas, *J. R. A. S.* 1916, pp. 362–6.

in the third century of our era—the name is given as Amitrochates.[1] Strabo has Allitrochades,[2] but it has been surmised that the last name may be a corrupt form, due to confusion between the Greek capitals ΛΛ and M—also that Amitrochates may represent the Sanskrit title Amitraghāta, meaning ' slayer of foes ', which is quoted in Pātañjali's commentary on Pāṇini's Sanskrit grammar, perhaps with reference to this king. According to Indian tradition, Bindusāra's reign lasted twenty-five, and that of his son, the great Aśoka, thirty-six or thirty-seven years. It is to the reigns of these three emperors that the main interest of the Maurya period belongs. The rise of Candragupta's power and his relations with Seleukos Nikator are thus briefly narrated by Marcus Junianus Justinus (Justin) in his epitome, composed in the second half of the second century A.D., of the lost *Historia Philippica*, which was published between 20 B.C. and A.D. 14 by Pompeius Trogus, a writer of Gallic origin, and based, probably, on a Greek work entitled περὶ βασιλέων by Timogenes of Alexandria (born between 80 and 75 B.C.): [3] **Justin.**

' Seleucus Nicator waged many wars in the east, after the partition of Alexander's empire among his generals. He first took Babylon, and then, with his forces augmented by victory, subjugated the Bactrians. He then passed over into India, which, after Alexander's death, as if the yoke of servitude had been shaken off its neck, had put his prefects to death. Sandrocottus was the leader who achieved their freedom, but, after his victory, he forfeited by his tyranny all title to the name of liberator; for he oppressed with servitude the very people whom he had emancipated from foreign thraldom. He was born in humble life, but was prompted to aspire to royalty by an omen significant of an august destiny. For when, by his insolent behaviour, he had offended Nandrus,[4] and was ordered to be put to death, he sought safety by a speedy flight. When he lay down, overcome with fatigue, and had fallen into a deep sleep, a lion of enormous size, approaching the slumberer, licked with his tongue the sweat which oozed profusely from his body, and, when he awoke, quickly took its departure. It was this

[1] Athenaeus, xiv. 67.
[2] Strabo, II. i. 9.
[3] Bk. xv, ch. 3.
[4] According to the reading Nandrum, adopted by McCrindle, in place of the common reading, Alexandrum.

prodigy, which first inspired him with the hope of winning the throne, and so, having collected a band of robbers, he instigated the Indians to overthrow the existing Government. When he was thereafter preparing to attack Alexander's prefects, a wild elephant of monstrous size approached him, and, kneeling submissively, like a tame elephant, received him on its back, and fought vigorously in front of the army. Sandrocottus, having thus won the throne, was reigning over India, when Seleucus was laying the foundations of his future greatness. Seleucus having made a treaty with him, and otherwise settled his affairs in the east, returned home to prosecute the war with Antigonus.'

Treaty with Seleukos.

Justin, it will be seen, represents Candragupta as having achieved the freedom of the Indians by overthrowing the Greek power in northern India. The evidence with regard to the treaty between Seleukos and Candragupta is thus summed up by Dr. Macdonald in chap. xvii, vol. i, of the *Cambridge History of India.*

'Invaders and invaded, we are told, concluded an alliance, and sealed it by a further compact, which Appian [1] (Syriake, 55) calls a *κῆδος*, Strabo (xv. 724) an *ἐπιγαμία*. . . . Not only did Seleucus acquiesce in his (Candragupta's) sovereignty over all the country beyond the Indus. He also transferred to him the satrapies of Arachosia (Kandahar) and the Paropanisadae (Kabul), with at least some portion of Gedrosia (Baluchistan) and of Aria (Herat). In other words, the frontiers of the Maurya Empire were extended so as to embrace the southern half of Afghanistan, and, perhaps, the whole of British Baluchistan. The expression 'presented' (*ἔδωκε*), which is used by Strabo (loc. cit.) to describe the transaction, does not preclude the possibility of the transfer having been made on conditions. A return gift of 500 war-elephants is, in fact, mentioned. But under no circumstances could that have been looked upon as an equivalent. We may take it that there were further stipulations as to the freedom of trade and the like, such as would naturally accompany an *ἐπιγαμία*. There may have been a nominal and unmeaning acknowledgement of suzerainty. It must be borne in mind that the written record contains nothing to show that Seleucus suffered defeat, nothing even to suggest that the

[1] Appianus, a native of Alexandria, who lived at Rome during the reigns of Trajan, Hadrian, and Antoninus Pius (A.D. 98–161), and wrote a history giving a separate account of the affairs of each of the countries comprised in the Roman Empire.

rival armies ever came to blows at all. The probability is that, while he was still endeavouring to gauge the magnitude of the task that confronted him, an urgent call for help reached him from the confederate kings across the 2,500 miles that separated him from Asia Minor. . . . It was only politic, therefore, to make the best terms he could with Candragupta, whose 500 elephants reached the theatre of war in time to play a conspicuous part in the final overthrow of Antigonus at Ipsus in the year 301.'

Evidently, at the time of his treaty with Seleukos, Candragupta acquired, if he had not acquired before, at least a suzerainty over the Panjab and Sind.

Extent of Candragupta's empire.

Although no monument of Candragupta's time has been found in India, an estimate of the extent of his empire may be formed from the inscriptions of his grandson, Aśoka, from the tenor of some of which it may be inferred that no conquest, except that of Kaliṅga, was made by the latter. As there is also no satisfactory evidence of any important conquest having been made by Bindusāra,[1] it is almost safe to infer that the whole of the empire over which Aśoka ruled, except, perhaps, Kaliṅga, had been handed down by Candragupta to his successors.

Aśoka's inscriptions will be discussed in detail in later chapters. With regard to the limits of his empire, as shown by them, it may be useful here to quote Professor Rapson's summary : [2]

'His edicts clearly show that there were certain well-defined grades in the influence which he claimed to exercise in different regions. There were, first of all, "the King's dominions", by which we must, no doubt, understand the provinces of the empire—the central government of Pāṭaliputra (the United Provinces and Bihar), and the vice-royalties of Takṣasīla (the Panjab), Avanti or Ujjayini (Western and Central India, north of the Tapti), and Kaliṅga (Orissa and the Ganjam District of Madras). Over all kingdoms and peoples in these provinces the emperor was supreme. He was the head of a great confederation of states, which were united under him for imperial purposes, but which, for all purposes of civil government and internal

[1] v. *infra*, p. 185.

[2] *Cambridge History of India*, vol. i, chap. xxi.

administration, retained their independence.... Beyond the "King's dominions", to the north-west and to the south, lay "the border peoples", whom the emperor regarded as coming within his sphere of influence. On the north-west, in the north-west Frontier Province, and in the upper Kabul Valley, they are called in the inscriptions Gandharas, Kambojas, and Yavanas (Yonas); and, on the south, beyond the limits of the provinces of Avanti and Kaliṅga, there were the Rāshtrikas of the Maratta country, the Bhojas of Berar, the Petunikas of the Aurangābād district of Hyderabad, the Pulindas, whose precise habitat is uncertain, and the Andhras, who occupied the country between the Godāvari and the Kistna.

'On the north-west Aśoka's sphere of influence ended at the frontiers of the Yavana king Antiochus, i.e. the Seleucid monarch Antiochus II, Theos; and on the south it probably did not extend much beyond the locality of his southernmost group of inscriptions, at Isila, the modern Siddapura, in the Chitaldroog district of N. Mysore.'

In the above enumeration there is no mention of Bengal, but the Greek evidence previously cited shows that the Ganges delta was included in Candragupta's empire, probably as a subordinate or feudatory kingdom.

Tārānātha, a Thibetan monk, who wrote a history of Buddhism early in the seventeenth century of our era, mentions that Candragupta's son and successor, Bindusāra, was born in the country of Gauḍa.[1] Himself a late author, Tārānātha may probably have derived his information from old tradition and early manuscripts stored in monastic libraries, and his evidence is not entirely unworthy of attention. The term Gauḍa, like so many other Indian geographical expressions, has had different meanings. It appears to have been used, primarily, for northern Bengal, and, perhaps, especially, for the tract of comparatively high land outside the Ganges delta, comprising portions of what are now the Malda, Rājshāhī, Dinājpur, Rangpur, and Bogra districts, which was also known as Varendra or Varendri, and is now called the Barind; sometimes it had an extended sense, covering the whole of Bengal and adjacent territory in Magadha and Aṅga (South Bihar). It

[1] Schiefner, *Tārānātha*, p. 88.

would seem that, in the passage quoted, Tārānātha means by Gauḍa, Bengal, or northern Bengal. In another passage he refers to Gauḍa as 'part of Bhangala'.[1] If we are to suppose that northern Bengal was the place of Bindusāra's birth, we may infer that the country was included in Candragupta's dominions, and, perhaps, that he had a royal residence there, but of this there is no other evidence. In later times, much of what is now northern Bengal was included in the separate kingdom of Kāmarūpa.

Feudatory states. That the Maurya empire was probably a confederation of states, each enjoying a certain degree of independence, is emphasized by Professor Rapson in the passage just quoted, and also by Dr. Thomas, who observes, in chap. xviii, vol. i. of the *Cambridge History of India*:[2]

'Indian conquerors do not, for the most part, displace the rulers whom they subdue, nor was the example of Alexander in India to the contrary. Accordingly we may assume that the empire of Candragupta included feudatory kingdoms; and even the presence of his viceroys would not necessarily imply, for example, in Taxila or Ujjain, the extinction of the royal dynasty. It has been acutely remarked by Lassen[3] that, in a number of cases, Megasthenes states the military power of particular provinces; and he infers that these are instances of independent rule.'

Professor Rapson, in his *Ancient India*, says:

'Alexander, in fact, carried into practice the traditional Indian policy recommended by Manu (viii. 202), and followed, wherever it has been possible or expedient, by conquering powers in India generally, both ancient and modern, that a kingdom which had submitted should be placed in charge of some member of its ancient royal family.... It was always regarded as a legitimate object of the ambition of every king to aim at the position of a cakravartin or "supreme monarch". If his neighbours agreed, so much the better; but if they resisted his pretentions, the question was decided by a pitched battle. In either case, the government of the states involved was usually not affected. The same prince continued to rule, and the nature of his rule did not depend on his position as supreme or vassal king. Generally

[1] Schiefner, *Tārānātha*, p. 82.
[2] p. 96.
[3] Lassen, *Ind. Alt.* ii, pp. 219–20.

speaking, the condition of the ordinary people was not affected, or was only affected indirectly, by the victories or defeats of their rulers. The army was not recruited from the tillers of the soil. The soldier was born, not made. It was just as much the duty of certain castes to fight as it was the duty of others not to fight. War was a special department of government, in which the common people had no share.'

This view of the traditional origin and structure of Indian empires, which, for the proper understanding of the early history of India, it is important to keep in mind, is borne out by the *Kauṭilīya Arthaśāstra*, where the model ruler is described as Vijigīṣu,[1] 'ambitious of conquest', and the 'virtuous conqueror' (*dharmavijayin*), as being satisfied with obedience.[2] In the same work occurs a verse to the effect that 'conquered kings preserved in their own territories, in accordance with the policy of conciliation, will be loyal to the conqueror and his descendants'.[3]

Bengal.

The fact that no inscription of Aśoka has been found in the Bengal delta is easily accounted for. The Aśoka inscriptions known were incised either on conspicuous faces of natural rock in or near cities, on main lines of communication, or at sacred spots frequented by pilgrims, or on stone pillars erected in such situations. In deltaic Bengal, natural rocks suitable for such inscriptions are not found at all, and pillars erected in an alluvial tract, traversed in every direction by erratic rivers, would be very likely, in the course of centuries, to be undermined and buried under river deposits. Ten pillars only bearing inscriptions of Aśoka have been found in the whole of India.

Kaliṅga.

As already mentioned, the term 'Kaliṅga' had various extensions in ancient, as 'Orissa' has had in modern, times. Versions of Aśoka's 'major rock edicts' inscribed at Dhauli, about seven miles south of Bhuvanesvar, in the Puri district, and at Jaugaḍha, in the Ganjam district, prove that in his time those places formed part of Kaliṅga. It is likely that

[1] *K. A.* Bk. VI, ch. ii, 322, 5, *inf.*, p. 133.

[2] *K.A.* Bk. XII, ch. i, 461, 1, *inf.*, p. 134.

[3] *K. A.* Bk. VII, ch. xvi, 381, 1, *inf.* p. 135.

the Godāvari river may have been the southern boundary of Kaliṅga, while the north-eastern may have been drawn at, or not far from, the Ganges' western branch. From the thirteenth Major Rock Edict we learn that Aśoka conquered Kaliṅga in the thirteenth year of his reign (the ninth reckoning from his coronation), but we need not necessarily infer from this that Kaliṅga had not previously formed part of the Maurya empire. It might have been included in the empire as a feudatory state, and its conquest by Aśoka might have resulted from its throwing off the Maurya allegiance.

While Aśoka's supremacy on the eastern seaboard of the Indian peninsula is thus attested by the inscriptions at Dhauli and Jaugaḍha, another version of his edicts inscribed on a rock at Girnar, near Jūnāgaḍh, in Kathiāwār, proves the extension of the Maurya empire to the coast of the Arabian Sea. On the same rock is found another inscription, of the satrap Rudradaman, of a date some four centuries later, which sets forth that the artificial lake named Sudarśana, 'The Beautiful', was made for purposes of irrigation, by Candragupta's viceroy, Puṣyagupta, the Vaiśya.

III

MAURYA INSTITUTIONS

THE *KAUṬILĪYA ARTHAŚĀSTRA*

Maurya institutions.

INQUIRY with regard to social conditions and institutions, laws, customs, administration, and polity in Bengal and Bihar during the Maurya period is beset with the difficulties which surround all similar research relating to ancient India. Much information under the above heads is supplied by the various branches of Indian literature which have been explored by European scholars—in the *Dharma*, *Artha*, and *Nītiśāstras*, and the didactic parts of the Epics, as well as from descriptions and allusions in the dramas and romances, and scientific and religious compositions of various classes. But in nearly every case, doubts arise as to the dates of the writings, and as to the periods and, sometimes, the regions to which different passages relate. Ancient texts have been changed by interpolations and additions, and, on the other hand, it may be found that very old traditions are embodied in relatively modern compositions. The criticism of Mayne on the Smṛtis—that 'maxims which have long since ceased to correspond with actual life are reproduced, either without comment, or with non-natural interpretation. Extinct usages are detailed without a suggestion that they are extinct',[1] probably applies to the *Arthaśāstras* and *Nītiśāstras* also.

The accounts of Greek and Latin authors purporting to be based on Megasthenes, are definitely assignable to the reign of Candragupta, but here doubts arise as to the accuracy of Megasthenes' observation and relation, and as to the fidelity with which his evidence has been reproduced by later authors.

On the epigraphic side, all that we have are the inscrip-

[1] Mayne, *Hindu Law and Usage*, ed. 1883, ch. ii, p. 13.

tions of Aśoka, the interpretation of which is, in parts, open to question, while they afford, in any case, but meagre evidence under the heads above referred to.

The *Kauṭilīya Arthaśāstra*, already quoted, purports to be the work of the Brahman minister named Kauṭilya, Viṣṇugupta, or Cānakya, who, according to tradition, helped Candragupta in overthrowing the last of the Nanda kings and placing himself on the throne of Magadha. Allusions to this tradition are found in several places in Sanskrit literature. Thus, in the *Viṣṇupurana*,[1] the following passage occurs : The *Kauṭilīya Arthaśāstra.*

'Mahāpadma, then his sons, only nine in number, will be lords of the earth for a hundred years. Those Nandas Kauṭilya, a Brahman, will slay. On their death, the Mauryas will enjoy the earth. Kauṭilya himself will instal Candragupta on their throne. His son will be Bindusāra, and his son Aśokavardhana.'

Kāmandaka, in his dedication of the *Nitisara*, says :

'To him who shone like a thunder-bolt, and before the stroke of the thunder-bolt of whose witchcraft the rich mountain-like Nandas fell down root and branch ; who alone, with the power of diplomacy, like Indra with his thunder-bolt, bestowed the earth on Candragupta, the moon among men ; who churned the nectar of Nitiśāstra from the ocean of Arthaśāstra, to him, the wise and Brahma-like Viṣṇugupta, we make salutation.'

Again, in the *Nītivākyāmṛta* by the Jaina author Somadeva (*cir.* 950 A.D.), a work which, from internal evidence, would appear to be based on the *Kauṭilīya Arthaśāstra*, there occurs a line mentioning the report that Cānakya caused the last Nanda king to be assassinated. The plot of the drama, *Mudrā Rakṣasa*, by Visākha Datta, of uncertain date, but perhaps not later than the seventh century A.D., is closely connected with the same tradition. In the play, *Daśakumāracarita*, by Dandin, of about the sixth century, there is a comic passage which turns to ridicule some precepts of the *Kauṭilīya Arthaśāstra*, and begins thus :

'Learn then the science of polity (*dandanītim*). This has

[1] iv. 24.

now been abridged in 6,000 ślokas by the teacher Viṣṇugupta for the Maurya's benefit.'

Later, in the same passage, the author of the work on daṇḍanīti is referred to, at one place, as Cāṇakya.

In the *Kauṭilīya Arthaśāstra*, as we have it, the name of Kauṭilya appears at the end of every book as the author, and the two final verses run :

> 'This Śāstra has been made by him, who, from intolerance of misrule quickly rescued the scriptures, and the science of weapons, and the earth, which had passed to the Nanda king. Having seen many discrepancies on the part of commentators (bhāśyakāra) on the śāstras, Viṣṇugupta himself has made this sūtra and commentary (bhāṣya).'

Authorship and date of *Artha-śāstra*.

The questions of the authorship and date of this *Artha-śāstra* have been the subject of exhaustive discussion by eminent scholars, a summary of which has been given by Dr. Otto Stein in his work *Megasthenes und Kauṭilya*, published in 1922, a most thorough, minute, and painstaking comparison between the *Arthaśāstra* and the accounts of Megasthenes, as handed down by different Greek and Latin authors. Dr. Otto Stein's conclusion is expressed in the following words :

> 'Nach all dem ist bei einer näheren Gegenüberstellung des Berichtes des Megasthenes mit dem Arthaśāstra von einer Übereinstimmung, wie sie manche Förscher behauptet haben, nicht die Rede. Damit wird die Gleichzeitigkeit der beiden Quellen unwahrscheinlich und die Autorschaft des Ministers Candraguptas für das Arthaśāstra zweifelhaft.'

Historical value of *Artha-śāstra*.

There is, however, sufficient evidence of a persistent tradition in India, ascribing to Candragupta's minister the authorship of the *Arthaśāstra* in question, and the very existence of such a tradition seems to support a presumption that, whether the whole treatise or any part of it be the work of Cāṇakya or not, it deals with social conditions and institutions which prevailed in the Maurya period, and especially in the regions nearest the centre of the Maurya dominion, namely, Bihar and Bengal. This does not mean that we should expect to find in the administration depicted agreement in all details with that which may have been observed by Megasthenes at Pāṭaliputra, when the Magadha state had grown into an empire. The government contemplated by the *Kauṭilīya Arthaśāstra* appears to be that of a relatively small state, such as Magadha may have been in the early period of Candragupta's reign, before his dominions had been much extended by conquest, and, although the Maurya empire, when fully developed through the policy of systematic aggression inculcated in this treatise, was of the decentralized Indian type, each of its outlying provinces enjoying a measure of independence, yet it is natural to suppose that, by the time Pāṭaliputra had become the centre of a great federal state, a somewhat more elaborate form of administration had developed in the home provinces, and especially in the capital, than had sufficed for the original kingdom of Magadha. We may expect, then, to find in this *Arthaśāstra*, not exactly the administration described by Megasthenes, but institutions which might have grown in the course of a quarter of a century or thereabouts into those described by him. The theory here adumbrated cannot be proved conclusively; for the interpretation of the *Kauṭilīya Arthaśāstra* presents many difficulties; Megasthenes's account is obviously superficial and inaccurate, and, when all allowances have been made, there remain discrepancies which it is difficult to explain. But, on the whole, it seems that this theory bears the test indicated above, and that, for the purposes of history, the best means of arriving at an idea of social conditions in Bihar and Bengal during the Maurya period will be by analysis of the *Kauṭilīya Arthaśāstra* and its comparison with the description attributed to Megasthenes and with the Aśoka edicts. There is evidence of the survival in those countries, in various forms and with diverse changes, through later centuries, of political institutions and theories of the Maurya age, and to the *Arthaśāstra* we may look for elucidation of expressions occurring in records of the Gupta period in the fourth and fifth centuries of our era, of the time of Harṣa's empire in the seventh, and of the Pāla and Sena kings.

Interpretation of the *Artha-śāstra*.

In the following abstract of the *Kauṭilīya Arthaśāstra*, Mr. Shamasastry's translation [1] will be followed generally with a few suggested emendations. Mr. Shamasastry is far from claiming finality for his interpretation. In a preface thereto he modestly remarks :

> 'As regards my translation, I am conscious of the fact that it is far from being perfect. Beset as the work is with difficulties, it would be sheer presumption on my part to hope that my translation presents a correct interpretation of the text in all cases. Still I shall feel highly rewarded for my labours if it proves a stepping-stone for others to arrive at a correct interpretation.

The 'sūtra' style.

Much of the *Kauṭilīya Arthaśāstra* is written in what is called the 'sūtra' style, sūtra being the name given to short sentences or verses used in the Indian system of *memoria technica*, to recall the subject-matter of oral discourses.

According to time-honoured Indian tradition, all teaching should, properly, be oral. Buhler [2] has observed that 'the Hindus, even at present, in spite of a long-continued use of writing, esteem the written word less than the spoken one, because they base their whole literary and scientific intercourse on oral communications, and because, especially in scientific works, writing and MSS. are mentioned very rarely. Though MSS., being "sarasvatīmukha", "the face of the goddess of speech", are held sacred, and are worshipped, the Veda and the Śāstras exist, even for the modern Hindu, only in the mouth of the teacher, whose word has more weight than a written text, and they can only be learned properly from a teacher, not from MSS. Even in our days the Hindus esteem only the 'mukastha vidyā', the learning which the Pandit has imprinted on his memory'. It is easy to understand that, while the tradition of oral teaching was preserved, and handed on intact, sūtras—strings of short sentences conveying by themselves no clear meaning, or merely hinting at successive heads or divisions of a subject which might easily be committed to memory—were very

[1] *Kauṭilīya's Arthaśāstra*, translated by R. Shamasastry, B.A., M.R.A.S., Bangalore, 1915.

[2] Indian Palæography. English version by Fleet. *Ind. Ant.* 1904, App.

useful both to teachers and pupils; but if the tradition were once lost, the *sūtras* by themselves, without authoritative explanation, would become unintelligible. As the use of writing extended, and schools with divergent teaching multiplied, there came into existence writings called *bhāṣya* which explained and expounded the *sūtras*, and thus served at the same time to preserve the sciences and make the teaching of different professors accessible to persons who could not attend their schools. The word *bhāṣya* is usually translated 'commentary', but it cannot be said, in general, with accuracy, that the *sūtra* is the text of a treatise and the *bhāṣya* the commentary thereon. Often it will be found that the *sūtra* by itself is unintelligible, and the *bhāṣya* is more properly the treatise. But, even of *bhāṣya* and *sūtra* combined, it is not expected, according to Indian ideas, that they will convey the whole teaching of a subject. It is assumed that there will be competent oral teaching too.

Fortunately the *Kauṭilīya Arthaśāstra* is not pure *sūtra*. In its final verse, quoted above, it claims to be *sūtra* and *bhāṣya* combined, and much of it is quite intelligible as it stands. And for a portion of the work (Book II.) there exists a commentary of unknown date, by one Bhaṭṭa-svāmin, which has been utilized by Mr. Shamasastry in his translation.

Daṇḍa-nīti in other works.

The subject-matter of the work—*daṇḍanīti*, or Political Science—is dealt with in others of the same class (*artha-* or *nītiśāstras*), and much of it is covered also by the *Dharma-śāstras* and didactic passages of the Epics, but apart from what they have in common with the *Kauṭilīya Arthaśāstra*, there is nothing to connect those compositions especially with the Maurya period. The opening sentence of the *Kauṭilīya* runs: 'This *Arthaśāstra* is made as a compendium of almost all the *arthaśāstras*, which, for gaining and preserving the world, have been composed by former teachers'—showing that *daṇḍanīti* had been cultivated and that several works on the subject already existed. As will be seen, a number of them are quoted by name.

IV

THE *KAUṬILĪYA ARTHAŚĀSTRA*

INTRODUCTION

Plan of the work.

THE *Kauṭilīya Arthaśāstra*, which may be referred to in future, for the sake of brevity, as 'the *Arthaśāstra*', comprises, including a *tantrayukti*, or summary of contents, at the end, fifteen books (*adhikaraṇa*), of which the first, entitled *Vinayādhikārikam* ('concerning Discipline'), after laying down general rules for the conduct of the king, gives injunctions for the appointment of ministers (*amātya*) and high priests (*purohita*), and then proceeds to describe the important institution of spies or secret agents. Then follow a chapter on the king's council, and one on the duties of ambassadors. The remainder of this book is concerned with rules for the king's sons and wives, for his daily routine of life, and for securing his personal safety.

The second book, entitled *adhyakṣapracāraḥ* ('Duties of Superintendents'), describes the duties of a great many classes of officials, but begins with interesting chapters on the formation of villages, the division of lands, fortification, and town-planning. The third book, *Dharmasthīyam*, is concerned with Civil Law, including Administration of Justice; the fourth, *Kanṭakaśodhanam*, with Police and Criminal Law. The next book has the title *Yogavṛttam*, which may be translated 'internal policy', and contains chapters on methods of dealing with seditious ministers and of replenishing an exhausted treasury; also a table of salaries for officials, chapters on the behaviour of courtiers, and general rules of policy directed towards strengthening the position and prestige of the throne. The remainder of the work is chiefly concerned with foreign policy and war, but in the first chapter of Book VI the constitution of the

State and the basis of the kingly power are briefly discussed, and Book XI, consisting of a single chapter, deals with the control and management of guilds and corporations.

Form of govern-ment. The ministers.

The form of government described is autocratic. In chapter i of Book VI it is said that the king, the minister (*amātya*), the country, the fort, the treasury, the army, and the ally are the ' elements of sovereignty ' (*prakṛtisampadas*). In the chapter[1] headed *amātyotpattiḥ* (' creation of ministers'), Kauṭilya, after quoting the opinions of different authors, expresses approval of the principle that ministers should be selected solely on the ground of their qualifications, as shown by their work. Evidently the appointment of ministers is to be made by the king. The concluding verse of this chapter is thus translated by Mr. Shamasastry :

> 'Having divided the spheres of their powers (*vibhajyāmātyavibhavam*), and having definitely taken into consideration the place and time where and when they have to work, such persons shall be employed, not as councillors (*mantrinas*) but as ministerial officers (*amātyas*).'

In the next chapter, headed *mantripurohitotpattih*, however, as in other parts of the book, the words *amātya* and *mantrin* appear to be used as synonymous, the functions of the minister being thus described :

> ' As works do not happen to be simultaneous, are various in form, and pertain to distant and different localities, the king shall, in view of being abreast of time and place, depute his ministers to carry them out (*amātyaiḥ karayet*). Such is the work of ministers (*ityamātyakarma*).'

In different parts of the *Arthaśāstra* ambiguity arises from the old Indian practice of giving the same title indifferently to lower as well as high officials of the same department. Thus, *amātya* and *mantrin* mean, in some places, ' prime minister ', elsewhere an ordinary ' councillor ' of the king, while, from other passages again, it appears that the title *amātya* was borne by a large class of civil officials of subordinate rank.[2] In the army, the commander-in-chief and a class of inferior officers are called alike *senapati*.[3] There

[1] Bk. I, ch. viii.
[2] Cf. p. 155.
[3] Cf. p. 78.

appears to have been a similar wide use of the titles *adhyakṣa*, *mahāmātra*, *antapāla*.

The Council.

The chapter[1] on 'Functions of the Council' (*mantrādhikāra*) lays down the rule that 'all administrative measures are preceded by deliberations in council' (*mantrapūrvāssarvārambhāḥ*).

After emphasizing the importance of secrecy in the deliberations of councils, the chapter proceeds to discuss the question how many ministers (*mantrinas*) should be consulted by the king on administrative measures. After quoting various opinions, Kauṭilya expresses his own—that the king should consult three or four ministers. Next, the chapter discusses what number of ministers should form the 'assembly of ministers', and quotes the opinion of the school of Manu that the number should be twelve :

'*mantriparisaḍaṁ dvādasāmātyānkurvīteti mānavāh.*'

The school of Bṛhaspati says sixteen, and the school of Usanas twenty, but Kauṭilya opines that the assembly (*pariṣad*) should comprise as many ministers as the needs of the dominion require. The following rule is laid down :

> 'In the case of important work (*ātyāyike kārye*) he (the king) shall summon and inform the ministers and the assembly of ministers (*mantrino mantripariṣadaṁ ca*). He should do whatever the majority (*bhūyiṣṭas*) there recommend.'

Apparently, the *mantripariṣad* were an executive council of ministers, each of whom had charge of a department of administration. In the ordinary business of government, the king consulted three or four of the ministers, presumably those in whose departments the matter lay, or whose special experience made their advice valuable, before taking action. In cases of special importance, besides consulting a few ministers specially, he summoned the whole council, and was guided by the opinion of the majority. In chapter i, Book VI, which deals with the salaries of officials, that allotted to the *mantrin* is 48,000 *paṇas* per annum, the highest salary given to any secular civil functionary, the salary of the

[1] Bk. I, ch. xv.

sannidhātṛ (chamberlain or treasurer), and *samāhartṛ* (collector-general), who, as appears from another passage, are both *mantrins*, is fixed at 24,000 *paṇas* each, while the other members of the *mantripariṣad* receive 12,000 only. Apparently, here, the *mantrin* or *āmātya* receiving the higher salary is the prime minister. Chapter x, Book I, lays down that, 'assisted by his prime minister (*mantrin*) and his high priest (*purohita*), the king shall, by offering temptations, examine the character of the ministers (*āmātya*) appointed to the charge of the ordinary departments (*sāmānyesvadhi-karaneṣu*)'.

The various temptations which may be offered to ministers are then detailed. They fall under the four heads—*dharma* ('religious duty' or 'sacred law'), *artha* (wealth), *kāma* (sensuality), and *bhaya* (fear).

In the first, a dismissed priest instigates ministers to rebel, on the ground that the king is unrighteous (*adhārmika*). In the second, a general dismissed for embezzlement offers the temptation of money; in the third, a female ascetic (*parivrā-jikā*), admitted to the queen's apartments, represents to each of the ministers—here called *mahāmātra*—in turn, that the queen is in love with him; in the fourth, ministers are tempted to enter into a plot against the king's life. The rule laid down is that those ministers who have resisted the *dharma* temptation shall be appointed to the office of judge (*dharmasthīya*), or to duties of *kaṇṭakaśodhana* ('removal of thorns'—i. e. police); those who resist money temptations shall be employed as collector-general (*samāhartṛ*) or treasurer (*sannidhātṛ*); those who resist temptations of sensual pleasure shall be employed in the superintendence of the outer and inner pleasure-grounds (*vihāra*); those who resist temptations falling under the head of 'fear' (*bhaya*) shall be appointed to offices immediately about the king's person (*āsannakārya*).

Those who have withstood every kind of temptation are eligible for the appointment of *mantrin* (prime minister ?); while those who have yielded to one or other may be appointed to the charge of mines, timber- or elephant-forests (*dravyahastivana*), or manufactories (*karmānta*). Evidently all the ministers were appointed by the king, and there is no trace of what we now call representative institutions of government. On the other hand, we find frequent mention of corporations and guilds—*saṅgha*, *śreṇī*—and it is clear, from numerous passages, that they were powerful and influential, and that it was necessary for the sovereign to conciliate them and gain them over to his side. As already mentioned, a whole chapter forming a book to itself is devoted to the subject of their control and management.

Guilds and corporations.

Spies.

Great importance is attached to the institution of spies and secret agents (*gūḍhapurūṣa*), who are relied upon to procure for the king confidential information on all matters affecting his government, and especially on the conduct of government servants of all classes, and also to spread reports and influence public opinion. Some are to be selected from among persons standing in a confidential relation to the person spied upon, as a religious disciple (*chātra*), a class-mate or colleague (*satrin*). Others are to adopt various disguises—as a recluse (*udāsthita*), an ascetic (*tāpasa*), a substantial cultivator (*gṛhapatika*), a merchant (*vaidehaka*). A subtle method of influencing the public is thus described :

'Spies (*satrin*) formed as opposing factions shall carry on disputations in places of pilgrimage, in assemblies, houses, and corporations. One spy may say : "This king is said to be endowed with all desirable qualities ; he seems to be a stranger to such tendencies as would lead him to oppress citizens and country people by levying heavy fines and taxes." Against those who seem to commend this opinion, another spy may interrupt the speaker and say : "People suffering from anarchy (*mātsyanyāyābhibhūtāḥ*)[1] first made Manu, the *Vaivasvata*, their king, and allotted one-sixth of the grains grown, and one-tenth of merchandise as his due shares. Being maintained by this payment, kings are responsible for the security of their subjects, and are answerable for their sins, if they do not punish them. Hence, even the hermits pay to the king his one-sixth share, saying :

[1] *mātsyanyāya* (lit. 'fish practice, or condition') is a proverbial expression signifying anarchy, which results in the strong destroying the weak, as large fish prey on small ones.

'We pay the share due to him, as he protects us.' The king, as dispenser of punishments and rewards, represents both Indra and Yama. Divine punishment also reaches those who despise kings. Hence, kings should not be despised."'

Secret agents thus employed, it appears, served the purposes of a controlled or inspired press, or 'publicity' department, in a modern state.

Other secret agents should be employed to assassinate people whom the king wishes to get rid of. Such murderers are of two classes—bullies or bravos, who use violent means, and are called *tīkṣṇa*, a word which Mr. Shamasastry translates as 'fiery', and poisoners (*rasada*).

Formation of villages.

Proceeding to the details of administration, the author of the *Arthaśāstra* first lays down rules for the settlement of waste lands and the formation of villages, recognizing, doubtless, the importance of the village as a social and administrative unit, having its origin in colonization, which, at a time when population was relatively scanty and waste land abundant, formed an important branch of the State activities. The areas available for the purpose may consist of virgin soil (*abhūtapūrva*), or of land formerly inhabited but abandoned (*bhūtapūrva*). In such areas, villages should be formed, each containing not less than 100 and not more than 500 families of *śūdra* (agriculturists), who may be either surplus population of the country, or immigrants from other countries. The boundaries of each village should extend to a *Krośa* or two, and the villages should be so arranged as to protect one another. Further protection should be given by fortified posts—a fort of the class called *sthānīya* (perhaps the origin of the modern '*thana*'), in the centre of every 800 villages, a *droṇamukha* fort for every 400, a *khārvaṭika* for every 200, and a *saṅgrahaṇa* for every ten villages. Besides these protective posts, there should be forts (*durgāṇi*) on the frontiers of the country manned by special guards (*antapāla*).

Forts.

Land settlement.

The distribution of the arable lands of the village is next dealt with. To certain classes of religious men—*ṛtvik, ācārya, purohita, śrotriya*—lands yielding sufficient produce are to be granted tax-free. To certain classes of officials, such as *adhyakṣa* (superintendent), *sankhyāyaka* (accountant), lands inalienable by sale or mortgage (*vikrayādhānavarja*), but not apparently revenue-free, are to be allotted, and similar allotments are to be set apart for the officials known as *gopa* (village accountant) and *sthānīka* (revenue supervisor),[1] as well as for veterinary surgeons (*anīkastha*), physicians (*cikitsaka*), horse-trainers (*aśvadamaka*), and messengers (*janghārika*). These different classes of officials will be further noticed below. To ordinary revenue-paying cultivators (*karada*), lands prepared for cultivation (*kṛtakshetrāni*) should be given for life only (*ekapurūṣikāṇi*). Lands not previously cultivated (*akṛtāni*) shall not be taken away from those who bring them under cultivation (*kartṛbhyo*). Lands may be taken away from those who do not cultivate them, and given to others, or they may be cultivated by village-servants or by traders.

The meaning of these rules, apparently, is that a cultivator who reclaimed waste land acquired a right to hold it as long as he continued to cultivate it; but if he ceased to do so the king might give it to another cultivator, or to a person of the trading class, who might be willing to undertake its cultivation and pay the revenue. Or failing such arrangement the king might have the land cultivated by hired labour. Any person to whom land reclaimed by another was given for cultivation had a right to enjoy it for his life only.

Cultivators who are good revenue-payers should be favoured with grain, cattle, and money: this apparently refers to advances. The king should allow remission of revenue on proper occasions.

State development.

(For the general improvement of the country, the king should work mines, carry on manufactures, exploit timber- and elephant-forests, encourage cattle-breeding and trade, maintain roads and water communications, and establish market-towns (*paṇyapaṭṭana*). He should construct reservoirs (*setu*) or provide sites, timber, and other requisites, and

[1] Cf. p. 80, *infra*.

roads for those undertaking their construction. This applies also to the maintenance of places of pilgrimage and sacred groves. Persons refusing to take part in any joint irrigation work (*sambhūyasetubandha*) shall be punished by being charged with the cost of labourers and bullocks employed on that account, and deprived of their share of the benefit of the work.

The king should exercise rights of ownership over artificial reservoirs in respect of fishing, navigation, and the like. He is enjoined to correct (*vinayaṁ grāhayet*) those who neglect their duty towards slaves and relatives (*dāsāhitaka-bandhunaśṛnvato*), and to make provision for orphans, the aged, the sick and infirm, and the destitute, poor women in confinement, and their babies. Of these injunctions we seem to find an echo in passages[1] of Aśoka's edicts inculcating kind treatment of relatives, slaves, and servants, and the reference in his second Major Rock Edict to provision for medical relief.

Village regulations.

The village elders should take care of the property of minor orphans till they attain majority.

Certain penal provisions designed for the welfare of village communities are here introduced. Persons neglecting without sufficient cause to maintain relatives dependent on them are liable to fine, and so is any person who embraces asceticism (*pravrājat*) without making provision for his wife and family, or who causes a woman to become an ascetic (*striyam pravrājayat*).

No ascetic (*pravrajitabhāva*) other than a *vānaprastha*, no corporation (*saṅgha*) other than one composed of natives of the place (*sajāta*), and no guild (*samayānubandha*) other than a *sāmutthāyika* shall be allowed in the village. The word *sāmutthāyika* is translated by Mr. Shamasastry 'local co-operative guild', but the precise meaning seems to be doubtful. Actors, dancers, singers, musicians, buffoons, and bards are not to be allowed to trouble the villagers and distract them from their work. The king is to protect agriculturists from oppressive fines, exactions of labour, and

[1] *R. E.* iii, ix, xi, xiii; *P. E.* vii.

taxes, and their cattle from thieves, tigers, poisonous creatures, and diseases; road-traffic from molestation by courtiers or subordinate officials (*kārmika*),[1] robbers, or boundary-guards (*antapāla*); the roads from damage by herds of cattle.

Forests. The next chapter is headed *Bhumicchidravidhānam* (disposition of land unfit for tillage), and prescribes the reservation of forests. Brahmans are to be provided with forests for *soma* plantations, and for the performance of austerities. Such forests were to be safe from all danger from living or inanimate things (*pradiṣṭābhayasthāvarajaṅgamāni*). A game-forest surrounded by a ditch (*khātaguptam*) is to be reserved for the king and another for the king's guests. Other forests are to be reserved for forest produce of different kinds, to be more particularly described in a later chapter, and factories should be set up for the preparation of the commodities obtained from them.

The greatest importance is attached to elephant-forests (*hastivana*), in view of the fact that 'the victory of kings depends mainly upon elephants; for elephants, being of large bodily frame, are capable not only of destroying the army of an enemy, his fortifications and encampments, but also of undertaking dangerous works'.

In a later passage[2] of the *Arthaśāstra* the value to the king of a timber-forest is compared with that of an elephant-forest: 'My teachers say that of the two forests, one productive of timber, and another of elephants, the former is the source of all kinds of works and is of immense help in forming a storehouse, the latter is of no value for these purposes.' 'Not so,' says Kauṭilya, 'for it is possible to plant any number of timber-forests; yet it is on elephants that the destruction of an enemy's army depends.' The elephant-forest is to be in charge of a superintendent (*nāgavanādhyakṣa*), with a staff of forest-guards (*nāgavanapāla*), who 'assisted by those who rear elephants, those who enchain the legs of elephants, those who guard the boundaries, those

[1] Shamasastry has 'workmen', but elsewhere *kārmika* is rendered by 'clerk'.

[2] Bk. VII, ch. xi.

who live in forests, as well as those who nurse elephants, shall, with five or seven female elephants to help in tethering wild ones, trace the whereabouts of herds of elephants. . . . Experts in catching elephants shall follow the instructions given to them by the elephant doctor (*anīkastha*), and catch such elephants as have auspicious marks and good character.'

The elephants of Kaliṅga and Anga, the eastern country, and Karūśa, it is said, are the best, those of the Daśārna and western countries are of middle quality; while those of Saurāṣṭta and Pañcajana are inferior.

The killing of an elephant is made a capital offence.

Fortification and town-planning.

The subject of fortifications is next dealt with. The king may either have forts on the frontiers of his kingdom in situations suitable for defence, or a fortified capital (*samudayasthānaṁ sthānīyam*). Elaborate directions for defensive works, as well as for the location of the palace, public buildings, inhabitants of different classes, trades, &c., in the fortified capital, are given.

The *Arthaśāstra* then proceeds to describe generally the functions of several categories of government officials, of whom the principal are the *samāhartṛ* and the *sannidhātṛ*. The *samāhartṛ* is the collector-general of revenue, and his duties are laid down in great detail. Those of the *sannidhātṛ* are not so clearly explained. The name is translated by Mr. Shamasastry as 'chamberlain', but it would seem that 'treasurer' or 'finance minister' would be more appropriate. It is said that the *sannidhātṛ* 'shall attend to the business of revenue collection' (*nicayān anutiṣṭet*), but the collection of revenue was evidently the business of the *samāhartṛ*. Apparently the *sannidhātṛ* was to receive and hold charge of revenue collected by the *samāhartṛ*. He had charge of the royal treasure of precious stones, and stores of grain and forest-produce, and seems also to have been entrusted with the construction of certain government buildings, viz. the treasure-house (*kośagṛha*), storehouses for agricultural produce (*koṣṭāgāra*) and forest produce (*kupyagṛha*), the royal trading-house (*paṇyagṛha*), the armoury (*āyudhāgāra*), the jail (*bandhanāgāra*), courts of justice

Duties of the *sannidhātr*.

(*dharmasthīya*), and the minister's office or secretariat (*mahāmātrīya*). All these buildings are to be provided with wells, privies, bathrooms, appliances for putting out fire (e.g. vessels of water, ladders, axes, hooks and pincers for pulling down walls, thatch, &c.), and cats and mongooses to keep down rats and snakes. The storehouse of agricultural produce should have a bowl with a mouth one *aratni* (twenty-four *aṅgulas*) wide for the measurement of rainfall (*varsamāna*).

Duties of the *samāhartṛ*.

Describing the duties of the *samāhartṛ*, the *Arthaśāstra* begins by saying that he should attend to (*aveksheta*) the fort (*durga*), the rural area (*rāṣṭra*), mines (*khaṇi*), irrigation works (*setu*), forests (*vana*), cattle (*vraja*), and communications (*vaṇikpatha*).

Under the heading *durga*, it is explained, are included tolls (*śulka*), fines (*daṇḍa*), weights and measures (*pautava*), the duties of the city superintendent (*nāgarika*), and the superintendents of coinage (*lakṣaṇa*) and passports (*mudra*), manufacture and sale of intoxicating liquor, cloth, oil, ghee, and sugar, and slaughter-houses, the state goldsmith, royal trade, courtesans, gambling, buildings, artisans' guilds (*kārūśilpigaṇa*), religious worship, dues collected at the city gates, or octroi (*dvāra*), and from *bāhirikas*, meaning perhaps, foreigners—in short, all matters connected with the administration of a city. *Rāṣṭra* includes cultivation of Crown lands (*sītā*), the royal share of the produce of other lands (*bhāga*), religious taxes (*bali*), tax paid in money (*kara*), traders (*vaṇik*), the superintendent of rivers (*nadīpāla*), ferries (*taras*), boats (*nāvaḥ*), market-towns (*paṭṭana*), pastures (*vivīta*), transit-dues (*vartani*), *rajjūśćorarajjūśca* (lit. 'ropes and ropes to bind thieves').

Gold, silver, diamonds, gems, pearls, coral, conch-shells, metals (*loha*), salt, and other minerals (*dhātu*), come under the head of mines (*khaṇi*). The heading *setu* apparently includes all cultivation of crops grown with the help of artificial irrigation, e.g. flower-, fruit-, and vegetable-gardens, wet fields (*kedāra*), and transplanted crops (*mulavāpa*).

Vana includes game-, timber-, and elephant-forests

(*paśumṛgadravyahasti*). *Vraja* includes cows, buffaloes, goats, sheep, asses, camels, horses, and mules. The heading *vaṇikpatha* covers communications by land and water (*sthalapatho vāripathaśca*).

This chapter concludes with a verse to the effect that a wise collector-general should bring about an increase of revenue and a decrease of expenditure. It will be seen, however, that the *samāhartṛ* was also concerned with certain branches of police work.

Accounts and records.

The *Arthaśāstra* then passes to the important subject of accounts. The first chapter on this subject is headed *Akṣapaṭale gāṇanikyādhikāraḥ*, which Mr. Shamasastry translates 'the business of keeping up accounts in the office of accountants'. It appears, however, from details given in this chapter, as well as from references to the *akṣapaṭala* in various land grants, that it served the purpose not only of an accountant's office, but also of a general record-room. It is laid down that the building should contain books well arranged by departments, relating not only to accounts, but also to the history of customs, professions, and transactions of countries, villages, families, and corporations, titles to possession of land and remission of taxes, and treaties with or ultimata issued to friendly or hostile kings.

Accountants (*gāṇanikya*) are to submit their accounts in the month of *Aṣāḍha*, and those who fail to furnish their accounts and pay the balances due from them at the appointed time are to be fined ten times the amounts due from them. There are elaborate instructions for the checking of accounts, and penalties are provided for a superintendent (*kāraṇika*) who does not proceed to check an account when the clerk (*kārmika*) concerned is ready, as well as for clerks who are not ready in time.

The subject of embezzlement by government servants is next dealt with. Thirty-six different forms of embezzlement are enumerated, and methods of detecting them indicated, as well as punishments prescribed. There is the following reflection :

'Just as it is impossible not to taste the honey or the poison that finds itself at the tip of the tongue, so it is impossible for a government servant not to eat up at least a bit of the king's revenue. Just as it is impossible to ascertain whether fish moving under the surface are drinking water or not, so it is impossible to detect government servants taking government money. It is possible to mark the movement of birds flying high up in the sky; but not so is it possible to ascertain the movements of government servants of hidden purpose.'

The final injunction under this head is that the king should force his servants to give up ill-gotten gains, and transfer them from one duty to another, so that they may be prevented from eating the substance of the state, and compelled to vomit what they have eaten.

Then follows a chapter on the drafting of official documents. Official letters (*lekha*) are classified according to their purport, as follows: blame (*nindā*), praise (*praśaṁsā*), inquiry (*pṛcchā*), narration (*ākhyāna*), request (*arthanā*), refusal (*pratyākhyāna*), censure (*upālambha*), prohibition (*pratiṣedha*), command (*codana*), conciliation (*sāntva*), promise of help (*abhyavapatti*), threat (*bhartsanā*), persuasion (*anunaya*). Writs or decrees (*śāsana*) are of eight kinds: notice (*prajñapana*), command (*ājñā*), gift (*paridāna*), remission (*parīhāra*), licence (*nisṛṣṭi*), instruction (*pravṛttika*), reply (*pratilekha*), general proclamation (*sarvatraga*).

The four kinds of stratagem (*upāya*), viz. negotiation (*sāma*), bribery (*upapradāna*), sowing dissension (*bheda*), and open attack (*daṇḍa*), are then enumerated, and minutely sub-classified. Finally, good qualities and defects of official style are pointed out.

V

THE *KAUṬILĪYA ARTHAŚĀSTRA*

DUTIES OF SUPERINTENDENTS

THE second book then proceeds to describe in detail the duties of twenty-six superintendents (*adhyakṣa*) in different departments, viz.: The *Adhyakṣas*.

The Treasury (*Kośa*).
Mines (*Akara, Khaṇi*).
Metals (*Loha*).
The Mint (*Lakṣaṇa*).
Salt (*Lavaṇa*).
Gold (*Suvarṇa*).
The Storehouse (*Koṣṭāgāra*).
Royal trade (*Paṇya*).
Forest produce (*Kupya*).
The Armoury (*Āyudhāgāra*).
Weights and measures of capacity (*Pautava*).
Measurement of space and time (*Māna*).
Tolls (*Śulka*).
Spinning and Weaving (*Sūtra*).
Cultivation of Crown lands (*Sītā*).
Intoxicating liquor (*Sura*).
Slaughter-houses (*Sūna*).
Courtesans (*Gaṇika*).
Shipping (*Nau*).
Cattle (*Go*).
Horses (*Aśva*).
Elephants (*Hasti*).
Chariots (*Ratha*).
Infantry (*Patti*).
Passports (*Mudrā*).
Pastures (*Vivīta*).

Besides the above, other *adhyakṣas* are mentioned elsewhere in the *Arthaśāstra*, namely, superintendents of

Elephant-forests (*Nāgavana*).
General trade (*Saṁsthā*).
Religious institutions (*Devatā*).
Gambling (*Dyūtā*).
Jails (*Bandhanāgāra*).
Ports (*Paṭṭana*).

From the range of the *samāhartṛ's* duties,[1] it would appear that all the *adhyakṣas* above mentioned were subordinate to him, except those of the treasury and storehouse, who

[1] Cf. p. 44.

were, presumably, under the *sannidhātṛ*, and those of the armoury, the infantry, horses and cavalry, chariots, and elephants, who would be under the *senapati*, or commander-in-chief.[1]

In the chapter on salaries, those of the superintendents of elephants, chariots, and infantry are set down at 4,000 *paṇas*, and of other *adhyakṣas* at 1,000 *paṇas* each.

In the same chapter there is a sentence indicating that an *adhyakṣa* should have charge of 100 or 1,000 communities (*varga*). It seems to be contemplated that, for the purpose of administration in the various departments, the country would be mapped out in circles of unequal size, each under an *adhyaksa*, subordinate, presumably, to the minister (*mantrin*, *āmātya*) in charge of his department.

In the polity described, much of the official agency is employed in the management and exploitation of Crown property. There were important royal estates and forests, and it seems that the State kept a monopoly of mines. The king carried on both export and import trade, and had State factories for working up the raw products of his country. Moreover, as a great part of the revenue was paid in kind, important establishments had to be maintained for dealing with the agricultural products received in payment of taxes, as well as those raised from the Crown lands. Of the general store, it appears part was kept as a reserve to meet years of famine, part went to the maintenance of the royal household and the remuneration of officials, who were paid in kind, and part as raw material for the royal manufactories.

The Treasury. Taking the chapters of Book II in their order, we find that the first is headed 'Examination of Jewels received in the Treasury' (*Kośapraveśyaratnaparīkṣā*), but, by a somewhat perplexing arrangement, the chapter deals not only with pearls (*mauktika*), gems (*ratna*), diamonds (*vajra*), and coral (*pravāla*), but also with certain perfumes, skins, and furs, and woven fabrics of different kinds.

These articles are classified according to the countries

[1] Cf. p. 78

from which they come, and, in some instances, the names of countries given in the *Arthaśāstra* have been explained by the commentator, Bhaṭṭasvāmin, as indicated below.

Pearls are classified as follows : Pearls.

Tamraparṇika, produced in the Tamraparni (a river in the Pāṇḍya country—Com.).

Pāṇḍyakavātaka, obtained in Pāṇḍyakavāta (a mountain known as Malayakoti in the Pāṇḍya country—Com.).

Pāsikya, produced in the Pāsa (a river—Com.).

Kauleya, produced in the Kūla (a river near the village Mayura, in the island of Siṁhala—Com.).

Chaurṇeya, produced in the Chūrna (a river near the village Murachi in the Kerala country—Com.).

Mahendra, that which is obtained near the mountain of Mahendra.

Kārdamika, produced in the Kardama (a river in Persia (*pārasika*)—Com.).

Srautasīya, produced in the Srotasi (a river falling into the Barbara Sea—Com.).

Hrādīya, produced in the Hrada (a gulf or bay of the Barbara Sea—Com.).

Haimavata, obtained near the Himalayas.

Defects of pearls (e.g. bad shape, roughness, bad perforation) and good qualities (e.g. size, weight, good spherical shape, and good perforation) are next enumerated. Several different kinds of pearl necklaces, distinguished according to the number of strings or otherwise, e.g. *śirṣaka,* composed of pearls all of one size, except a larger one in the centre; *yaṣṭi,* a string of pearls with a gem (*maṇi*) in the centre; *apavartaka,* a string made of pearls and gold beads (*hemamaṇi*), are also mentioned.

Gems (*maṇi*) are classified as those found in the Kūṭa and Mūleya mountains, and *pārasamudraka,* brought from beyond the sea; also by colour, e.g. *saugandhika* (? ruby), having the colour of the red lotus, the *parijāta* flower (*erithrina Indica*), or the rising sun; *vaiḍūrya,*[1] having Gems.

[1] Bhaṭṭasvāmin notes that the mountains such as the Vindhya, the Vidura, and that part of the Malaya which possesses the same

the colour of the blue lotus flower; the *śirīsa,* water, young bamboo, or parrot's feathers (? emerald); *indranīla* (? sapphire).

Diamonds. Diamonds are said to be found in the countries of Sabhārāṣṭra (Vidarbha—Com.), Madhyamarāṣṭra (Kosala—Com.), Kaśmaka (Benares—Com.). They are also described as *Śrikaṭanaka* (found near the mountain Vedotkaṭa—Com.); *maṇimantaka* (found near the mountain Manimān or Manimanta—Com.); and *indravānaka* (found in Kaliṅga—Com.). Diamonds, again, are distinguished according to colour and quality.

Coral. Coral is of two kinds: *alakandaka* (obtained in the mouth of the river of Barbara—Com.) and *vaivarṇaka* (of Vivarṇa, the ocean near the island of Yavanas—Com.).

Perfumes. Under the head of perfumes, we have sandal-wood (*candana*) of sixteen kinds, of which two (*joṅgaka* and *taurupa*) are said by the commentator to be products of Kāmarupa and one *nāgaparvataka,* of the Naga mountains; three kinds of *agaru* (*Agallochum*) wood, *joṅgaka* (from Kāmarupa—Com.), *pārasamudraka* (available in the island of Siṁhala—Com.), and *dongaka,* a black kind; and *tailaparnika,* a perfume, or class of perfumes not identified, of which seven kinds (*aśokagrāmika, joṅgaka, grameruka, sauvarṇakuḍyaka, pūrṇadvīpaka, paralauhityaka,* and *antarvatya*) are said by the commentator to be obtained from Kāmarupa, one kind, *kaleyaka,* is noted (in the text) as coming from Svarṇabhūmi, and one as produced in northern mountains (*auttaraparvataka*).

Furs. The furs, of which several kinds are enumerated, appear to be skins of small animals (fox, marten, &c.) found in the Himalayas. Thus, *bisi* and *mahābisi* furs are said, in the text, to be twelve *aṅgulas* (inches) long, and products of 'twelve villages', which, according to the commentator, are situated in the Himalayas, and inhabited by Mlecchas. Five kinds of skins are said to come from Aroha, and three from

characteristics as the Vindhya, and the Strīrājya, Malabar, are the sources of *Vaidurya* and other gems. The name Strīrājya ('women's realm'), applied to Malabar, evidently refers to the matriarchal custom of that country.

Bāhlava, also, according to Bhaṭṭasvāmin, places in the Himalayas. The best furs are soft, smooth, and thick. *Satina, nalatula*, and *vṛttapuccha* are skins of aquatic animals (*audra*, ? otters).

Fabrics. The enumeration of woven fabrics is detailed, but in parts, not quite clear, as the text stands. Under the head of woollen fabrics we have *kambala* (a coarse blanket—Com.), *Kaucapaka* (v. l. *Kucelaka*—usually worn by cow-herds—Com.), *kulamitika* (v. l. *kathamitika*—a head-dress—Com.), *saumitika* (bullock-covering—Com.), *turagastarana* (horse-blanket—Com.), *varṇaka* (v. l. *varṇa kambali*—a coloured blanket—Com.), *talicchaka* (blanket—Com.), *vāravāna* (coat—Com.), *paristoma* (large blanket—Com.), *samantabhadraka* (elephant-covering—Com.), *bhingisi* (said to be rain-proof) and *apasāraka*, products of Nepal.

The following fabrics of hair (*mṛgaroma*) are mentioned: *samputika* (*jaṅghatrana*, trousers—Com.), *caturaśrika, lambara* (*pracchadapata*, a curtain or wrapper—Com.), *katavānaka* (the same, but coarser—Com.), *pravāraka* (the same, another variety—Com.), *sattalika* (carpet—Com.).

In the next passage it is said that the *dukūla* of Vaṅga (*Vāngaka*) is white and soft, that of Puṇḍra (*pauṇḍraka*) black and 'gem-soft' (*maṇisnigdha*, rubbed with a gem while being woven—Com.), *suvarṇakuḍya*, gem-soft and wet-woven (*udakavānam*), and this applies also to *kaśika*, and the *kṣauma* of Puṇḍra. On this Bhaṭṭasvāmin notes that '*dukūla* is a fine fabric and *kṣauma* is a little coarse'. The word *kṣauma* is ordinarily translated 'linen', but more probably, here, it means jute.[1] The use of jute clothing by the poorer classes in Bengal was common before cotton cloth became cheap through trade with England.

Then there is a somewhat obscure reference to fabrics produced in Magadha, Puṇḍra, and Suvarṇakuḍya from certain trees—the *nāgavṛkṣa*, the *likucha* (*artocarpas lakucha*), the *vakula* (*mimusops elengi*), and the *vaṭa* (*ficus indica*). Probably silks spun by worms fed on these trees are here referred to, for the next sentence says that 'this

[1] Cf. Watters, *Yuan Chwang*, i. 149.

applies to *kauśeya* and China silk (*cīnapatta cīnabhūmija*)'. The cotton fabrics (*kārpāsika*) of Madhura (southern Madhura—Com.), Aparānta (*koṇkana*—Com.), Kāśi, Vaṅga, Vatsa (Kausambi—Com.), and Mahiṣa (the country called Mahiṣmati—Com.), are said to be the best.

Discussion of the names of places and countries in this list would be out of place here, but it may be mentioned that Vaṅga, in its more restricted sense, applied to central and sometimes to northern, and Puṇḍra to northern and eastern Bengal.

Mines. In the chapter on mining and connected industries (*ākarakarmāntapravartana*) it is said that the superintendent of mines (*ākarādhyakṣa*) should have a knowledge of the science of minerals, or be assisted by persons with such knowledge, and be provided with a staff of miners and necessary tools. Instructions are given for recognizing and classifying ores. The rule is laid down that 'mines yielding minerals from which vessels are made (*bhāṇḍopakārin*), and those requiring large outlay to work should be leased for a share of the output or a fixed rent (*bhāgena prakrayeṇa vā*). Those which are cheap to work should be exploited directly by the king.' The *Lohādhyakṣa*, it is said, should carry on the manufacture of copper, lead, tin, brass, &c. The commentator explains that '*loha* is a general name of metals, except gold and silver'.

Mint. The coins to be minted by the *Lakṣaṇādhyakṣa* (*Taṅkaśālādhikārin*, mint superintendent—Com.) are next specified. It is said that he should cause to be made the following: *rūpyarūpa*, with four parts of copper and the weight of a *māsa* seed of any of the metals, *tīkṣṇa* (?), tin, lead, or antimony added—*paṇa*, half, quarter, and one-eighth *paṇa*; *pādājīvam tāmrarūpam*—*māṣaka*, half *māṣaka*, *kākani* (one-quarter *māṣaka*), and half *kākani* (one-eighth *māṣaka*).

The commentator notes that *rūpyarūpa* is the same as *karṣapaṇa* and that *pādajīvam tāmrarūpam* means 'made up of four parts of silver, eleven parts of copper, and one part of *tīkṣṇa* or any other metal'.

'Having described coins received into the treasury (*kośa-praveśya*),' Bhaṭṭasvāmin says, 'the author goes on to describe coins of general currency (*vyavahārika*).'

If Bhaṭṭasvāmin's commentary is right, two kinds of coin were minted, viz. (1) *rūpyarūpa*, of an alloy mainly composed of silver, (2) *tāmrarūpa*, of an alloy mainly composed of copper—and the *rūpyarūpa* only were received in the public treasury. This passage may be compared with the following extract from Rapson's *Indian Coins*:

'The most ancient coinage of India, which seems to have been developed independently of any foreign influence, follows the native system of weights, as given in Manu VIII, 132 ff. The basis of this system is the *rati* (*raktika*) or *guñja* berry, the weight of which is estimated at 1·83 grains or 0·118 grammes. Of the gold standard coin, the *suvarṇa* of 80 *ratis* = 146·4 grains or 9·48 grammes, no specimens are known, but of the silver *purāṇa* or *dharaṇa* of 32 *ratis* = 58·56 grammes, or 3·79 grammes, and of the copper *karṣa-paṇā* of 80 *ratis* (same weight as the *suvarṇa*), and of various multiples and subdivisions of them, numerous examples have been discovered in almost every part of India. . . .

The shape of these coins is approximately square or oblong, the silver coins having been, as a rule, cut from a flat sheet of metal, and the copper coins from a bar. These primitive coins are little more than weights of metal, on which was stamped, from time to time, the symbol of the authority responsible for their correctness and purity.'

It will be noticed that, in the *Arthaśāstra*, there is no mention of the minting of gold coins by the *Lakṣaṇādhyakṣa*. The table of weights given is as follows:

10 *māṣa*-seeds or 5 *guñja*-seeds = 1 *suvarṇa māṣa*, 16 *māṣas* = 1 *suvarṇa* or *karṣa*, 4 *karṣas* = 1 *pala*.

88 white mustard seeds (*gaurasarṣapa*) = 1 *rūpya māṣa*.

16 *rūpya māṣas* or 20 *śaibya* seeds = 1 *dharaṇa*.

The commentator's note on *rūpyarūpa*, that it is 'the same as *karṣapaṇa*', would apparently mean that the *paṇa* coin of that alloy should have the same weight as the *suvarṇa* or *karṣapaṇa*, namely, 16 *suvarṇa māṣas* = 80 *ratis* or *guñja* seeds = 160 *māṣa* seeds.

In the Jātaka and other early Buddhist literature, the coin

most often referred to is the *kahapaṇa* (Sansk. *karṣapana*). Other instruments of exchange mentioned are the *nikkha* (Sansk. *niṣka*—originally a gold ornament), and the *suvaṇṇa* of gold, and the *kaṁsa, pāda māṣaka*, and *kākaṇika* of bronze or copper.[1] An official called the *rūpadarśaka* is charged with the regulation of currency (*paṇayātra*). Certain mint charges are mentioned, viz. :

Rūpika, 8 per cent.—apparently a seignorage.

Vyājī, 5 per cent.—a device frequently mentioned for securing a profit on transactions between government and the public by the use of special weights or measures.

Pārīkṣika, $\frac{1}{8}$ per cent.—testing charge. There is also mention of a fine (*atyaya*) of 25 *paṇas*, 'except in the case of the maker, the buyer, the seller, and the examiner', but the meaning is not clear.

The next official mentioned is the *khaṇyadhyakṣa*, who looks after the collection of conch-shells, pearls, and coral, the working of diamonds and other precious stones, the manufacture of salt, and commerce in such articles. His title, also, would mean, literally, 'superintendent of mines', and Mr. Shamasastry translates it 'superintendent of ocean-mines'. His duties are concerned with articles obtained from the sea, but he is entrusted also with the working of diamonds and other precious stones, apparently because they are grouped with pearls.

Salt. Salt manufacture is supervised by a special officer, the *Lavaṇādhyakṣa*, and carried on, it seems, under a system of licences, on payment of a fixed fee, or a share of the output, the salt received by government as its share being sold by the superintendent. In these government sales of salt, it is said, the *vyājī* of 5 per cent. should be realized through the difference between the royal measure and the measure generally used—in other words, the actual price charged to the public was 5 per cent. more than the nominal price.

[1] Cf. *Cambridge History of India*, vol. i, chap. viii : 'Economic conditions according to early Buddhist Literature', by Mrs. C. F. Rhys Davids, M.A., D.Lit., Fellow of University College, London.

Of all imported salt one-sixth is to be made over to the king, and this royal share of imported salt is also to be sold by the superintendent. In respect of it he is to realize a *vyājī* of 5 per cent., both when measuring the share—in other words, he is to take 5 per cent. more than one-sixth—and when selling the salt, the price realized for which should cover the *vyājī*, a premium (*rupika*) of 8 per cent., the toll (*śulka*), and an amount calculated as covering the loss which the king's revenue would otherwise sustain through the use of imported instead of home-made salt.

Gold and silver.

Working in gold and silver is under the supervision of the *suvarṇādhyakṣa*, who holds his office in a building called the *akṣaśāla*. This word is explained by the commentator, Bhaṭṭasvāmin, as meaning ' the place where superior work in gold, silver, &c., is carried on '. It is laid down that the *suvarṇādhyakṣa* shall establish a goldsmith (*suvarṇika*) of good family and honest character on the high road (*visikhāmadhye*). Apparently the intention is that the finer kinds of gold- and silversmiths' work should be carried out in royal factories, while ordinary goldsmiths' shops, where the business of making or converting common gold and silver ornaments would be carried on, should be established under royal sanction or licence in the streets of towns and in the villages. It was doubtless thought important that such licences should be given to men of good character only, on account of the opportunities for fraud which the business affords.

The chapter on the work of the *suvarṇādhyakṣa* in the *akṣaśāla* contains instructions on the methods of testing and recognizing different qualities of gold, processes of manufacture of gold and silver articles and setting of jewels, and elaborate precautions against fraud and theft by workmen in the factory.

The next chapter, which deals with the work of the ' goldsmith on the high road ' (*viśikhāyām sauvarṇikapracāraḥ*), is not very clear. It lays down that the goldsmith shall employ artisans to work up the gold and silver of town and country people. He is to return the same quality and weight as what he receives, but there is a rule that the loss (*kṣaya*) on a *suvarṇa* is one *kākaṇi*, which apparently means that a loss of weight in manufacture of one *kākaṇi* (one-fourth of a *māṣa*) for every *suvarṇa* of 16 *māṣas*, or one-sixty-fourth may be allowed. There is, finally, an elaborate account of frauds, which may be committed in goldsmith's work.

The storehouse.

The chapter on the superintendent of the storehouse (*koṣṭhāgārādhyakṣa*) makes him responsible for agricultural produce of Crown lands (*sītā*) and that which is received in payment of taxes and government dues of different kinds, as well as for salt received through the *lavaṇādhyakṣa*. It is laid down that, of the store received under these heads, half shall be kept in reserve for public calamities, and half used. From other passages it appears that the use contemplated is in allowances for the maintenance of the royal family, servants, and dependents, as well as in sale and barter.

The chapter contains a classified catalogue of agricultural products, other than grains, which are dealt with in another chapter, under the head *sītādhyakṣa*, and salt.

It is not possible to discuss this list in detail here, but a few examples will give an idea of its arrangement.

Under the heading *sneha* (oil and grease) are included *sarpis* (clarified butter, ' ghee '), oil, animal fat, and marrow : under the heading *kṣāra*, the following forms of sugar—*phāṇitā*, *guḍa*, *matsyaṇḍika*, *akhaṇḍa*, *śarkara*.

The ' pungent ' class (*tiktavarga*) includes long pepper (*pippalī*), black pepper (*marīca*), ginger (*śṛngibera*), cummin-seed (*ajājī*), *kirātatikta* (chirayta), white mustard (*gaura-sarṣapa*), coriander (*kustumburu*), *damanaka* (*artemisia indica*), *maruvaka* (*vangueria spinosa*), *sigru* (*hyperanthera moringa*).

The following descriptions of salt are enumerated : *saindhava*, *sāmudra* (sea-salt), *biḍa*, *yavakṣāra*, *sauvarcala udbhedaja*. There are calculations of the amounts of food obtainable from given quantities of grain of different kinds cooked or treated in various ways, of oil that can be pressed from the different oil-seeds, and of thread that can be spun from given quantities of cotton and *kṣauma* (flax or jute) fibre. Rations are laid down for different classes of men, women, and children, and animals other than horses and elephants (to be dealt with in the special chapters devoted to them). The utensils and appliances to be kept in the storehouse are enumerated.

Royal trade.

The *paṇyādhyakṣa* seems to have been chiefly concerned with the trade in various articles which the king himself carried on,[1] as explained above, and his business was to see that this trade proved profitable to the government. How he was to do this is described in a few terse sentences, though the precise meaning of some of the terms used is uncertain. Mr. Shamasastry translates :

'The superintendent of commerce shall ascertain demand or absence of demand for, and rise or fall in the price of various kinds of merchandise, which may be the products of either land or water, and which may have been brought in by land or by water path. He shall also ascertain the time suitable for their distribution, centralization (*vikṣepasaṁkṣepa*), purchase, and sale. That merchandise which is widely distributed (*pracuram*) shall be centralized, and its price enhanced (*ekīkṛtyārghamāropayet*). When the enhanced rate becomes popular (*prāpterghe*), another rate shall be declared. That merchandise of the king which is of local manufacture shall be centralized (*ekamukham vyavahāram sthāpayet*) ; imported merchandise shall be distributed in several markets (*anekamukhamukham*).'

Apparently the superintendent was to enhance the price of the king's merchandise by restricting sales, when this could be done profitably. At the same time, he was not to aim at an excessive profit. It is laid down that both local and imported merchandise should be sold at a rate favourable to the people (*prajānām anugraheṇa*), and the superintendent should avoid an oppressive (*aupaghātikam*) profit. The sale of articles, for which there is frequent demand, should not be hampered by restrictions of time and place.

[1] Private trade was supervized by another official, the *saṁsthādhyakṣa*, discussed in a later chapter, cf. p. 112.

An alternative method indicated for disposing of the king's merchandise is to have it sold at a fixed price by private traders in many markets (*bahumukham*). In that case, the traders should pay a compensation (*vaidharaṇa*). Apparently a licence fee was charged to the traders under the name of compensation for the loss which the king sustained by not trading direct. It is next laid down that the *vyājī* on commodities sold by measure is one-sixteenth, on those sold by weight one-twentieth, and on those sold by number one-eleventh. This *vyājī* was an exaction made or attempted in sales and purchases on behalf of the king, by the device of using measures and weights different from those in common use, or by over- or undercounting goods sold by number, as the case might be. The superintendent should show favour to foreign merchants, and grant them such remissions as may enable them to make a profit. The commentator's note on this passage indicates that favour should be shown to the merchants by protecting them from oppression by frontier and provincial officials, and by exemption from *vyājī*. The chapter concludes with instructions for pushing export of the king's merchandise to foreign countries.

Forest produce. The chapter on the superintendent of forest produce (*kupyādhyakṣa*) prescribes that he shall collect timber and other products of forests, establish factories for working them up, and fix the fines to be levied for damage to productive forests (*dravyavana*) except in case of calamity. In those days as now, it seems, forest regulations were relaxed in times of scarcity and famine. There follows an exhaustive list of forest products. It includes timbers and bamboos of different kinds, canes and other creepers, barks and fibres, leaves and flowers, medicinal roots and fruits, hides and skins, bones, sinews, teeth, horns, hoofs, and tails of various animals, utensils of cane, bark, and clay, charcoal, ashes, firewood, and fodder, wild beasts and birds for menageries. Certain metals—iron, tin, lead, copper, &c.—already mentioned under the head of mines, are also, oddly, included here.

The armoury. The superintendent of the armoury (*āyudhāgārādhyakṣa*) is required to employ experienced and competent workmen in manufacturing, in accordance with regulations as to time, wages, and output, wheels, weapons, armour, and other appliances for use in battle (*sāngrāmika*), in connexion with forts (*daurgamika*), or in destroying an enemy's defences (*parapurābhighātika*). There are instructions for the arrangement and care of such military equipment, followed by a long and interesting list of war engines and weapons, of which a few examples, with the commentator's explanations, must suffice.

Sarvatobhadra: a cart with wheels capable of rapid revolution, which, when rotated, throws stones in all directions. Some call it *bhumarikayantra*.

Bahumukha: a tower situated on the top of a fort, provided with a leather cover, and facing all directions. From this place a number of archers direct their arrows.

Viśvāsaghāti: a cross-beam above a ditch at the entrance of a fort and so placed as to be caused to fall down and kill enemies when approaching.

The above are classed as fixed engines (*sthirayantra*).

Among movable engines (*calayantra*) we find the following:

Pāñcālika: a big wooden board with sharp points on its surface. This is put in the midst of water outside the fort wall to arrest the onward march of an enemy.

Devadaṇḍa: a long pole with iron nails attached to it, placed on the top of a fort wall.

Sūkarika: a leather cover or bag filled with cotton or wool to protect the towers, roads, &c., against stones thrown by enemies. Some say that it is a bamboo mat covered with leather (Com.).

Eleven descriptions of weapons, including *sakti*, a metallic weapon four hands long, like the leaf of a *karavira*, and provided with a handle; *prāsa*, a weapon 24 *angulas* long with two handles; *varāhakarṇa*, a rod with edges shaped like a boar's ear, are comprised in a class called *hulamukhāni*. Bows made of *tāla* palm, *chapa* (a kind of bamboo), *dāru*-wood, and horn, are called *kārmuka*, *kodaṇḍa*, *drūṇa*, and *dhanu*, respectively. *Nistriṁśa*, *maṇḍalāgra*, and *asiyaṣṭi* are varieties of swords. Swordhilts are made of horn, ivory, wood, and bamboo-root.

The class of razor-like weapons (*kṣūrakalpa*) includes various kinds of battle-axes, and also the disk (*cakra*).

Jālika, a coat covering the whole body, *paṭṭa*, an armless coat, *kavaca*, a coat made of detached pieces, to cover the head, trunk, and arms, and *sūtraka*, covering the hips and waist only, are varieties of armour (*varma*) made of chain-mail, or of hides, hoofs, and horns of porpoise, rhinoceros, bison, elephant, or cow. Other pieces of armour and shields of different kinds are included in the class *āvarāṇi*.

VI

THE *KAUṬILĪYA ARTHAŚĀSTRA*

DUTIES OF SUPERINTENDENTS (*continued*)

Weights and measures of capacity.

THE superintendent of weights and measures of capacity (*pautavādhyakṣa*) is charged with the preparation of standard weights and measures, of which tables are given, and the stamping of those used by private parties, for which a fee was charged. Weights, it is said, should be made of iron, of stones from Magadha and Mekala, and of substances not affected by moisture or heat. There are also directions for the making of balances and scales.

Measures of space and time.

The *mānādhyakṣa* is required to have a knowledge of the measurement of space and time (*deśakālamāna*). Tables of linear and square measure and measures of time are given. It may be presumed that the *mānādhyakṣa* was responsible for standards of linear measure and for the calendar.

Śulka.

An important part of the king's revenue is derived from tolls on sales of goods, called *śulka*, the collection of which is in charge of the *śulkādhyakṣa*. From the fact that, in the classification of the duties of the collector-general (*samāhartṛ*), *śulka* is placed under the head *durga*, it may be inferred that it was levied on goods sold in the cities, and it may also, from the context, be assumed to have applied to wholesale, not retail transactions. It is an *ad valorem* duty levied in the city, and calculated on the price for which goods are sold there. To facilitate collection and prevent evasion, it is laid down that sales of goods shall be made at an appointed place, and that 'commodities shall never be sold where they are grown or manufactured (*jātibhūmiṣu paṇyānām avikrayaḥ*)'. Probably the latter rule referred to rural produce brought into the city. It can hardly have applied to all sales throughout the country. Goods are classified as *bāhya*, brought into the city from the country, *abhyantara*, produced in the city, and *ātithya*, imported from abroad.

Rates of *śulka*.

The rules as to rates of *śulka* toll are not quite clear. A general rule—*niskrāmyam praveśyam ca śulkam*—appears to mean that goods exported and imported are liable to toll, or to indicate some difference between rates of duty on imported and exported goods. Another rule appears to subject all imported (*praveśya*) goods to a uniform toll of one-fifth of their value: it is not clear, however, whether *praveśya* had the same meaning as *ātithya*. *Śulka* is levied also on sales of immovable property, as will be seen.[1]

Besides the *śulka* toll, imported goods are liable to a transit due (*vartanī*) levied by the *antapāla* (frontier guard, or warden of the marshes), viz. $1\frac{1}{4}$ *paṇa* for each cart-load of merchandise, 1 *paṇa* for each single-hoofed animal (i. e. horses, mules, asses), $\frac{1}{2}$ *paṇa* for each head of cattle, $\frac{1}{4}$ *paṇa* for every minor quadruped, and one *māṣa* for every head-load of merchandise. The *antapāla* is required to examine the quality of all imported goods, and stamp them with his seal (*mudra*). The following *ad valorem* scale of *śulka* is laid down:

One-sixth flowers, fruit, vegetables, roots (*mūla, kanda*), seeds, dried fish, and meat.

One-tenth or one-fifteenth fabrics of *kṣauma* (flax or jute ?) *dukūla* (cotton ?), and silk, mail armour, arsenic (*haritāla, manaśśilā*), vermilion (*hiṅgulaka*), metals, colouring ingredients, sandal-wood, *agaru* wood, pungent substances, ferments, pieces of armour (*āvaraṇa*), raw *kṣauma*, raw *dukūla*, carpets, curtains, raw silk, wool, and goat's hair.

One-twentieth or one-twenty-fifth bipeds and quadrupeds, cotton thread, perfumes, drugs, timber, bamboos, bark, hides, pottery, grain, oil, sugar, salt, intoxicating liquor, cooked rice, and the like. Conch-shells, diamonds, precious stones, pearls, and coral to be specially assessed by experts.

A gate due or octroi (*dvāradeya*) of one-fifth of the *śulka*

[1] Cf. p. 101. The term *śulka* is used also for bride-price, cf. p. 92.

appears to have been levied on articles brought into the city. This might be remitted in special cases. The rules on the subject lay down that the *śulkādyakṣa* shall erect the toll-house flag near the chief gate of the city, and that when merchants arrive in caravans (*sārthopayāta*), four or five toll-collectors (*śulkādāyin*) shall write down their names, whence they come, what goods they have brought, and where the goods have been stamped or sealed (*abhijñānamudrakṛta*). This rule evidently refers to goods brought into the city by merchants from the country or from abroad. Goods imported by land from beyond the frontiers are to be stamped by the *antapāla* with his seal, as already mentioned. Where or by whom other goods brought into the city were stamped does not appear.

Collection of *śulka*.

The rules prescribe that those whose merchandise has not been stamped shall pay twice the amount of toll: for using counterfeit stamps the penalty is a fine of eight times the toll. If the stamp has been effaced, the merchant should be required to stand in the *ghatikāsthāna*, which, the commentator explains, was a room where people were confined for walking in streets or roads at improper hours. He adds that, as an alternative penalty, they might be made to wait for a day in the toll-house.

The goods having been placed near the toll-house flag, the merchants must offer them for sale by proclamation, thus: 'Who will purchase this quantity of merchandise for this price?' If the price be enhanced owing to competition among purchasers, the amount by which the price paid exceeds that at which the goods were offered must be paid to the king's treasury, together with the toll. On the other hand, if, to avoid this risk, the merchant should price his goods too high, the amount of excess in the price is equally to be appropriated by the treasury. Again, if the quantity or price of the goods be understated, in order to evade payment of toll (even though the price be not raised by competition), the merchant concerned must pay to the king the difference between the price stated and the proper price, or, as an alternative penalty, eight times the toll. The same punishment is to be imposed when the price of goods packed (in bags, &c.) is lowered by showing an inferior sample.

By such provisions, practically involving a regulation of wholesale prices, was the *śulka* revenue protected.

Tolls should be remitted on goods intended for use at weddings, and certain other social and religious ceremonies. Persons making false representations in order to obtain such remissions should be punished as thieves. Acts of smuggling are punishable by fine. For purchasing minerals from mines a fine of 600 *paṇas* is to be imposed. For purchasing flowers, or fruit, or vegetables from gardens, and grass or grain from fields, fines varying from 52 to 54 *paṇas* are prescribed, presumably, where the goods are brought into the city after purchase. There appears to have been, also, a fixed fine or tax (*atyaya*) on purchases of agricultural produce of one *paṇa* on the purchaser and a *paṇa* and a half on the seller.

Spinning and weaving.

The royal factories, in which spinning, weaving, and manufacture of clothing, as well as of mail armour and ropes are carried on, are in charge of an officer called the *sūtrādhyakṣa*. In these factories, women of the lower classes, including widows, cripples, girls who have not been able to find husbands, religious mendicants (*pravrajita*), convicts, old courtesans,[1] and female slaves of the king (*rājādāsi*) and temple-slaves (*devadāsi*) who have completed their term of service should be employed, chiefly, it appears, in spinning. Spinning is also to be given out to women of a more respectable class, to be done at their own homes. A *sutrādhyakṣa* who looks at the face of any such woman, or speaks to her about any subject except her work, is liable to fine. Wages are paid by regulation, according to the quantity and quality of work, and the time occupied, and there are allusions to special rewards or prizes in addition to wages. Thus, spinners may be given presents of oil, and an ointment made of myrabolams, which the commentator notes was

[1] *rūpājivāmātṛkā*, translated by Shamasastry as 'mothers of prostitutes', which is the literal meaning, but the term seems to have been applied to all elderly women of the *ganikā* or *rūpājivā* class, who were relegated to menial or manual work (cf. p. 70). For the meaning of *rājādāsi*, cf. p. 70.

a balm to keep the head and eyes cool, and an inducement to others to work in earnest'. Weavers, who make cloth of *kṣauma* (flax or jute ?), *dukūla* (fine cotton ?), silk, *rānkava* (the hair of a kind of antelope), are to be rewarded with presents such as perfumes and garlands. There is also mention of special remuneration (*prativāpadānāmāna*) for working on holidays (*tithi*).

Cultivation of Crown lands.

The *sītādhyakṣa* is concerned with the management and cultivation of Crown lands. Such lands may be cultivated by means of free hired labour or by slaves or convicts, or, if this is not convenient, by persons paying one-half of the produce (*ardhasītika*). Independent cultivators (*svavīryopajīvin*), it is said, should pay one-fourth or one-fifth, or whatever amount they can without hardship. Apparently, those who paid half the produce were provided with plough-cattle, seed, or implements by the *sītādhyakṣa*, and tenants providing their own plough-cattle, &c., were charged a lower rent.

The following shares of produce payable as water-rate or irrigation-tax (*udakabhāga*) are laid down :

hastaprāvartima—when the water has to be raised by manual labour—one-fifth ;

skandhaprāvartima—when the water is raised by water-lifts worked by bullocks—one-fourth ;

srotoyantraprāvartima—when the water is supplied by irrigation-channels (*kulya*—Com.)—one-third ;

nadīsarastatākakūpodghata—when the water is supplied by rivers, lakes, ponds, or wells—one-fourth.

It is not clear whether these shares were payable as water-rate in addition to rent, but it seems more probable that they represent the higher rent payable on land which enjoyed a perennial water-supply, as distinguished from that which was wholly dependent on rainfall (*devamātṛka*). Instructions are given as to the collection of seeds, treatment of seed before sowing, seasons for sowing, selection of land for different crops, storage of crops after harvest, and rainfall.

The germination of seeds (*vījasiddhi*) may be forecasted, it is said, from the appearance of the sun, the formation of grain (*stambakaritā*) from the planet Jupiter (*vṛhaspati*), and the rainfall from the movements of Venus (*Sukra*).

Intoxicating liquor. The manufacture of intoxicating liquor, which was controlled by the *surādhyakṣa*, seems to have been carried on by state agency in royal breweries or distilleries, and also by private persons under licence. There is a rule that those who deal in liquor other than that of the king shall pay a toll (*śulka*) of five per cent., and a verse which says that, having ascertained the daily sale of different kinds of liquor, and the *vyājī* from the difference between royal and public measures, the *surādhyakṣa* shall fix the proper amount of compensation (*vaidharaṇa*). This word appears to have been used generally in the sense of a tax realized from dealers in articles sold by the government, by way of compensation for the loss caused to the State trade by private competition. By other rules families may be allowed on certain occasions to manufacture white liquor (*śvetasura*), *ariṣṭa* in case of sickness, and other kinds of liquor. On the occasions of festivals, fairs, and pilgrimages, licences to make liquor for four days were given, on payment of a daily fine or fee (*daivasikamatyayam*).

Generally speaking, the rules on this subject seem to have been designed, as in a modern state, to raise revenue, and at the same time check intemperance and prevent disorders. Thus it is laid down that liquor shops shall not be close one to another, not more than a certain quantity of liquor shall be sold to one customer at a time, and only persons of approved character shall be allowed to take liquor away from the shop. Liquor shops shall have several rooms provided with couches and seats, and shall be provided with perfumes, garlands of flowers, and other attractions appropriate to the season. Spies are to be employed in them for the detection of criminals. Instructions are given for the preparation of different kinds of liquor.

Slaughter-houses. Slaughter-houses are under the supervision of an official called the *sūnādhyakṣa*.

There is a general rule prohibiting, subject to penalty.

the slaughter or capture of (1) any animal declared to be under State protection (*pradiṣṭābhaya*), (2) any animal living in a 'sanctuary-forest' (*abhayavana*). (*Abhayavana* forests seem to have been the same as the forests for brahmans referred to in the chapter on *Bhūmicchidravidhāna*, which, it will be remembered, were '*pradiṣṭābhaya*'.)[1]

Householders (*kuṭumbin*) trespassing in an *abhayavana* are liable to fine, and there is a rule that one-sixth of all animals (presumably harmless ones) caught alive should be let loose in such forests. Another rule lays down that one-sixth of all beasts of prey, and one-tenth or more (but less than one-sixth?) of other beasts, birds, and fish captured shall be made over to the *sūnādhyakṣa* as toll (*śulka*). The animals referred to as *pradiṣṭābhaya* were evidently animals protected by special decree, the slaying or capture of which was punishable with a fine of from 500 to 1,000 *paṇas* (the *uttamasāhasadaṇḍa*, or 'highest amercement' of the penal code, to be noticed later).[2]

A list of animals is given, the molestation of which in any way is prohibited, subject to the 'first amercement' (*pūrvasāhasadaṇḍa*), or a fine of from 48 to 96 *paṇas*. The first items in the list are unintelligible, perhaps owing to corruption of the text. They appear to represent certain kinds of fish and other aquatic animals, and are followed by birds: *krauñca* (a kind of heron, *ardea jaculator*), *utkrośaka* (osprey), *dātyūha* (*gallinula madraspatana*), *haṁsa* (wild goose or swan), *cakravāka* (ruddy goose or 'brahmany duck'), *jīvañjīvaka* (pheasant), *bhṛngarāja* (*Lanius Malabaricus*), *cakora* (red-legged partridge), *mattakokila* (a kind of cuckoo), peacock, parrot, *maina* (*Gracula religiosa*). The list concludes with the general description, 'all auspicious (*maṅgalya*) birds and beasts'. It is not known what they were.

Then there is a rule that calves, bulls, and cows are not to be killed, disobedience of which is punishable with a fine of 50 *paṇas*. There was evidently no general prohibition

[1] Cf. p. 42. [2] Cf. p. 98.

against the slaughter of oxen or eating beef. This is made more clear in the chapter on the superintendent of cattle,[1] and it is curious that the penalty for killing a cow is less than the maximum penalty for killing several other protected animals.

There is a rule making liable to a fine of 26¾ *paṇas* a person who traps, kills, or injures any bird or fish, and to a fine of double the amount any person killing, trapping, or molesting any deer or other beast, which does not prey on living creatures (*apravṛttabadha*). This evidently applied to wild animals.

Courtesans. The chapter on the *gaṇikādhyakṣa* begins by laying down that he shall engage a girl endowed with beauty, youth, and accomplishments, of *gaṇikā* origin (*gaṇikānvayā*) or otherwise, as *gaṇikā* on a salary of 1,000 *paṇas* a year, or as *pratigaṇikā* (apparently a *gaṇikā* of lower rank) on half that amount.

Another rule lays down that the *gaṇikās* employed in holding the king's umbrella, golden pitcher, and fan, and in attendance on the royal litter, throne, and chariot, shall be graded as of lowest, middle, and highest rank, according to their quality, and shall have salaries and adornment corresponding to their grade. It is also laid down that the *gaṇikādhyakṣa* shall provide masters to teach *gaṇikās*, female slaves, and actresses, music and singing, dancing, acting, reading, writing, painting, thought-reading, the making of perfumes and garlands, massage, and the arts of fascination. On the death of a *gaṇikā*, her daughter or sister, or a girl adopted by her mother, may succeed to her salary and property ; in the absence of such a successor, her property goes to the king. (The commentator notes that a *gaṇikā's* son does not inherit her property.) Sons of *gaṇikās* are to be brought up as actors. When a *gaṇikā* grows old, and loses her looks, she becomes a *mātṛkā* (' mother '). Another rule says that a *gaṇikā* and a female slave, when incapable of giving enjoyment (*bhagnabhogā*), shall work in the storehouse or kitchen.

[1] Cf. p. 73.

A *gaṇikā* shall pay 24,000 *paṇas*, and a *gaṇikā's* son 12,000 to obtain liberty (*niṣkraya*).

A *gaṇikā* living away from the king's court, under the protection of a private person, shall pay a *paṇa* and a quarter per mensem to the king.

A *rūpājīvā* shall pay each month twice the amount of a day's earnings to the king.

A *gaṇikā* who does not yield her person to a man according to the king's order shall receive 1,000 lashes with a whip or pay a fine of 5,000 *paṇas*.

A *gaṇikā* who murders her paramour is to be burned alive or drowned.

Cheating of her paramour by a *gaṇikā*, or vice versa, is punishable with fine. A *gaṇikā* is to supply information about her fees and income and her paramour.

From the above rules it would appear that the term *gaṇikā* was applied to courtesans of the palace as well as those outside, and that all were under the control of the *gaṇikādhyakṣa*. It is not clear whether he was concerned with *devadāsīs* (female slaves attached to temples).

Palace *gaṇikās*.

As regards the palace *gaṇikās*, it appears that some were educated and accomplished women, while others were employed in various menial offices about the king's person, but all were alike slaves. On the other hand, it is not clear whether all the female slaves of the palace were classed as *gaṇikās*. In a later chapter, which deals with the law relating to slaves,[1] there are rules which imply that the master of a female slave had no sexual rights over her. It is laid down that violation of the chastity of a female slave by her master entitles her to liberty, and that if a female slave have a son by her master she must be set free with her child. It appears that the *gaṇikā's* person, on the other hand, was, in theory at any rate, absolutely at the king's disposal. Probably there were among *gaṇikās* and female slaves different degrees of status to which various social conventions and legal rules, of which we are ignorant, attached, but in some of its rules, as we have seen, the *Arthaśāstra* groups together

[1] Bk. III, ch. xiii.

gaṇikās and all female slaves of the palace, including actresses, dancers, musicians, and other artists, and educated women corresponding to the Greek *hetairai*, placing all under the control of the *Gaṇikādhyakṣa.*

Outside *gaṇikās.* On the status of *gaṇikās* outside the palace some light is thrown by a rule in a later chapter to the effect that a woman resorting to prostitution [1] shall become the king's slave (*rājadāsyam gacchet*). The theory that all courtesans were slaves of the State, was, perhaps, a convenient legal fiction, which gave the government control over women of this class, and enabled it to use them for purposes of espionage and obtain a revenue from them. Whether the *rūpājīvās* were a particular class of *gaṇikā*, or the two terms are equivalent, is not clear.

The *mātṛka.* When a *gaṇikā* grew old, she was called a *mātṛka* ('mother') probably because then, as now, in India, superannuated courtesans were supported by daughters, natural or adoptive, whom they brought up to follow the same calling. If an old *gaṇikā* had no such means of support, she would be employed in a royal spinning and weaving factory,[2] or in the palace kitchen, storehouse, &c.

Succession to *gaṇikās'* property. The rule regarding succession to a *gaṇikā's* property on her death is different from that which applies to the property of other slaves. In the chapter on slaves it is laid down that, on the death of a slave, his property passes to his kinsmen; in the absence of any kinsmen to his master. On the death of a *gaṇikā*, only her daughter (natural or adoptive), or sister, or a girl adopted by her mother—in either case, presumably, a *gaṇikā*—can succeed to her property; in the absence of such a successor, the property passes to the Crown. This rule probably applied to *gaṇikās* outside the palace as well as to those on the royal establishment. To this day, in Bengal, property left by prostitutes is often escheated for want of a claimant, because no respectable person wishes to acknowledge relationship to a prostitute or succeed to her earnings.

[1] This seems to be the meaning of *svayaṁ prakṛtā* in Bk. IV, ch. xii.
[2] Cf. p. 64.

A *gaṇikā's* daughter would, ordinarily, follow her mother's profession. The *gaṇikā's* son, although, according to Bhaṭṭasvāmin, he could not succeed to his mother's property, inherited, it appears, her servile status, and was a royal slave, his ransom being fixed at 12,000 *paṇas*. Sons of *gaṇikās* were employed as actors (*raṅgopajīvī*), which term, we may assume, included dancers, musicians, &c. These rules are intelligible as applying to sons of palace *gaṇikās*. Outside the palace, possibly, sons of *gaṇikās* found salaried employment as actors, musicians, dancers, &c., the fiction that they were royal slaves being maintained to give the government control over them. A later chapter refers to the wages of hired musicians, buffoons, &c. *Gaṇikās'* children.

A *gaṇikā* who had not a daughter of her own might adopt a minor girl, obtained from necessitous parents, and bring her up as a *gaṇikā*. Girls thus adopted would presumably be reckoned as *gaṇikānvayā*. Outside the palace, a woman who was not *gaṇikānvayā* might become a *gaṇikā* by prostituting herself. The *gaṇikādhyakṣa*, it appears, recruited *gaṇikās* for the palace by voluntary engagement; perhaps also by acquisition, through purchase or gift, of girls from their relatives and of female slaves from private owners. Recruitment of *gaṇikās*.

VII

THE *KAUṬILĪYA ARTHAŚĀSTRA*

DUTIES OF SUPERINTENDENTS (*continued*)

Shipping. THE *nāvadhyakṣa* appears to have been concerned with all navigation by sea, river, and lake, including fishing and ferry boats.

From the chapter describing his duties it appears that there were royal ships (*rājānau*) on which passengers were carried on payment of passage-money (*yātrāvetana*), and others which were hired to private adventurers for the collection of conch-shells and pearls. It is laid down that such traders shall either pay ship-hire (*nauhātaka*) or use their own ships. Fishermen are to give a sixth of their catch as boat-hire (*naukahātaka*). Perhaps this was exacted from those who used government boats. Merchants are to pay a toll (*śulkabhāga*) as port-due (*paṭṭanānuvṛtta*).

The *nāvadhyakṣa* is required to maintain the customs of commercial ports (*paṇyapaṭṭanacāritra*) and the regulations of the port-superintendent (*paṭṭanādhyakṣanibandha*). The functions of the last-named officer are not stated. The *nāvadhyakṣa* is enjoined to 'show fatherly consideration' to vessels in distress, and to allow to pass on payment of half toll (*śulka*), or exempt altogether, merchandise damaged by water.

There are a number of ferry regulations. On large rivers not fordable even in the winter and hot seasons, large boats, properly equipped, shall be maintained, and smaller boats on rivers flowing in the rainy season only.

The ordinary rates of ferry toll are—for a small beast, or a man carrying a load, one *māṣa*; for a head-load,[1] a load carried on the shoulders, a cow, or a horse, two *māṣas*; for

[1] Another rule, however, seems to fix the toll for a head-load of merchandise at ¼ *māṣa*.

a camel or buffalo, four *māṣas*; for a light cart (*laghuyāna*), five *māṣas*; for a medium-sized buffalo cart (*goliṅga*), six *māṣas*; for a large cart (*śakaṭa*), seven *māṣas*. On large rivers these rates are doubled. Persons crossing rivers otherwise than at the appointed places and times are liable to fine, but several classes of people whose occupations require them to cross rivers without delay, such as fishermen, carriers of firewood, grass, flowers, fruit, and vegetables, messengers, and persons pursuing suspected criminals, are exempted from this rule. Brahmans, ascetics (*pravrajita*), children, aged and infirm persons, royal messengers, and pregnant women should be given ferry passes free of toll. Various categories of suspicious persons using the ferries are to be arrested.

The duties of the *go'dhyakṣa* are elaborately set forth under eight heads, which need not be repeated. He seems to have been concerned with the king's cattle, and also with private herds, which were placed under his charge for protection from cattle-lifters in return for a share of their dairy produce. Among the classes of cattle enumerated is that of *sūna*—beasts fit for slaughter, and there is a rule that cow-herds may sell meat either fresh or dried. Rules are also laid down for the grazing and stall-feeding of cattle, horses, mules, asses, and camels, and as to the milking of cows and the quantities of clarified butter to be obtained from a *droṇa* of milk of cows, buffaloes, goats, and ewes. Cattle.

The *aśvādhyakṣa* has charge of the royal stables, for the construction of which elaborate directions are given. Mention is made of officials and servants of different classes connected with the stables: *aśvavāha* (head groom ?), *sūta sūtragrāhaka* (charioteer), *aśvabandhaka* (tetherer), *yāvasika* (grass-supplier), *keśakara* (groom), *stānapāla* (watchman), *vidhāpācaka* (cook), *cikitsaka* (veterinary surgeon), *janga-līvid* (applier of remedies against poisons). There is a scale of rations for horses of different ages and sizes. The breeds of the countries of Kāmbhoja, Sindhu, Araṭṭa, and Vanāyu are said to be the best, those of Bāhlika, Pāpeya, Sauvira, and Taitala of middle quality, and other breeds ordinary or Horses.

inferior. Horses of these breeds may be trained for war, or for ordinary riding or driving, according as they are spirited (*tīkṣṇa*), quiet (*bhadra*), or sluggish (*manda*).

Under the head of training of horses, a bewildering variety of movements is given, falling under the five heads of *valgana* (circular movement), *nicairgata* (slow movement), *laṅghana* (jumping), *dhoraṇa* (gallop), and *nāroṣṭra* (movement by signal). Of circular movement six, and of slow movement sixteen different kinds are mentioned. The explanation of each of these movements is given by the commentator—in some cases, unfortunately, his explanation is not easily intelligible. Among circular movements we have *apaveṇuka*, turning in a circle of a cubit diameter; *ālīḍhapluta*, running and jumping simultaneously; *vrithāṭṭa*, movement of only the front portion of the body; *tṛvacāli*, movement of only the hind portion of the body.

Among slow movements: *niṣanna*, a movement in which the hind portion of the body is kept steady; *pārśvānuvṛtta*, movement sideways; *ūrmīmārga*, movement up and down like a wave. Jumping (*laṅghana*) includes jumping like a monkey (*kapipluta*), like a frog (*bhekapluta*), &c. Different kinds of gallops are likened to the movements of a vulture, a wild duck, a peacock, a mongoose, and a wild boar.

Elephants.

Seven different kinds of trot (*vikrama*) are also mentioned. The superintendent of elephants (*hastyadhyakṣa*) is required to take proper steps for the protection of elephant-forests (this was also the duty of the *nāgavanādhyakṣa*, previously mentioned in the chapter on *bhūmicchidravidhāna*),[1] and to supervise the elephant stables and the training of elephants. Among the establishments under his control we find mention of elephant-doctors (*cikitsaka*), trainers of war-elephants (*anīkastha*), riders or mahouts (*ārohaka*), cooks (*vidhāpācaka*), grass-suppliers (*yāvasika*), tetherers (*pādapāśika*), watchmen (*kuṭirakṣaka*), &c.

Rules are given for the construction of elephant stables, and times for feeding, bathing, rest, and exercise, with a scale of rations for elephants according to size and age.

[1] Cf. p. 42.

The training of elephants, it is said, falls under four heads—*damya* (breaking-in of wild elephants), *sānnahya* (training for war), *aupāvahya* (training for ordinary riding), *vyāla* (taming of rogue elephants).

Breaking-in (*damya*) is of five kinds—*skandhagata* (ridden), *stambhagata* (tied to a post), *vārigata* (taken to water), *avapātagata* (fallen into a pit), *yūthagata* (with the herd). These perhaps represent in reverse order the stages through which a newly caught elephant passes, i. e. (1) with the wild herd, (2) caught in a pit, (3) taken to water (between two tame elephants), (4) tethered to a post, (5) ridden.

Four kinds of military training are specified, viz. *upasthāna* ('such as rising, bending, and crossing fences and lines drawn'—Com.); *samvartana* [1] ('lying down, sitting, and crossing pits and lines drawn'—Com.); *samyāna* ('going straight and transverse, and making serpentine movements'—Com.); *vadhāvadha* ('trampling down the horses and chariots, and killing the infantry'—Com.); *hastiyuddha*, fighting with elephants; *nāgarayana*, assailing forts and cities; *sāṅgrāmika*, general fighting.

Eight classes of riding-elephants are specified by names, which appear to indicate the extent of training, but the meaning of which is doubtful.

The *rathādhyakṣa* has charge of the king's chariots, of which the following kinds are specified: *devaratha* (chariots of gods); *puṣyaratha* ('used on festive occasions, such as coronation, &c.'—Com.); *sāṅgrāmika* (war chariots); *pāriyānika* (travelling chariots); *parapurābhiyānika* (used in attacking forts, &c.); *vainayika* (training chariots). He has also to supervise the training of troops in fighting from chariots. Chariots.

The next official mentioned is the *pattyadhyakṣa*, or superintendent of infantry, who, it is said, should be acquainted with the strength and weakness of hereditary troops (*maula*), hired or mercenary troops (*bhṛta*), military corporations Infantry.

[1] The sounds 'butt', 'sumbutt' used by a mahout when directing an elephant to kneel, may be connected with this word.

(*śreṇī*), as well as of the armies of friendly and unfriendly foreign powers, and of wild tribes (*āṭavī*). He should also be familiar with the practices and exercises for fighting on low and high ground, open fighting, stratagem, trench-fighting, and fighting from heights, by day and by night.

The Army.

The hereditary troops (*maula*) seem to have been levies of men among whom the profession of fighting was hereditary, and who held land subject to military service, and the term *āyudhiyā* in the chapter on land revenue, to be discussed presently, may have reference to such land. These levies were probably very numerous, but imperfectly trained and equipped, and a parallel to them may be found in the great armies of *paiks* raised under the Moghals. The *bhṛta* soldiers, no doubt, were purely mercenaries, voluntarily engaging for pay—fewer in number, but better trained and provided.

The nature of the military corporations, here referred to by the description '*śreṇi*', commonly applied in literature to trade-guilds, is obscure. In the chapter headed *Saṅghavṛttam*, meaning 'Conduct' or 'Management of corporations', occurs the passage *Kāmbhojasurāṣṭrakṣatriyaśreṇyādayo vārtāśastropajīvinaḥ Licchivikavṛjikamallakamadrakakukurakurupāñcālādayo rājaśabdopajīvinaḥ*, which Mr. Shamasastry translates—' The corporations of warriors of Kāmbhoja and Surāstra, and other countries live by agriculture, trade, and wielding weapons. The corporations of Licchivika, Vṛjika, Mallaka, Madraka, Kurura, Kurū, Pāñcāla, and others live by the title of a Rāja.'

The names Kāmbhoja, Surāstra, Licchivika, &c., suggest that the passage has reference to populations or communities rather than guilds ; on the other hand, it is clear, from many other passages, that the words *śreṇī* and *saṅgha* in the *Arthaśāstra* both mean corporation or guild. In the same chapter, the word used for the head of a corporation is *saṅghamukhya*, while in the chapter on salaries the *śreṇīmukhyas* are grouped with the *mukhyas* of elephants, horses, and chariots, and allowed the same salary—8,000 *paṇas* per annum. Probably the military *śreṇīs* were special troops, composed of men of different fighting races who enlisted in the royal army under their own chiefs. They would be called *śreṇī* from analogy to trade-guilds, and, no doubt, served for pay, perhaps under a contract made between the king and the *śreṇīmukhya*. Dr. Otto Stein likens them to the Italian *condottieri*,[1] and parallels for them may be found in Indian states at different periods. The meaning of the expression, 'live by the title of a rāja', is not clear.[2]

In a later chapter, comparison is drawn between the three descriptions of army, the conclusions arrived at being that a *maula* force, from hereditary aptitude and loyalty, is better than a *bhṛta* force, and the latter, from being readily available and well disciplined, superior to a *śreṇi* force. In the same chapter, the following passages occur:

'That army, which is numerous, composed of men of various castes (*anekajātīyastha*), which is eager to set out, bidden or unbidden, without subsistence or pay, in the hope of plunder, which can protect itself against unfavourable weather (?), which can easily be disbanded (*bhedya*), but not easily dispersed by the enemy (*paresāmabhedya*), which is equal in excellence in respect of nationality, race, and training (*tulyadeśajātiśilpaprāya*), is a great and compact army.'

'Some teachers say that, of armies composed of brāhmans, kṣatriyas, vaiśyas, and śudras, the first is better than the second, the second than the third, and the third than the fourth, in regard to bravery. "No," says Kauṭilya, "the enemy may win over the army of Brahmans by submission and prostration (*pranipātena*). An army of kṣatriyas is to be preferred for their training and skill in the use of arms, or an army of vaiśyas or śudras for their great numbers."'

From these extracts it is clear that fighting was not the business of the *kṣatriya* caste only.

On the other hand, the following passage is found in another part of the *Arthaśāstra*:[3]

'Coming down from father and grandfather, constant, obedient, able to maintain their families in comfort, not discouraged by lengthy sojourns abroad, everywhere invincible, enduring hardships, experienced in many wars, and skilled in the use of all kinds of weapons, sharing loyally the king's

[1] *Megasthenes und Kauṭilya*, p. 155, note 1.
[2] Cf. p 156.
[3] Bk. VI, ch. i.

good and evil fortune, and composed solely of kṣatriyas (*kshātraprāyam*) is the best army.'

It seems that armies were collected for a campaign, and disbanded afterwards, and no doubt the *maula* troops were called out for such temporary service only, while some of the *bhṛta* and *śreṇī* troops were permanently entertained.

Pay of soldiers. In the chapter on salaries, the pay of trained foot soldiers (*śilpavantaḥ pādātāḥ*) is set down as 500 *paṇas* per annum.

Probably such pay was given only to the best trained of the *bhṛta* and *śreṇī* troops. It seems high, as compared with the salary of 1,000 *paṇas* a year allowed to *adhyakṣas* of civil departments, but the king is advised to recoup himself by the sale of provisions to the troops.

'When starting on an expedition the king should mobilize his army. Then his agents, in the disguise of merchants, should supply food to the soldiers at double price. Thus will there be sale of the royal wares, and recovery of the pay disbursed.'

It seems probable that the cavalry soldier received the same pay as the infantryman, with an additional allowance for the upkeep of his horse. The pay of the chariot-driver is fixed at 2,000 *paṇas*, and that of elephant-drivers at from 500 to 1,000 *paṇas* per annum, according to merit.

Army officers. The classes of military officers mentioned, and salaries allotted to them, are as follows :

Senapati . . .	48,000 *paṇas*
praśāstṛ	24,000 ,,
nāyaka	12,000 ,,
mukhya	8,000 ,,

adhyakṣas of infantry, cavalry, elephants, and horses 4,000 *paṇas* each.

Another passage lays down that every ten units of each *aṅga* should be under a *padika*, every ten *padikas* under a *senapati*, every ten *senapatis* under a *nāyaka*.

It thus appears that the term *senapati* was applied to the commander-in-chief, and also to officers of lower grade subordinate to the *nāyaka*. In some inscriptions the commander-in-chief is called *mahāsenapati*.

In the Arthaśāstra, the commander-in-chief belongs to the highest group of functionaries, drawing the same salary as the chief ecclesiastics, *ṛtvik*, *ācārya*, and *purohita*, and the chief minister, namely, 48,000 *paṇas* a year, the same amount being allowed to the heir-apparent (*yuvarāja*), the king's mother, and the chief queen (*rājamahiṣī*). The *senapati* is frequently mentioned in conjunction with the heir-apparent, and it is laid down that a prince endowed with good qualities should be installed as heir-apparent [1] or appointed as commander-in-chief. As Dr. Otto Stein has pointed out,[2] according to the *Arthaśāstra*, the *adhyakṣas* of infantry, cavalry, elephants, and chariots would be administrative officers charged with the recruitment and training of troops, the provision and training of horses and elephants, and the construction and upkeep of war chariots, while the duty of leading the troops in the field devolved on the other officers mentioned. It is laid down that infantry, cavalry, chariots, and elephants shall be exercised daily at sunrise, except on holidays, in the king's presence.

Ambulance.

From the following passage, in a description of the order in which an army should be drawn up for battle, it appears that the military organization included medical and ambulance departments:

'Physicians with surgical instruments and appliances and healing ointments and bandages (*sastrayantrāgadasnehavastrahastāḥ*), and women with food and drink should stand behind encouraging the fighting men.'

Passports.

Every person entering or leaving the country is required to have a passport (*mudrā*), the issue of which is entrusted to the *mudrādhyakṣa*.

Pastures.

The *vivītādhyakṣa* (superintendent of pastures), has charge of all desert or uncultivated common lands, other than those reserved as forests. He is required to preserve the boundaries of timber- and elephant-forests, to keep roads in repair, to arrest thieves and secure the safety of caravans of merchants, and to protect cattle.

[1] Bk. I, ch. xvii.

[2] *Megasthenes und Kauṭilya*, pp. 271–3.

In waterless tracts, wells and tanks, as well as shelters for travellers, and flower- and fruit-gardens should be provided.

Land revenue.

A chapter on the duties of the revenue-collector (*samāhartṛpracāra*) gives some idea of the land-revenue system. A country (*janapada*) should be divided into four parts or districts, and the villages classified as of first, second, and third class. They should also be distinguished according as they are *parihāraka* (wholly or partly exempt from taxation); or *āyudhīya* (villages which supply contingents of soldiers), or pay their revenue in money, or in grain, cattle, or other raw material, or in the form of labour on public works.

Village accountants.

For every five or ten villages there is a village-accountant (*gopa*), whose duty it is to keep the *cadastre*, numbering plots as cultivated and uncultivated, dry (*sthala*) and wet (*kedāra*) fields, gardens, woods, homesteads, shrines (*caitya*), temples (*devagṛha*), irrigation works, cremation grounds, charitable institutions (*sattraprapā*, i. e. places where food and drink was supplied free to travellers), places of pilgrimage, grazing grounds, and roads, and maintaining a record of boundaries of villages, fields, forests, and roads, of areas, of gifts and sales, and of tax-remissions. He is also to keep a record of the number of tax-paying and tax-free houses, of inhabitants of each village belonging to each of the four castes, of cultivators, cow-herds, traders, artisans, labourers, slaves, and domestic animals, and to assess money-taxes, labour in lieu of taxes, as well as tolls and fines. He is also to keep a record of families, of their history and occupations, income and expenditure.

Supervisors.

The work of these village-accountants appears to have been supervised by officers with the title of *sthānika*. It is said that a *sthānika* should look after (*cintayet*) one-fourth of the *janapada*. This word is commonly applied to the whole country or kingdom, but it seems to be used also in the sense of a province or district. The office of *sthānika* may have been connected with the *sthānīya* fort, which, as suggested above,[1] may have been the origin of the *thāna*. The *Artha-*

[1] *Supra*, p. 39

śāstra lays down that there should be a *sthanīya* for every 800 villages. As we have seen, *gopas* and *sthānikas* had allotments of land,[1] perhaps revenue-free, or on favourable terms. It does not appear that they received any other remuneration. Over the *gopas* and *sthānikas* are commissioners (*pradeṣṭṛ*), who, besides their duties of supervision, appear to have been entrusted specially with the collection of the religious tax known as *bali*. The pay of a *pradeṣṭṛ* is 8,000 *paṇas*.

The amount and rates of taxation levied on the land are not clearly stated, but with regard to them some indications may be found in different passages. The traditional royal share of the produce of cultivated lands was, as is well known, one-sixth, and this is alluded to in a passage already quoted.[2] From the chapter on the *sītādhyakṣa* [3] it would appear that on irrigated lands a share, varying from one-fifth to one-third of the produce (*udakabhāga*), was levied as water-rate, whether in addition to, or in lieu of, the general one sixth share is not clear, but most probably the latter. On the other hand, it is laid down in another chapter that on the construction of new irrigation works, such as tanks, tax shall be remitted for five years—for repairing ruined or neglected works of the kind, four years' remission shall be allowed, for improvements in them three years' remission. Assessment.

There is a chapter, entitled 'Replenishments of the Treasury', which sets forth additional taxes which may be imposed on land when the king is in special need of money. It illustrates what, no doubt, were from time immemorial the two main features of the Indian land-revenue system, namely, the fixed share of produce due to the king, and the varying additional demands, which were, ostensibly, intended to meet special and occasional necessities, but probably came to be exacted habitually to a greater or less extent. These two divisions of the land revenue came to be known under Muhammadan rule as the *asal* and the *abwāb*, respectively, and, as is well known in those parts of India where successors to the land-revenue collectors of the Additional taxes.

[1] *Supra*, p. 40. [2] Cf. p. 40. [3] Cf. p. 65.

Moghul government have come to be recognized as landlords, various cesses bearing the name of *abwāb*, though expressly prohibited by law, are still exacted from the cultivators—such is the force of ancient custom—in addition to the legal rent.

> 'The King', it is laid down, 'who is in straits for money, may make the following collections. In a country which depends solely on rain (*devamātṛka*) and is rich in grain, he may demand a one-third or a one-fourth share of the crop; but he should not make this demand from land of middle or low quality, not from people who render help in the construction of forts or other public buildings, or of gardens or roads, in reclaiming waste lands, or in the exploitation of mines or of timber or elephant forests, nor from frontier tracts.'

This passage apparently means that, in case of necessity, the king may assess the revenue of land dependent on rainfall at one-third or one-fourth of the crop—the rate prescribed for irrigated land—instead of the traditional one-sixth; but this extra demand is to be made only where the harvest has been good, and certain tracts and classes of people are exempt from it. There follows a somewhat obscure passage which apparently refers to extra crops sown by the cultivators in the summer-time, at the instance of the land-revenue collectors. The chapter continues:

> 'They (the revenue officials) may collect from the cultivators one-fourth of their grain and one-sixth of forest produce (*vanya*), silk-cotton, lac, *kṣauma* (flax or jute), bark, cotton, wool, silk, drugs, perfumes, flowers, fruit and vegetables, firewood, bamboos, and meat fresh or dried; and one-half of ivory and hides. . . . Fowls and pigs should pay half, small (*kṣudra*) beasts one-sixth, and cows, buffaloes, horses, mules, asses, and camels one-tenth. . . . In other cases, the collector-general may beg (*bhikṣeta*) money from people of town and country, representing that some work has to be carried out (*kāryamapadiśya*).'

To this day, *zemindars* in Bengal sometimes levy *abwābs* from their tenants under the names of *cāndā*, subscription, and *māngani* or *bhikṣa*, begging.

In the chapter on the superintendent of the Storehouse,

already referred to,[1] there is a list of the taxes levied in kind, and a brief, and unfortunately, not very lucid, explanation of each tax named has been given by the Commentator, Bhaṭṭasvāmin. They are:

Various land-taxes.

piṇḍakara—'taxes levied on whole villages' (Com.)—apparently a name given to assessment in a lump sum on the village;

ṣaḍbhāga—one-sixth share;

senābhakta—'such as oil, rice, salt, &c., which are to be supplied while the army is marching or preparing for expeditions' (Com.);

bali—religious tax—'such as taxes of ten *paṇas*, twenty *paṇas*, &c.' (Com.);

kara—'such taxes as are collected every year during the months of *Bhadrapada* and *Vasanta*' (Com.);

utsanga—taxes collected on the occasion of the birth of a prince;

pārśva—'Margin-tax'—perhaps, what the tax-payer can afford over and above what has been collected;

pārihīṇaka—tax on crops that are grown on uncultivated ground. In addition to the collection of land revenue, the Collector-general and his subordinates are responsible for police duties in rural areas, as appears from the chapters relating to police. Spies, under the guise of cultivators, are to be employed in checking the accounts and returns of the village-accountants, and their work generally.

Devices for raising money.

It will be convenient to notice here, before leaving the subject of land revenue, certain other devices for raising money in times of financial stringency, which are recommended in the *Arthaśāstra*.

It is suggested that advantage may be taken of the weaknesses of ostentation and ambition; thus:

'Persons acting in collusion shall publicly pay handsome donations, and, with this example, the king may make demands on his subjects. Spies passing as citizens shall revile those who pay less. Wealthy persons may be requested to give as much of their gold as they can. Those who for their own advantage, or spontaneously offer their wealth to

[1] Cf. p. 56.

their king, shall be honoured with precedence (*sthāna*), an umbrella, a turban, or some ornaments.'

In the modern state, it is sometimes alleged, money obtained by the sale of honours does not find its way into the public treasury. Covert or open spoliation of religious establishments seems to be inculcated :

'Spies, under the guise of overseers, shall abstract the property of a religious corporation (*pāṣaṇḍasaṅgha*), or institution other than property assigned for the maintenance of brahmans (*śrotriyabhogyam*), alleging that it is property of a dead man or of one whose house has been burnt, entrusted to their care. The superintendent of religious institutions (*devatādhyakṣa*), having collected the property of the local deities of towns and rural areas (*durgarāṣṭradevatānām*), shall carry it off to the treasury.'

Various devices are suggested for taking fraudulent advantage of religious or superstitious impulse :

'Having on some night set up an idol or a shrine (*caitya*) or holy place, money may be collected by holding religious processions or gatherings. Or the arrival of a god may be augured from flowers or fruit being produced out of season on a tree in a *caitya* grove. Spies under the guise of ascetics may obtain money by means of a man hidden in a tree who similates an evil spirit (by making noises), and causes terror to the people.'

Money may be collected by exhibiting a serpent with many heads in a well, or a cobra in a hole made in the image of a snake, or in a shrine, or in an ant-hill. Incredulous persons may be sprinkled with, or given to drink, water which is drugged, and told that the effects are due to a divine curse. Or, having caused an outlaw (*abhityakta*) to be bitten by a snake, money may be collected to avert the omen. Other forms of fraud, too, are shamelessly advocated.

'A secret agent, disguised as a merchant, may become partner in business of a rich man. When a sufficient sum has been collected as sale-proceeds of goods, deposits, and loans, the former may cause himself to be robbed. A secret agent in the guise of a merchant may borrow gold and silver from individuals or from corporations for investment in his business, and allow himself to be robbed at night.'

'Women assuming a respectable appearance may be employed to entrap seditious men, who may be arrested in the women's houses, and all their property confiscated. On a quarrel being brought about among members of disloyal families, poisoners may be engaged to give poison to members of one party, and the other party, being accused of the offence, may be deprived of their property.'

'A man of straw, under a guise which inspires confidence, may make a claim on a disloyal person for recovery of a deposit, or a debt, or a share of an inheritance, or he may pretend to be his slave; or claim the disloyal man's wife, daughter, or daughter-in-law as his female slave, or as his wife. Then an assassin may be employed to murder the claimant at night, when he is lying at the king's enemy's door, or on some other occasion, and the enemies of the king may be accused of the crime of murdering a man who was only claiming what belonged to him, and deprived of their property.'

Other ingenious schemes for procuring the condemnation and ruin of the king's enemies to the advantage of the king's treasury are indicated, and the chapter concludes with the injunction that such measures are to be adopted only against seditious and wicked persons, and not against others.

The city.

The City superintendent (*Nāgaraka*) is to look after the affairs of the capital, as the *samāharta* does for areas outside. In the City a *gopa* should supervise ten, twenty, or forty households. He should know the names, castes, and *gotras* of both men and women of these households, as well as their occupations, income, and expenditure.

Four *sthānikas* should be in charge, each of a fourth part of the town area.

Managers of charitable institutions for the accommodation of wayfarers (*dharmāvasathin*) shall report the arrival of *pāṣaṇḍas* (buddhist mendicants—Com.) and travellers, and shall be responsible for the character of professed ascetics and scholars (*śrotriya*) whom they lodge. Similarly, artisans and traders are responsible for persons of their respective callings, whom they allow to stay in the quarters assigned to them. Merchants are bound to report cases of irregular or dishonest trading which come to their notice. Sellers of liquor and cooked food and courtesans shall put up only people whom they know, and shall report any extravagance or evil conduct on the part of their hosts.

Generally, householders are made responsible for reporting crimes, and travellers for detaining persons of suspicious conduct or appearance.

Police regulations.

There are a number of police regulations for cities made in the interests of public safety and convenience.

Several of these relate to the prevention of fires. Apparently, during the hot season, between certain hours in the middle of the day, the kindling of fire indoors was prohibited, and persons were required to do their cooking out of doors.

Every householder is required to have in his possession appliances for putting out fires—certain water vessels, a leather water-bag (*dṛti*), a ladder, an axe, a winnowing tray (' to blow off smoke '—Com.), hooks and grapplers for pulling down burning thatch, &c. Persons using fire in their trade (*agnijīvin*, e.g. smiths) must live in a separate quarter of the town.

Thousands of water-vessels are to be kept arranged in rows, in good order, along the main-streets, at street-crossings, and in front of public buildings. Any owner-occupier of a house failing to help promptly in extinguishing a fire is liable to a fine of twelve *paṇas*, and the fine for similar failure on the part of a tenant is six *paṇas*. The punishment for setting fire to a house through negligence is a fine of 54 *paṇas*, for wilful arson, death by burning. Fines are also set down for throwing dirt or causing mud or water to collect in streets, for committing nuisances in places of pilgrimage, reservoirs, temples, and public buildings, throwing out carcases of animals, and disposing of human remains otherwise than in the prescribed burial-places and cremation grounds.

There is a mild curfew regulation, prohibiting movements in the city during the time between six *nālikas* (2–3 hours),[1]

[1] According to the *Arthaśāstra*, a *nālika* = $\frac{1}{30}$ part of the day or night, varying according to the season.

after sunset, and the same interval before dawn, but from this persons holding passes, and those going out for urgent reasons, such as doctors, midwives, and persons going to put out a fire, or to visit the city-superintendent (*nāgaraka*), are exempt.

The City-superintendent is required to inspect reservoirs, roads, and the secret approaches and fortifications of the city. He is also to take charge of lost and unclaimed property.

Jail delivery.

On the king's birthday, and on days of full moon, prisoners who are young, old, sickly, or helpless, and those who are ransomed by charitable persons, should be released from jail. There should also be gaol-deliveries once a day or every five days, of prisoners who have gained their freedom by their work, who have paid their fines, or on whom corporal punishment has been inflicted.

VIII

THE *KAUṬILĪYA ARTHAŚĀSTRA*

CIVIL LAW

Distinction between Civil and Criminal Law.

THE third book of the *Arthaśāstra* has the title *Dharmasthīyam,* which may be translated 'Civil Law', although, as will be seen, the book covers matters which would now be regarded as falling within the province of criminal law. In the Maurya state the line of distinction between these two departments of law was not drawn as in modern Europe. As to where exactly it was drawn, some doubt arises, chiefly because of the different meanings attaching to the word *daṇḍa.* It meant punishment of any kind, and included punishments inflicted by the State, e. g. death, corporal punishment, and fines payable to the king, as well as sums of money decreed by the courts to be paid as damages, &c., to private parties. It seems that imprisonment was not employed as a specific and independent punishment for offences. A person on whom a sentence of fine was imposed, if he failed to pay the fine, was imprisoned and made to work as a slave until he had worked it off. Similarly, a person against whom a decree was given in a civil action, if he failed to satisfy the decree, was handed over to the judgement creditor as his slave, in which condition he remained until he worked off or paid the amount. From the general arrangement of the *Arthaśāstra,* however, it would appear that the third book is intended to deal mainly with civil law and civil actions, although certain penal provisions are introduced in it as in other parts of the work not mainly concerned with the criminal law.

In many cases where a rule which defines a right or obligation is stated, the penalty for breach of the rule is given, and sometimes it is not certain whether by *daṇḍa,* a fine payable to the State or damages due to the injured party is meant. The fourth book deals with criminal law as well as police, but there also in some instances doubt arises as to the meaning of the word *daṇḍa,* and certain cases of civil damage or compensation are mentioned.

Some apparent discrepancies, redundances, and inconsistencies in the *Arthaśāstra* may be due to its being, as explained in its Introduction, a compilation from a number of works—others to corruption of the text and the loss of passages, which might have given a clue to its arrangement.

The courts.

The third book begins with a chapter headed *Vyavahārasthāpanā vivādapadanibandhaḥ* ('Forms of agreement and determination of disputes'). The first sentence runs: *Dharmasthāstrayastrayomātyā janapadasandhisangrahadroṇamukhasthānīyesu vyavahārikānarthān Kuryuḥ,* which Mr. Shamsastry translates:

'In the cities of *saṅgrahana, droṇamukha,* and *sthānīya,* and at places where districts meet, three members acquainted with sacred law, and three ministers of the king, shall carry on the administration of justice.'

Among the meanings of the word *vyavahāra* are 'contract', 'trade and business', and 'legal procedure' or 'administration of justice', but the first part of this chapter discusses licit and illicit contracts. It will be remembered that *saṅgrahaṇa, droṇamukha,* and *sthānīya* were the names of different classes of forts, and it has been laid down in a previous chapter [1] that there should be a *sthānīya* fort in the centre of every 800 villages, a *droṇamukha* for every 400, and a *saṅgrahaṇa* for every ten villages. We have also seen that among the posts which might be held by a *mantrin* or *amātya* was that of *dharmastha* or judge.[2] It is obvious that a court composed of three ministers, who were members of the King's Executive Council, could not have been held at every place where there was a fort of any kind. Possibly, only one or two such courts may have been contemplated, and the sentence may be taken to indicate the kind of place which should be chosen as the site of such a court. But

[1] Cf. p. 39. [2] Cf. p. 37.

a more probable conjecture seems to be that the word *amātya* may have had a second extended sense, covering a large class of subordinate officials, and that courts of different grades for adjudicating cases relating to trade or business, or arising out of contracts, were established in large and small towns, each such court being composed of three *amātyas* holding the office of *dharmastha*. *Artha* may mean a legal suit or action.

Illicit contracts. Certain kinds of agreements are prohibited, namely, those which are (1) *tirohita*, made in seclusion; (2) *antaragāra*, made indoors (i. e. in private houses ?); (3) *nakta*, made at night; (4) *āraṇya*, made in a forest; (5) *upadhya*, fraudulent; and (6) *upahvara*, secret. Parties, and also witnesses, to such contracts are liable to fine.

Under each of the above classes, however, there are exceptions. Agreements made in a remote place (*tirohita*) seem to have been valid if made in the presence of witnesses, and not otherwise open to objection. Agreements made in a private house are valid if they relate to inheritance, or to marriage, or deposits, or concern women who are in bad health, or do not leave their houses. Agreements made at night by persons who transact business in the first part of the night are valid, and so are those made in forests by traders, cowherds, hermits, and hunters who live in forests. We seem to have here an example of an old legal rule which, in course of time, was found inconvenient and so modified by exceptions and dispensations that very little was left of it. There is the remarkable rule that fraudulent agreements entered into by spies or secret agents (*gūḍhājīvī*) are valid. So are secret agreements made by members of an association (*samavāya*) among themselves.

Those agreements are void which are made by unauthorized persons, such as a member of a joint family (as, for instance, a father having a son or sons, a son having his father alive, or a brother) not authorized to act for the family, a woman who has a husband or a son, a servant, a person too young or too old or physically incapacitated for carrying on business. So also is one made by a person under the influence of anger, or pain, or intoxication, or insane, or possessed.

Procedure.

The chapter then passes to legal procedure. The trial of a civil action should begin by registration of the names of the parties, the date, and the matter in suit. The pleadings and interrogatories of the parties are then taken down. Examples are then given of certain breaches of rules of procedure falling under the head *parokta*.

The meaning is not very clear, but among the examples given are—shifting or changing the question at issue (*deśa*), inconsistent averments, introducing irrelevant statements of third parties, irregular communication with witnesses.

The penalty for *parokta* is said to be *pañcabandha*, which Mr. Shamasastry translates as 'five times the amount'. A fine of five times the amount in suit would seem an excessive penalty, but it was perhaps a maximum.

A few words appear to indicate rules for the payment of expenses of witnesses, but they are not clear. The defeated party in the case is to bear the costs on this account.

The cases in which alone a counterclaim is admitted are specified. They are cases arising out of *kalaha*, riot or affray, and *sāhasa*—a word translated by Mr. Shamasastry as 'robbery', but which, as explained in another chapter,[1] covers all cases of open and violent, as opposed to fraudulent (*steya*), taking possession of property or person—and cases arising among companies and guilds of traders (*sārthasamavāyebhyaḥ*).

When the defendant in a suit has answered the claim, the plaintiff must make his rejoinder on the same day. This is considered reasonable, because the plaintiff is acquainted beforehand with the subject-matter of the suit. The defendant who has not such previous knowledge is allowed from three to seven nights to make his defence. If he takes longer than that he is liable to a fine of from three to twelve *paṇas*. If he does not reply within six weeks he is liable to the penalty for *parokta*, and the amount of the plaintiff's claim (where the suit is not one for specific performance)

[1] Cf. p. 106.

shall be recovered from his property. The result is the same if the defendant, having made his reply in good time, afterwards fails in his case. A plaintiff failing in his case is liable to the penalty for *parokta*. In certain circumstances, it seems, the defeated plaintiff was required to pay the defendant's funeral expenses, but the passage is obscure.

Marriage.

The book then proceeds to deal with the subject of marriage. Eight kinds of marriage are enumerated, of which the first four are said to be in accordance with morality and religion (*dharmya*). The giving in marriage of a maiden provided with ornaments (1) is called *Brāhma*. Marriage by joint performance of a religious ceremony (*sahadharmacarya*) (2) is *prajāpatya*. The giving of a maiden for a couple of cows (*gomithuna*) (3) is called *ārsa*, after a sacrifice, to the officiating priest, (4) *daiva*. The voluntary union of a girl with her lover (5) is called *gāndharva*, the giving of a maiden for a price (*śulka*) (6) *āsura*, the abduction of a maiden (7) *rākṣasa*, the abduction of a maiden when asleep (8) *paiśāca*. Marriages of the first four kinds require the consent of the bride's father: those of the last four kinds must be made with the consent of both the bride's parents who receive her price (*śulka*). On the death of both her parents, the woman herself becomes entitled to the *śulka*, the payment of which, it appears, might be deferred. There is a general rule that any form of marriage is permissible which is pleasing to all (i.e. presumably approved by custom in the class to which the parties belong).

Married women's property.

Married women's property (*strīdhana*) may consist of means of subsistence, i.e. property producing an income (*vṛtti*) or jewellery. A wife may make use of her *strīdhana* for her own maintenance, and that of her son and daughter-in-law, in the absence of her husband, if he has made no provision for their maintenance. Her husband may spend it in case of disease, famine, or other calamity, or on a pious object.

In *dharmiṣṭa* marriages, i.e. those of the first four kinds, when husband and wife, by mutual agreement, have been using the *strīdhana* property for three years, no complaint shall be made if there have been two children of the marriage. In *gāndharva* and *āsura* marriages, if the wife's property is used by the husband, even with the wife's consent, it must be restored with interest (presumably to the wife's parents). In *rākṣasa* and *paiśāca* marriages the use of the wife's property by the husband is treated as theft (from her parents).

On the death of her husband, a woman intending to lead a pious life (*dharmakāmā*, i.e. not intending to remarry) is entitled to at once receive her property and also any balance of *śulka* due to her. If not vowed to a religious life she is entitled, on remarriage to a relative of her deceased husband, with her father-in-law's consent, to receive whatever has been given to her by her father-in-law or her first husband. If she remarries without her father-in-law's consent, she forfeits what has been given to her by them. A widow is not entitled to the property of her deceased husband. She has the usufruct of it if vowed to a religious life (i.e. not to remarry). A widow who has a son has not an absolute right even to her own property. It must pass to her son or sons. If she hold it for the maintenance of her sons, she must preserve it for them. A widow without a son, who is faithful to the bed of her deceased husband, may enjoy her property for her life, under the protection of her spiritual guide (*gurū*). Afterwards, it passes to her heirs. The sons and daughters of a wife who predeceases her husband should divide her property. If she has left no sons her daughters take it. If she has left no children, her husband succeeds to her property, except what has been given to her by her relations, which returns to them.

Re-marriage.

As regards the remarriage of males, the principle is laid down that a man may marry any number of women in succession, if he gives adequate compensation to the wife or wives previously married and provides them with subsistence. Without paying compensation, a man may remarry, if his wife has had no children, after waiting eight years; if she has brought forth a dead child only, after ten; and if she has had daughters only, after twelve years. Remarriage of a woman to a brother or other relative of her husband is also allowed in certain circumstances. A general rule lays down that a woman, whose husband has died, has gone to live abroad permanently (*dīrgha-pravāsin*), or has become a homeless ascetic (*pravrajita*) may, after seven months, if she be childless, and after a year if she have a child, marry a brother of her husband. If there are a number of brothers, she should marry the next in age to her former husband, or one who is virtuous and capable of supporting her, or a younger unmarried brother. If there is no brother of the deceased husband she should marry his nearest surviving male relative.

The wife of a man who is living abroad temporarily (*hrasvapravāsin*) should wait for him a year before re-marrying if she has not given birth to a child, but more than a year if she has had a child. She should wait twice as long if she has been provided with maintenance (by her husband ?). If she has not been so provided, and has relatives (*jñāti*) who are well-to-do, they should maintain her for four or eight years, and then leave her free to remarry, taking (from her new husband ?) what they have given. (The passage is obscure.) If the husband is a Brahman studying abroad, his wife should wait for him ten years if she has no issue, and twelve years if she has a child, before remarrying. The wife of a *kṣatriya* temporarily absent should not remarry, but if she marry and bear children to a man of the same *gotra* as her husband she shall not be disgraced. Other rules lay down that the wife of an absent husband, who is without means of subsistence and abandoned by her well-to-do relatives, may marry a man of her choice who is able to support her. In a marriage of any of the first four kinds (*dharmavivāha*) a bride (*kumārī*) whose husband has gone abroad, but is heard of, shall wait for him for seven months without remarrying if she has not published his name, but for a year if she has published it. If the husband has not been heard of she shall wait five months ; if he has been heard of, ten months. If the *śulka* has not been fully paid, should the husband not be heard of, she shall wait three months, if he is heard of, seven. If the whole *śulka* has been paid and the husband is not heard of, she shall wait five months, if heard of, ten. Then, with the permission of the judges, she may marry whom she likes. These rules, in which *śulka* is mentioned, evidently refer to marriages of the last four classes—*gāndharva, āsura, rākṣasa,* and *paiśāca.* Divorce (*mokṣa*) is not allowed if the marriage is of either of the first four kinds. In other marriages it is allowed by mutual consent.

Punishment of wives. A man may reprove a disobedient wife by calling her such names as 'naked one', 'cripple', 'fatherless', or 'motherless', or he may inflict on her corporal punishment to the extent of three strokes with a bamboo rod, a cord, or the palm of the hand. Should he exceed these limits he is liable to punishment for cruelty. Women are to be punished similarly for cruelty to their husbands.

Various punishments are prescribed for indecorous conduct of different kinds on the part of women, including whipping by a *caṇḍāla* in the middle of the village, which may, however, be remitted on payment of fine at the rate of one *paṇa* for each stroke.

Twelve years is laid down as the age of majority (*vyavahāra*) for a woman, and sixteen for a man.

Inheritance. We then pass to the subject of division of Inheritance (*Dāyavibhāga*). The principle is laid down that sons, whose parents or higher ascendants are alive, cannot be independent owners of property (*anīśvarāḥ*). Where there is no parent or higher ascendant the division of inheritance is made *pitṛtaḥ* ('by fathers', i. e. *per stirpes*). Self-acquired property is not to be divided, except that which has been earned by means of the paternal property.

The interpretation of the detailed rules as to shares in inherited property must, in the absence of a commentary, be uncertain, and in any case the subject is one for discussion in a treatise on Hindu Law. There is a rule that a father dividing his property in his lifetime shall not favour any son nor deprive any son of his share without reason.

Sons. A chapter is devoted to the different kinds of sons.

Besides the natural legitimate son (*aurasa*), there are the adopted son given by his parents (*datta*), and the adopted son who offers himself (*upagata*). There are also the *kṣetraja* or son begotten on a man's wife by another man appointed for the purpose by the husband, and the *gūḍhaja*, or son begotten on a man's wife by another man secretly in the house of relatives, and recognized by her husband. A natural legitimate son is heir to his father and his father's family (i.e. may claim to succeed to a share of the family property of his father). An adopted or recognized son is heir to his father by adoption or recognition only (i.e. may claim to succeed to the self-acquired property only of the father by adoption or recognition).

Mixed castes.

With regard to mixed castes (*antarāla*) it is said that the begetting of sons by men of lower on women of higher caste (*pratiloma*) has resulted from kings transgressing religion and morality. Sons begotten by a *Śūdra* on women of higher caste are *Ayogava, Kṣatta*, and *Caṇḍāla*; by a *Vaiśya, Māgadha* and *Vaidehika*; and by a *Kṣatriya, Sūta*. Sons begotten by men of higher on women of lower castes are called *anuloma*. The son of a *Brāhmana* by a *Vaiśya* woman is called *Ambaṣṭa*, by a *Śūdra* woman, *Niṣāda* or *Pāraśava*; of a *Kṣatriya* by a *Śūdra* woman, *Ugra*; of a *Vaiśya* by a *Śūdra* woman, *Śūdra*. The son of an *Ugra* by a *Niṣāda* woman is called *Kukkuṭa*; of a *Niṣāda* by an *Ugra* woman, *Pulkasa*; of an *Ambaṣṭa* by a *Vaidehaka* woman, *Vaiṇa*; of a *Vaidehaka* by an *Ambaṣṭa* woman, *Kuśilava*; of an *Ugra* by a *Kṣatta* woman, *Śvapāka*. A *Vaiṇya* (*Vaiṇa*, offspring of an *Ambaṣṭa* by a *Vaidehaka* woman ?) becomes a *rathakāra* or chariot-maker by profession.

The rules of succession conclude with a verse which says that 'the partition of inheritance shall be made in accordance with the custom of the country, caste, corporation, or guild (*sangha*), and the village'.

Slaves.

The chapter on slaves (*dāsakalpaḥ*) throws light on the institution of slavery in ancient India, and is of special interest in connexion with statements by certain Greek writers that slavery did not exist among the Indians.

Kinds of slaves.

According to the *Arthaśāstra* it appears a person might become a slave (*a*) by being born a slave (*udaradāsa*), (*b*) by being sold, (*c*) by being mortgaged (*āhitaka*), (*d*) by sentence or decree of a court (*daṇḍapratīkārin daṇḍapraṇīta*), (*e*) by being taken a prisoner of war (*dhvajāhṛta*). Under heads (*b*) and (*c*) a minor might be sold or mortgaged into slavery by his or her relations, or a person might sell or mortgage himself or herself (*ātmavikrayin ātmādhātṛ*). It also appears that the owner of a slave might sell or mortgage him or her. From the master's point of view a slave might be born in his house (*gṛhejāta*), inherited (*dāyāgata*), purchased (*krīta*), or obtained (*labdha*) by mortgage, decree of a court (e.g. in satisfaction of a debt), or capture in war.

Ārya and *mleccha.*

A general rule is laid down that no *ārya* should be a slave—*na tvevaryasya dāsabhāvaḥ*—but this is subject to exceptions. The term *ārya*, in different passages of the *Arthaśāstra*, is opposed to *mleccha*, but the exact meaning of the latter term is not clear. From a maxim in Book IX, chapter ii, that 'the army of the enemy under the leadership of an *ārya* is better than the army of wild tribes (*aṭavībala*)', we may infer that the wild or forest tribes (*aṭavika*), who are frequently mentioned in the *Arthaśāstra*, were regarded as *mleccha*. Non-Indian races would also be *mleccha*. In the *Periplus Maris Erythraei*, already quoted, among the imports received at the port of Barygaza (Broach), 'good-looking girls, πρὸς παλλακίαν', are mentioned. These would be slave-girls. In the *Arthaśāstra* there is no mention of European or other non-Indian slaves. It would appear that all free *śūdras* were regarded as *ārya*, and that an *ārya* of any caste might in certain circumstances be reduced to slavery, and in that case lost his *ārya*-hood, but regained it on again becoming free.

It is laid down that the selling or mortgaging into slavery by his kinsmen of a minor *śūdra* who is not a born slave, but is an *ārya*, is punishable with a fine of twelve *paṇas*; in the case of a *vaiśya* the fine is double, in that of a *kṣatriya* treble, and in that of a brahman quadruple. In the case of sale or mortgage into slavery of a minor *ārya* by any one but his relatives, sellers and purchasers, or mortgagors and mortgagees, as well as any abettors of such transactions, are alike liable to much heavier punishment—the *pūrva*, *madhyama*, and *uttamasāhasadaṇḍa* [1] in the cases of a *śūdra*, a *vaiśya*, and a *kṣatriya* respectively, and in the case of a brahman, death. For *mlecchas* to sell or mortgage their offspring is no offence. But, it is added, if to meet some family necessity an *ārya* should be mortgaged by his relatives, they should redeem him as soon as possible.

Slave's property.

A slave is entitled to keep any property that he acquires without prejudice to his master's work, or that he inherits. On his death his kinsmen inherit his property; in the absence of kin, his master.

Redemption.

An *ārya* sold into slavery is entitled to recover *ārya*-hood on payment of his price, and this applies also to a born or mortgaged slave. A person enslaved by decree of a court shall work off the amount of his price or of the decree against him. An *ārya* taken prisoner in war, it seems, might claim release on payment of half his value, or after doing an equivalent amount of work. From these rules it would appear that a brahman, *vaiśya*, *kṣatriya*, or *śūdra* would be born a slave if his father was a slave at the time of his birth. The relatives of a minor *ārya* might mortgage him or her as a slave in case of family necessity, but in that case they should redeem him as soon as possible. If they sold or mortgaged him without sufficient cause they were liable to fine, but the purchaser or mortgagee was not liable to punishment, the sale or mortgage held good, and the slave, if not redeemed, remained a slave. An *ārya* of any caste might sell or mortgage himself into slavery, or be enslaved by order of a court, or when taken prisoner in war. There is a rule which says that the offspring of a man who sells himself into slavery shall be regarded as *ārya*. This apparently means that the children born in freedom of an *ārya*, who afterwards sells himself into slavery, do not thereby become slaves.

A slave of *ārya* origin may claim his freedom on payment

[1] For the meaning of these terms, see p. 107.

of his price, if he has been sold as a slave; of his value if a born slave; if mortgaged as a slave, on payment of the amount of the mortgage; if a prisoner of war, on payment of half his value or by equivalent work.

The position of *mleccha* slaves was, perhaps, different. *Mlecchas* might freely sell their offspring into slavery, and it does not appear that *mleccha* slaves enjoyed the same rights of redemption as those of *ārya* blood.

It is not clear whether the provision that a person enslaved by decree of a court (*daṇḍapraṇīta*) must work off the amount of the fine or decree means that this kind of slave has not the right to claim release on payment of the fine or decree, as the case may be, but must, if required to do so, work it off as a slave. If this be the meaning, it would explain provisions of the penal code making serious offences punishable by fine only, since a fine might really mean penal servitude for a long term.

Protection of slaves.

There are various provisions for the protection of slaves. A master is liable to fine—apparently half the fine for improperly selling or mortgaging an *ārya* into slavery—if he misappropriates the belongings of a slave of *ārya* descent or deprives him of his status as an *ārya* (*āryabhāva*). This rule seems to imply that such a slave was entitled to certain privileges (e.g. not to be employed on degrading work, required to eat improper food, &c.).

According to another rule, the employment of a slave in carrying a dead body, filth, or leavings of food, keeping him naked, beating, or reviling him, and violation of a female slave entail forfeiture of value (*mūlyanāśa*), entitling the slave apparently to liberty. The next rule distinctly says that the violation (*atikramaṇa*) of female slaves gives them liberty (*mokṣakara*). A master failing to set a slave at liberty on receipt of the legal ransom is liable to a fine of twelve *paṇas*. So is a master who keeps a slave in confinement without sufficient cause. This seems to imply that a master might punish his slave by confinement for certain offences. If a master have a child by a female slave, both she and the child are entitled to freedom. If, for the sake of subsistence, she prefers to remain a slave, her brother or her sister may be set free. The position of female slaves has been discussed above in dealing with the *gaṇikādhyakṣa*.[1]

Hired servants.

As regards hired servants, the general rule is that wages should be paid as previously agreed upon. In the absence of previous agreement, a ploughman should receive one-tenth of the crop, a herdsman one-tenth of the clarified butter (*sarpis*), a person employed in selling goods, one-tenth of the sale proceeds. Artisans, musicians, physicians, buffoons, cooks, &c., should be paid according to current rates, or such wages as may be determined by experts. Failure to pay the proper wages is punishable with a fine of five times the amount due, or of six *paṇas*; in case of fraud the fine is doubled.[2]

A person who fails to do work for which he has received wages is liable to a fine of twelve *paṇas*, and to be compelled to complete the work. An employer failing to give work as agreed upon is liable to a similar fine. Some authorities held that work which the workmen were willing to do, but were prevented from doing by the employer, should be paid for as work done. But Kauṭilya would not lay down this as an absolute rule, as circumstances may have changed: for instance, the work done may not be satisfactory.

Workmen's corporations.

There is a special rule for corporations or associations of workmen (*sanghabhṛta*). Apparently they took contracts for work with a time limit. If they exceeded the time agreed upon they were allowed seven days' grace, after which the employer might have the work carried out by other agency. Such corporations, or any other associations doing work in co-operation (*sambhūya samutthātāraḥ*), should divide their earnings, either equally or in such manner as they may agree upon among themselves.

Special rules are given for dividing the remuneration for performance of a religious ceremony or sacrifice among a body of priests (*yājaka*) carrying it out jointly.

[1] Cf. p. 68.

[2] The words 'five' and 'ten' appear to have been erroneously interchanged in the text.

IX

THE *KAUṬILĪYA ARTHAŚĀSTRA*

CIVIL LAW (*continued*)

Three chapters are devoted to the law of immovable property (*vāstu*), which is defined as including houses, fields, gardens, irrigation works of all kinds (*setubandha*), tanks, and ponds. At the outset the rule is laid down that disputes about *vāstu* are to be decided by or on the evidence of the neighbours (*sāmantapratyaya*). **Immovable property.**

The alienation of immovable property is regulated by a provision that ' wealthy kinsmen and neighbours shall, in succession, be allowed to purchase land and other immovable property '. Apparently the meaning is that an owner of immovable property wishing to sell it must give the option of purchase first to his kinsmen and next to the neighbours. There is another rule that ' taxpayers ' (*karada*) shall sell or mortgage lands to taxpayers only, and brahmans the lands bestowed on them (*brahmadaya*) to brahmans only. **Sale.**

A sale of immovable property must be made publicly, in the presence of forty respectable persons of the neighbourhood, besides the purchasers. The price at which the property is offered for sale should be fixed beforehand (perhaps as estimated by the neighbours), and an *ad valorem* duty (*śulka*) on the sale paid to the State. An exact description of the boundaries of fields and gardens, and of the buildings, tanks, &c., included in the property, having been proclaimed, it is offered for sale by crying : ' Who will purchase this at such and such a price ? ' As in the case of public sales of other goods, if the price is enhanced by bidding, the excess over the published price goes to the State, as well as the duty on the sale.

There is a curious series of building regulations, for the most part not very clear. Some relate to foundations and **Buildings.**

stability, and some are sanitary. Every house must be provided with a proper water-supply and privy, as well as drainage. There are regulations regarding intervals between houses and the construction of windows, but these matters may be settled by agreement between neighbouring householders, provided that no injury is caused. Persons causing nuisance through faulty construction of their houses, tenants remaining in occupation of houses, and landlords evicting their tenants wrongfully are liable to penalties.

Boundary disputes. A dispute about the boundary between two villages is to be decided by people of five or ten adjacent villages, in accordance with the natural or artificial boundary marks. Disputes about fields are to be decided by the neighbours and the village elders. If they do not agree, the opinion of a number of respectable (pure) people should be sought, or the parties may agree to divide the disputed land. If these methods fail, the king should take possession of the disputed land. The king may also take possession of any immovable property for which there is no claimant, or, for the public advantage, he may distribute it. Wrongful occupation of immovable property is to be punished as theft. A person occupying the property of another justifiably shall pay such amount as may be proper, allowing for his labour and subsistence.

Penalties are provided for encroachment on boundaries and damage to boundary marks.

Damage. There are a few rules relating to damage to immovable property. One of them seems to fix the relative importance of acts interfering with the use of pasture, dry and wet cultivation, gardens, threshing floors, dwellings, and stables respectively, but the meaning is doubtful. Persons using paths through dry fields for the purpose of access to tanks, rivers, and wet fields must compensate the owners for damage done to crops. Owners of wet fields, gardens, and buildings causing damage to similar property belonging to others must pay twice the value of the damage as compensation. **Irrigation.** A tank must not be made below one already existing in such a way as to submerge any irrigated field.

The flow of water from a higher tank to a lower one shall not be stopped, unless the latter has been out of use for three consecutive years. The emptying of a tank is punishable with fine. The ownership of any private irrigation work which has been neglected for five years shall lapse, except in the case of public calamity. Persons making use of irrigation works belonging to others on payment of a lump sum, an annual rent, or a share of the produce shall keep the works in repair or pay twice the cost of putting them in repair. The penalty for letting water out of a tank otherwise than by the proper sluice (*apāre*) or obstructing a sluice (*pāra*) through negligence is six *paṇas*; for wilfully obstructing irrigation, the *pūrvasāhasadaṇḍa*.[1]

Trespass.

Any person establishing on a site belonging to some one else a place of pilgrimage, shrine, or temple, or alienating by sale or mortgage a building devoted to religious use, is liable to the *madhyamasāhasasaṇḍa*.[1]

A scale of fines is laid down for obstructions to roads according to their importance. A series of regulations deal with cattle-trespass. Any person allowing cattle to stray is liable to penalty, but this does not apply to bulls let out in the name of the village deity, or those used in crossing cows. If crops be damaged by stray cattle, the owners are liable to pay as compensation twice the value of the damage done. Cattle found trespassing should be driven out without injuring them.

Co-operative works.

In the same place are introduced some rules on the subject of work undertaken by village communities. A labourer engaged from outside for such work, if he fails to perform it, shall forfeit to the village twice the amount of wages paid to him and twice the value of food and drink that he has received. A villager who does not perform his share in the preparation of any public spectacle shall, with his family, forfeit their right to enjoy the show. Should he be present at it he is liable to pay twice the value of his share of the work. The same rule applies to all cases of refusal to help in work beneficial to the village, and also to all co-operative

[1] Cf. p. 107.

undertakings of districts, castes, families, and corporations (*saṅgha*).

Recovery of debts. Interest.

On the subject of recovery of debts (*Ṛṇādāna*), it is laid down that interest at the rate of 1¼ per cent. per month (15 per cent. per annum) is just (*dharmyā*). Five per cent. per month is commercial interest (*vyavahāriki*), 10 per cent. prevails among forest-dwellers (*kantaraka*), and 20 per cent. among seafarers (*samudra*). Interest on grain shall not exceed half the value of the loan in money. This presumably refers to loans of grain at sowing-time repayable after the harvest. Interest on trading stocks shall be half the profit, and be payable annually. If interest is allowed to accumulate, the amount recoverable shall not exceed the principal. (This is the rule now known by the name of *dandupat.*)

Transgression of these laws is punishable with fine. A person claiming interest which is not due, or representing as principal the amount of the principal debt with interest added (a common device to evade usury laws), is liable to be fined four times the amount in dispute. Another rule says that in such cases the creditor shall pay three-fourths of the fine and the debtor one-fourth. This probably applied to cases where the debtor abetted a breach of the law by acknowledging receipt of a fictitious amount of principal.

Interest should not accumulate on a debt due from a person long engaged in any sacrificial ceremony or studying in the house of his teacher (*gurū*), or from a minor or a poor person.

A creditor refusing payment of a debt without reasonable cause is liable to a penalty of twelve *paṇas*. If he have a reasonable ground for refusal the amount may be deposited with a third party, and interest does not accrue on it subsequently.

Limitation.

A debt neglected for ten years becomes irrecoverable, except where the creditor is a minor, an aged or sick person, or has gone abroad, or in times of civil commotion. The debts of a deceased person may be recovered from his heirs, or from a partner or surety. There is a curious rule that, except in the case of a debtor going abroad, a person shall not be sued at the same time by two or more creditors. In all cases a debtor should satisfy his different creditors in the order in which the debts were incurred, but debts due to the king or to brahmans should take precedence of others. Debts incurred to one another by husband and wife, father and son, or brothers of undivided interests are irrecoverable. Cultivators and government servants shall not be arrested for debt while at work. A wife shall not be arrested for her husband's debt, but the husband is liable to arrest for his wife's debt.

Rules of evidence.

Some rules as to evidence are introduced here. A debt may not be proved by the evidence of one witness only. Ordinarily, the evidence of three respectable witnesses is required, but that of two may be accepted with the consent of parties. Various categories of persons are mentioned as excluded from giving evidence: wives' brothers, co-partners, creditors, debtors, enemies and dependants of parties, and '*ahamvādins*', which perhaps means those having a personal interest in the case, for presumed partiality; minors and other persons incompetent to do business; the blind, the deaf, and the dumb, for incapacity; outcasts, *caṇḍālas* and persons engaged in degraded occupations; prisoners and convicts, for presumed untrustworthiness; lepers and persons with loathsome diseases, on sanitary grounds; brahmans learned in the Vedas (*śrotriya*), on account of their dignity; women, in deference to social conventions; village servants and government officials, perhaps to avoid interruption of their duties. The rule is qualified by the words '*anyatra svavargebhyaḥ*', which Mr. Shamasastry translates: 'excepting in the case of transactions in one's own community'. In cases arising out of assault, theft, or abduction, persons other than wives' brothers, enemies, and co-partners of parties, and in those relating to secret transactions, a single male or female witness may give evidence.

Witnesses are to be adjured before a brahman, a vessel of water, and fire. A brahman witness should be told simply to tell the truth. Others should be threatened with the consequences of false evidence. The imprecation addressed to a *kṣatriya* or *vaiśya* is, 'May thou not attain the fruit of thy good deeds, but, having broken thine enemy's strength, go begging, skull in hand'; to a *śūdra*: 'On thy death, may the fruit of thy merits go to the king, and the consequences of his sins fall on thee. If thou speak falsely, punishment will surely befall thee, that which is now unseen and unheard will, one day, surely be revealed.' It does not appear that witnesses were required to take any form of oath. The rules regarding open deposits (*upanidhi*), pledges (*ādhi*), and sealed deposits (*nikṣepa*) do not call for special remark.

Prescription. Regarding prescriptive titles to property, two rules are laid down. A person who for ten years neglects his movable property (*dravya*) while it is in the enjoyment of others loses his title to it, unless he be a minor, an aged person, a person living abroad, or one who left his country in consequence of civil disturbance.

Title to immovable property (*vāstu*) is acquired in similar circumstances by twenty years' possession. A passage mentioning exceptions to these rules is obscure. In certain circumstances occupation of immovable property by relatives, *śrotriya* brahmans, and religious men of different denominations (*pāṣaṇḍa*) does not give title; and title cannot be acquired by prescription to deposits or pledges or movable property belonging to the king or to *śrotriyas*.

Sāhasa. We then come to a chapter on *sāhasa*, which, as defined at the beginning of the chapter, means 'open and violent action' (*anvayavatprasabhakarma*). From the context, however, it appears that the term *sāhasa* was applied to forcible seizure of property or persons. As *sāhasa* is contrasted with *steya* or theft, it would seem that the former term as applied to property, covered wrongful, but not fraudulent, taking of possession.

For *sāhasa* of small articles, such as flowers, vegetables, fruit, cooked rice, onions, bamboos, and earthen pots, the penalty ranges from 12 to 24 *paṇas*; in the case of articles of greater value, such as iron, wood, ropes, flocks of small animals, from 24 to 48 *paṇas*; in the case of articles of copper, brass, bell-metal, glass, ivory, from 48 to 96 *paṇas*. The penalty last mentioned is called *pūrvasāhasadaṇḍa*. The seizure of cattle, men, fields, houses, gold, fine fabrics, renders liable to penalty ranging from 200 to 500 *paṇas*, called *madhyamasāhasadaṇḍa*. For keeping by force in confinement, or releasing from prison men or women, the penalty is the *uttamasāhasadaṇḍa*, or from 500 to 1,000 *paṇas*. These three degrees of fine or damages—*pūrva-*, *madhyama-*, and *uttamasāhasadaṇḍa*, or first, middle, and highest punishments for *sāhasa*—are frequently referred to in the *Arthaśāstra* as scales of penalty for offences and torts of different kinds.

Defamation and insult.

The next subject dealt with is *vākpārūṣya*, which is defined as including *apavāda* (defamation), *kutsana* (contemptuous talk or insult), and *abhibhartsana* (abuse and threatening). All abusive expressions, whether true or false, are actionable. If addressed to a person of superior rank the penalty should be double, if to an inferior, half of what it would be in the case of equals. Addressing a person with an expression which refers to a physical defect, as 'blind one', 'lame one', &c., renders liable to a penalty of 3 *paṇas* if the description be true, and of 6 *paṇas* if it be false. For the use of an ironical offensive expression, such as 'fine eyed' addressed to a blind man, the penalty is 12 *paṇas*. Threatening with an injury renders liable to half the penalty for inflicting the same injury. If the person uttering the threat be an enemy of the person threatened and in a position to do him harm the former is required to give security for the safety of the latter for his lifetime.

Threats.

Assault.

Daṇḍapārūṣya (assault) is defined as 'touching, striking, or hurting'. Touching the body of another person below the navel with the hand, or with mud, dust, or ashes, renders liable to a penalty of 3 *paṇas*; with the leg or spittle, 6 *paṇas*; with excrement, 12 *paṇas*. For touching the body above the navel the penalty is doubled, for touching on the head, quadrupled. The above are the penalties for wilfully touching a man of equal rank; for touching one of superior rank or a woman the penalty is doubled; for touching a man of inferior rank, halved. If the act be due to carelessness or intoxication, the penalty is halved. For seizing a person by his legs, clothing, hand, or hair the penalty is '6 *paṇas* or more' (perhaps 6 to 12 *paṇas*); for squeezing, throwing the arms round, pushing, pulling, or sitting on a person's body, the *pūrvasāhasadaṇḍa.* For causing a person to fall, the penalty seems, curiously, to have been half as much.

It is laid down that the limb with which a *śūdra* strikes a brahman shall be cut off. Further rules provide that for striking with a stick, a clod, a stone, iron or a rope, without drawing blood, the penalty should be 24 *paṇas*; for drawing blood, except bad blood (i.e. treatment by bleeding), double that amount; for breaking an arm, leg, or tooth, and cutting the ear or nose, or any organ, except in surgery, the *pūrvasāhasadaṇḍa.* For causing injury to the thigh or neck, or any injury resulting in impediment to speech, movement, or eating, the penalty is the *madhyamasāhasadaṇḍa* and payment of compensation equal to what is required to effect a cure.

Riot and affray. For seizing property in an affray a penalty of 10 *paṇas* is laid down. This perhaps refers to the taking of property to which the offender has some claim, as distinguished from robbery. The destruction of property in an affray is punishable with fine, in addition to payment of compensation.

Mischief. Penalties are also provided for different degrees of mischief by damaging walls, throwing harmful or dangerous things into houses, and injury to domestic animals, trees, and plants.

Gambling Notice of offences connected with gambling and betting is preceded by regulations for gambling, which is controlled by a superintendent (*dyūtādhyakṣa*), and allowed only at places licensed for the purpose. The superintendent is to collect from winners 5 per cent. on their winnings, also rent and licence fees for the gambling premises. At the same time he is allowed to carry on sale and mortgage transactions, i. e. presumably to buy and sell gamblers' property and lend money to them on mortgage. Any player using dice other than those supplied by the superintendent incurs a fine. A player who cheats is liable to the *pūrva-sāhasadaṇḍa*, as well as the penalty for theft or fraud, and to restore the amount of his winnings. The same penalties for cheating apply to all bets and wagers.

Miscellaneous offences.

Penalties are laid down here for a variety of miscellaneous offences, such as failing to restore property borrowed, hired, or received on trust at the appointed place and time, failing to deliver property to a third person in accordance with a trust, evading payment of tolls by pretending to be a brahman, violating the chastity of a widow who lives independently, touching an *ārya* woman by a *caṇḍāla*, failing to hasten to the help of a person in danger, entertaining at a ceremony in honour of *devas* or ancestors, *śākyas* (buddhists), *ājīvikas*, low caste (*vṛṣala*) persons, or *pravrajitas*, examination of any one on oath by an unauthorized person, doing of official acts (*yuktakarma*) by one who is not an official (*ayukta*). At the end of this chapter the following general principles are laid down.

Punishments should vary according to the persons concerned and the nature of the offence. Consideration should be shown to pilgrims, ascetics, sick persons, those suffering from hunger, thirst, or the fatigue of a journey, people from remote districts, those who have suffered punishment, and the destitute.

Judges should take up, without a complaint being lodged, cases affecting *devas*, brahmans, ascetics, women, minors, and aged, sick, and helpless persons. In such cases technical pleas and pleas of limitation shall not be admitted.

Honour should be shown to persons distinguished for learning, intelligence, valour, high birth, or great actions.

X

THE *KAUṬILĪYA ARTHAŚĀSTRA*

POLICE AND CRIMINAL LAW

THE fourth book, entitled *Kaṇṭakaśodhanam* (Removal of Thorns), mixes up in a confusing manner regulations for police and public safety, criminal procedure, and punishments for petty as well as serious offences. It does not contain the whole of the criminal code, penalties for various offences being provided, as already mentioned, in other books. Some of the provisions in this book appear to be in conflict with others, and it seems that certain of them may have been obsolete at the date when the *Arthaśāstra* was compiled.

Police control.

The book begins by laying down that the removal of thorns should be the duty of three commissioners (*pradeṣṭaraḥ*) or three *amātyas*. It is not clear whether these commissioners were the same as those entrusted with the supervision of village accountants,[1] under the general control of the collector-general, but probably this was the case, since it appears that the collector-general was responsible for certain branches of police work in addition to his revenue duties. As in regard to the appointment of judges,[2] a doubt arises as to the interpretation of *amātya* here. Then follow regulations applicable to different classes of artisans and professional men, which begin with a somewhat obscure

Guilds.

reference to guilds (*śreṇī*). Apparently the guilds' funds were kept in deposit with trustworthy persons, and were available for relief of distress among their members in times of calamity.

Artisans generally are subject to fine and forfeiture if they fail to carry out agreements as to time, place, and quality of work, and also for loss of or damage to materials.

[1] Cf. pp. 43, 44, 80. [2] Cf. pp. 35 ff.

Weavers.

For weavers rules are laid down as to the proportions of cloth to thread for different materials—cotton, silk, wool, jute, &c.

Washermen.

Washermen are required to beat clothes on wooden boards or smooth stones. For selling, mortgaging, or letting for hire clothes entrusted to them they are liable to a fine of 12 *paṇas*, for substituting clothes, to a fine of twice the value of the clothes taken, besides making restitution. Apparently to prevent their wearing customers' clothes, washermen are required to have their own clothes marked with a certain mark: for wearing any clothing not so marked they are to be fined 3 *paṇas*. With the same object, the time for returning clothes sent to them to be washed is fixed at one night, or five, six, or seven nights, according to the value and amount of washing to be done. A goldsmith privately buying a gold or silver article from a person of doubtful character is liable to a fine of 12 *paṇas*; if he should melt the article down the fine is 24 *paṇas*; if he should buy an article at a low price and melt it down secretly, or commit any fraud in the manufacture of articles, he is liable to the punishment for theft.

Goldsmiths.

Charges for manufacture of gold and silver articles are fixed in proportion to the weight of the metal. For silver, one *māṣa* per *dharaṇa*, for gold, one-eighth of a *suvarṇa* per *suvarṇa*. Similarly, the fees for manufacture of articles of brass, copper, iron, lead, tin, and other metals, and the loss of metal in manufacture to be allowed are laid down.

Coin.

An examiner of coins (*rūpadarśaka*) [1] who passes bad or rejects good coin is to be fined 12 *paṇas*. Any one causing counterfeit coin to be made or passed is to be fined 1,000 *paṇas*. For causing counterfeit coin to be received in the treasury the punishment is death.

Treasure trove.

Scavengers who find valuable things other than precious stones in the course of their work are allowed to keep one-third of their value and required to give up two-thirds to the State. If they find precious stones, they must surrender the whole to the State on pain of the *uttamasāhasadaṇḍa*.

[1] Cf. p. 54.

A finder of treasure, if he proves it to be his ancestral property, may keep the whole of it. Otherwise, on reporting the find, he may keep one-sixth if the total value is less than 100,000 *paṇas*. If the value is 100,000 *paṇas* or above, the whole goes to the king.

Physicians.

Apparently a physician who treated a patient for any dangerous disease was bound to report to some authority. If he failed to do so and the patient died, or if a patient grew worse owing to careless treatment, the physician was liable to fine.

Musicians, &c.

The object of a rule requiring musicians to remain at one place during the rainy season is not apparent. They are prohibited from making exorbitant charges on pain of a fine of 12 *paṇas*. Similar rules apply to dancers and beggars, but the latter, in lieu of fine, are to be punished with whipping at the rate of one lash for each *paṇa*.

Private trade.

The superintendent of trade (*saṁsthādhyakṣa*) is charged with the prevention of fraud in private trade.[1] It appears that he was required to control specially the trade in old or second-hand articles, examining the proofs of ownership.[2] He is also to have an eye on weights and measures.[3] A difference of half a *pala* in the measures *parimāṇi* and *droṇa* may be disregarded: the use of such measures differing by a *pala* from the standard is punishable with a fine of 12 *paṇas*. Similarly, no offence is involved in the use of a *tulā* balance with an error of a *karṣa*: if the error should amount to two *karṣas*, the trader concerned is liable to a fine of 6 *paṇas*. In an *āḍhaka* measure a difference of half a *karṣa* may be overlooked: an excess or a defect of a *karṣa* makes the trader liable to a fine of 3 *paṇas*. For greater errors in weights, measures, and balances proportionately larger fines are inflicted.

The offences of false description and adulteration of goods sold, and all combinations of traders to lower the quality of artisans' work or to hinder the purchase or sale or lower

[1] The royal trade was in charge of the *panyādhyakṣa*, cf. p. 57.

[2] Cf. p. 117.

[3] The maintenance of standard weights and measures was the duty of the *pautavādhyakṣa*, cf. p. 61.

the quality or raise the price of goods, are punishable with fine. There is a somewhat obscure passage which appears to refer to middlemen, and to lay down that the difference between their buying and selling prices should be merely a brokerage enough for their subsistence and not a profit.

A permit or licence to buy up grain for the market from cultivators is required. If any one should do so without permission, the stock of grain collected by him should be confiscated to the king by the superintendent of Royal Trade (*paṇyādhyakṣa*). We have seen that wholesale prices were fixed for the purpose of calculating the *śulka* toll.[1] Traders are allowed to make a profit of 5 per cent. of the fixed price on goods produced in the country, and 10 per cent. on foreign goods. If they make more profit they are liable to a fine of 5 per cent. (whether calculated on the profit or on the gross price is not stated).

In the case of goods long in stock or brought from a distance, the price should be fixed on consideration of the quantity and the outlay, interest on outlay, and other expenditure.

There follow certain regulations for public safety. Public safety.

Divine or providential dangers (*daivāni mahābhayāni*) are said to be eight in number, namely: fire, flood, pestilence, famine, rats, tigers, serpents, and demons.

The precautions against fire prescribed in the chapter on the City superintendent [2] are repeated, and it is enjoined that fire should be worshipped at the moon's changes. Fire.

As precautions against floods, villagers living on the banks of rivers should remove to higher ground on rainy nights. They should provide themselves with planks of wood, bamboos, and boats, and rescue, by means of gourds, inflated leather bags, trunks of trees, or bamboos, those who are being carried away by a flood. Failure to rescue a drowning man by a person having the means to do so is punishable with a fine of 12 *paṇas*. Incantations against rain are to be made by persons versed in *māyā*, *yoga*, and the Vedas. Flood.

[1] p. 61.

[2] v. p. 86.

During droughts, *Sacīnātha* (Indra), the Ganges, the mountains, and *Mahākaccha* should be worshipped.

Pestilence. Epidemics are to be combated by physicians with drugs and by holy ascetics with purificatory rites. A variety of religious or magical practices are also recommended. Against cattle disease the only remedies suggested are the ceremony of waving lights in cowsheds and worship of household deities.

Famine. In times of famine the king should provide the people with seeds and food. He may have recourse to allied states for help, may start relief works, or force the miserly rich to give up their hoards. Migration from the famine-stricken area to a district where the harvest has been good, or to the sea-coast or the shores of lakes, is also recommended. Catch-crops of grain or vegetables, roots or fruit may be grown on irrigated land, or hunting expeditions may be organized.

Rats may be kept down by means of cats and mongooses, as well as by the ministrations of holy ascetics. Rats also should be worshipped at the changes of the moon. Similar means may be employed to prevent damage by birds, and locusts and other insects.

Snakes. Snakes may be exorcized by incantations or destroyed.

Tigers. Tigers may be killed by means of carcases poisoned with the juice of the madana plant, caught in nets, or attacked with weapons by men protected with armour. A reward of 12 *paṇas* should be given for killing a tiger.

Demons. Demons should be exorcized by persons learned in the *Atharva Veda* and in the *māyā* and *yoga*. At changes of the moon *caitya* worship should be celebrated by placing on a terrace (*vitardi*) offerings such as an umbrella, the picture of an arm, a flag, and the flesh of a goat.

Prevention and detection of crime. For the prevention and detection of crime extensive use is made of spies, who in some cases act as *agents provocateurs*.

The collector-general (*samāhartṛ*), it is said, should employ throughout the country spies disguised as holy men (*siddha*), ascetics (*tāpasa*), friars (*pravrajita*), vagabonds, bards, jugglers (*kuhaka*), mystics (*pracchandaka*), astrologers (*kār-*

tāntika), fortune-tellers (*naimittika*), soothsayers (*mauhūrtika*), physicians, lunatics, the dumb, the deaf, idiots, the blind, traders, artists, artisans, musicians, dancers, vintners, confectioners, and sellers of cooked food. These men should make inquiry as to the character of villagers and *adhyakṣa* (i. e. private persons and officials of different departments). If a person is suspected of evil conduct, a suitable spy should be told off to shadow him. If the person suspected be a judge or commissioner (*pradeṣṭṛ*), the spy should say to him: 'My friend, so-and-so, has had a charge or claim brought against him. Please get him out of trouble, and accept a sum of money.' If the other agrees to the proposal, he may be denounced for corruption and banished. Or a spy may say to a *grāmakūṭa* (village head ?) or *adhyakṣa*: 'This wealthy man of bad character has got into trouble. Let us take advantage of it to deprive him of his wealth.' If the official so approached agrees to the proposal, he may be denounced for extortion and banished.

Agents provocateurs.

A spy, pretending to be implicated in a case, may tempt people with money to give false evidence. If they yield to the temptation they may be banished as false witnesses.

A person suspected of enamouring women by means of charms and spells may be offered money by a secret agent to gain the affections of some woman with whom the agent professes to be in love; if the former agrees, he may be denounced as a sorcerer and banished.

Similarly, a man suspected of poisoning may be offered money by a spy to poison some one, and, on his accepting, be banished as a poisoner.

Where a man is suspected of making false coin by reason of his purchases of metals and alkalis, and implements such as bellows, pincers, and stamps, and of his clothes and hands being soiled with ashes and smoke, a spy may enter his service as an apprentice and then denounce him, and he may be expelled.

For the special purpose of entrapping young men inclined to commit robbery and adultery, spies are to be employed who profess to be able, by means of a spell, to escape capture, to disappear from view, to open closed doors, or to enamour women. They will entice the young men to a village and there, after pretending to open doors of houses and cause the guards to fall asleep by means of incantations, introduce the young men to women personating other men's wives. Then the youths may be instructed in the art of incantation, and encouraged to test their power by plundering houses of articles previously marked. They may be arrested, either in the act of plundering, or afterwards while selling or mortgaging the marked property, or when they have been intoxicated with drugged liquor. When they have been arrested, information may be obtained from them about their past lives and their associates.

By similar devices detectives, posing as experienced thieves, shall associate with thieves and cause them to be arrested, and the *samāhartṛ* shall exhibit them to the public, announcing: 'The king has studied the science of arresting thieves. In accordance with his instructions I have arrested these thieves, and will arrest others.'

Another device is for spies masquerading as thieves to associate with criminal forest tribes, and arrange with them to attack caravans or villages stocked beforehand for the purpose with spurious gold and other goods. On the attack taking place, the assailants may be slain by armed forces lying in wait for them, or they may be arrested while asleep or intoxicated with drugged food or drink provided for them.

Suspicious characters.

Instructions with a view to the prevention and detection of crime by means other than the employment of spies are also given. There is a long list of classes of persons who may be arrested on suspicion based on their manner of life and conduct. It includes: persons who change their residence, caste, or name; those addicted to the luxuries of eating meat, drinking liquor, using perfumes, wearing garlands, expensive dress, and ornaments; the extravagant; those who associate with profligate women, gamblers, and vintners; those who are often away from home at places or on business not known; who travel alone in forests, hold secret meetings, have fresh wounds treated with secrecy and haste, hide themselves in their houses, are attached to women or unduly inquisitive about the wives or property of other men, keep bad company, or loiter in the dark, behind walls, or in the shade of trees; those who sell goods under suspicious circumstances, are of low occupation and caste, whose conduct is notorious; a town superintendent who, on seeing a *mahāmātra*, hides himself or absconds, a man who shows fear by irregular breathing, whose face is pale and dry and utterance halting; one who goes accompanied by armed men and has a threatening aspect. All these, it is said, may be suspected of being murderers, thieves, men guilty of misappropriation of treasure-trove or deposits, or otherwise men of evil life.

Stolen property.

For the detection of thefts it is enjoined that notice of articles lost or stolen should be given to dealers in similar articles. A dealer who conceals any article of the loss of which he has received notice shall be considered guilty as an abettor of theft. A dealer who comes into possession of a lost or stolen article without knowing that it has been lost or stolen shall be acquitted on giving it up.

No one shall sell or mortgage an old article without giving notice to the superintendent of trade (*saṁsthādhyakṣa*).[1] On receipt of such information, the superintendent shall ask the person in possession of the article how he came by it. If his explanation is found on inquiry to be correct and satisfactory, he shall be released; otherwise he shall be required to restore the property, and may, according to circumstances, be fined or punished as a thief. An honest person who has been in possession of an article lost by another for a long time may retain possession of it.

House-breaking.

In cases of housebreaking and theft from a building, it is said, it should be ascertained from appearances—such as appearances of entry or exit otherwise than by doors, breaking of doors and windows, ascent or descent of stairs, piercing and tunnelling of walls, and methods of removing property—whether the crime has been committed by internal (*abhyantara*) or external (*bāhya*) agency, or by both. It

[1] Cf. p. 112.

appears that this maxim refers to crimes committed in cities, the description *abhyantara* applying to thieves who belong to the town, and *bāhya* to those from outside, for the chapter in which it occurs concludes with a verse which says that the commissioner (*pradeṣṭṛ*), with his staff of *gopas* and *sthānikas*, shall take steps to find out external (*bāhya*) thieves, and the city superintendent (*nāgaraka*) those within the town (*antardurge*).

A further list is given of persons who may be suspected in such cases, such as: a neighbour in miserable circumstances, a woman of poor condition or engaged in some intrigue, a servant of bad character, a person who is very sleepy or shows signs of want of sleep or fatigue, whose face is pale and dry and speech broken, whose appearance shows that he has been climbing (walls or other obstacles), whose body is scratched or clothing torn, hair and nails dirty, or nails broken; one who has just bathed and anointed himself, or just washed his hands and feet; one whose footprints resemble those which have been found of a person entering or leaving the building.

Homicide. Next follow instructions for the investigation of cases of suspected homicide.

They lay down that, in all cases of sudden death, the corpse shall be smeared with oil and examined. Detailed lists are given of the symptoms of death by suffocation, hanging, drowning, beating with sticks or ropes, throwing down, poisoning, and snakebite. In the case of poisoning, the remains of a meal should be examined in milk, or the undigested food found in the stomach may be thrown on a fire. If it makes a 'chitchit' sound and turns the colour of the rainbow, poison may be inferred.

When in the burning of a corpse the belly remains unburnt, servants should be examined as to ill-treatment (they may have received from the deceased). Inquiry should also be made as to any other person in the dead man's family or household who may have had cause for enmity against him, such as a person in distress, a woman engaged in an intrigue, the adviser of a woman who has been deprived of her inheritance. Generally, in cases of apparent suicide by hanging, inquiry should be made as to injury caused by the deceased to any one.

Homicide, it is said, results from anger, and anger may arise from one or other of the following causes: women, succession to property, professional competition, hatred between rivals, disputes about trade or the affairs of guilds, and lawsuits.

Instructions are given as to inquiries to be made from relatives of the deceased and persons who happened to be near the scene of the occurrence where a man has been killed by his own hirelings, by thieves for the sake of money, or by enemies of another man whom he resembles.

If a person under the influence of love or anger commits suicide by rope, weapon, or poison, his or her corpse shall be dragged along the public road by a *caṇḍāla*, with a rope, and deprived of funeral rites. Suicide.

The next chapter has for its title *Vākyakarmānuyogaḥ*, meaning 'the questioning of an accused person by word and by act', i.e. without or with torture. As in ancient Europe, torture appears to have been applied to elicit a confession from an accused person whose guilt had been established by other evidence—a practice based on the view that, as the best and most conclusive evidence of guilt, a confession should be obtained, where this is possible, to clinch and confirm other proof. To this day, as is well known, Indian police officers investigating cases are prone to attach undue importance to the object of procuring a confession, and, with this object, sometimes resort to questionable expedients. It is prescribed that if the defendant's answers to the questions addressed to him are corroborated by reliable witnesses, he shall be acquitted: otherwise he shall be subjected to torture. Torture.

There is an obscure rule which seems to mean that after an interval of three days from the commission of an offence no one shall be arrested except on strong proof of his guilt: the idea being, perhaps, that the fact of suspicion falling at once on a man is, in itself, evidence against him. Other Protection of the innocent.

provisions are that any one who charges an innocent man with theft shall himself be liable to the punishment for theft. An accused person who proves that the complainant is actuated by hatred or enmity towards him should be acquitted. Any one who keeps an innocent man in confinement should be punished with the *pūrvasāharadaṇḍa.* The guilt of a suspected person should be established by the production of such evidence as the instruments used in committing the crime, accomplices and abettors, the stolen article, and persons concerned in its sale or purchase. In the absence of such evidence the accused should be acquitted. For sometimes an innocent person has been arrested as a thief in consequence of his accidental presence near the scene of the theft, or resemblance to the thief in appearance or dress, possession of arms similar to those carried by the criminal, or possession of articles similar to those stolen; as in the case of one Māṇḍavya,[1] who, though innocent, confessed to a theft through fear of torture. Having clearly laid down that only those whose guilt has been proved shall be subjected to torture, and then only if they persist in denying their guilt, the chapter proceeds to enumerate certain categories of persons on whom torture is not to be inflicted. They are: children, the aged and infirm, persons of weak intellect, lunatics and intoxicated persons, the weakly, and those suffering from hunger, thirst, or fatigue, women who are pregnant or have been delivered within the preceding month, and brahmans.

Persons exempt from torture.

Kinds of torture.

The different kinds of torture are next enumerated. There were, it appears, four ordinary (*vyavahārika*) tortures, namely: (1) the 'six punishments' (*ṣaḍḍaṇḍaḥ*—meaning uncertain); (2) seven kinds of whipping; (3) two kinds of tying or hanging up; (4) the water-tube torture—perhaps by allowing water to drop slowly on the victim's head.

For serious offences the tortures are, nine kinds of caning, two kinds of suspension, burning a finger-joint after the accused has drunk rice-gruel, heating for a day the body

[1] Apparently a 'leading case'.

of a person who has drunk oil, making the accused lie out on grass on a winter's night. Different kinds of torture, it is said, may be employed on successive days. A brahman, instead of being tortured, should be branded with a symbol indicating his offence and banished. There follow rules providing punishments for various forms and degrees of theft. These rules may be taken as applying to theft as distinguished from *sāhasa*, a term which, as suggested above, may cover cases of wrongful taking possession of property amounting to civil tort, not crime. It is not certain, however, whether this interpretation is correct, as discrepancies and redundances in existing texts of the *Arthaśāstra* might be accounted for in various ways (cf. *supra*, p. 28).

Theft of royal property.

Regarding theft of royal property, it is provided that those who steal precious stones or other articles of value from mines or important manufactories shall be beheaded. Theft of articles of less value from factories is punishable with the *pūrvasāhasadaṇḍa*. Theft from the royal store-yards (*paṇyabhūmi*) of things valued at from 1 *māṣa* ($\frac{1}{16}$ *paṇa*) to 1 *paṇa* is punishable with fines ranging from 12 to 48 *paṇas*, of things from 1 to 2 *paṇas* in value with the *pūrva*, from 2 to 4 *paṇas* with the *madhyama*, from 4 to 8 *paṇas* with the *uttamasāhasadaṇḍa*, from 8 to 10 *paṇas* with death. For theft of goods from royal warehouses and armouries the fine in proportion to value is doubled, for thefts from the treasury and *akṣaśāla* (royal goldsmith's office [1]) multiplied eightfold.

Theft of private property.

For thefts of private property from fields, threshing-floors, dwellings, or shops the scale of punishment according to values is as follows:

$\frac{1}{16}$ to $\frac{1}{4}$ *paṇa*, 3 *paṇas* fine or the culprit to have his body smeared with cow-dung and be proclaimed (as a thief). Another alternative punishment—*śarāvamekhalā* (lit. dish-skirt)—is mentioned, the meaning of which is uncertain.

$\frac{1}{4}$ to $\frac{1}{2}$ *paṇa*, 6 *paṇas* fine or the culprit to have his head shaved and be banished.

$\frac{1}{2}$ to $\frac{1}{3}$ *paṇa*, 9 *paṇas* fine or to be smeared with cow-dung

[1] Cf. p. 55.

or ashes and proclaimed, or the *śarāva* (earthen dish) punishment.

$\frac{1}{3}$ to 1 *paṇa*, 12 *paṇas* fine or the culprit to have his head shaved and be banished.

1 to 2 *paṇas*, 24 *paṇas* fine or the culprit to have his head shaved with a piece of brick and be banished.

2 to 4 *paṇas*, 36 *paṇas* fine.

4 to 5 *paṇas*, 48 *paṇas* fine.

5 to 10 *paṇas*, the *pūrvasāhasadaṇḍa*.

10 to 20 *paṇas*, 200 *paṇas* fine.

20 to 30 *paṇas*, 500 *paṇas* fine.

30 to 40 *paṇas*, 1,000 *paṇas* fine.

40 to 50 *paṇas*, death.

For theft accompanied by force, the above rates of fines in proportion to value are doubled; for robbery under arms quadrupled.

Forgery.

For forging a deed or using a counterfeit seal, a head of a family (*kuṭumbādhyakṣa*) or chief owner of joint property (*mukhyasvāmin*) is liable to either of the three *sāhasadaṇḍas* or to the death penalty, according to the gravity of the offence.

Misconduct of judges and court officials.

Then come clauses dealing with a number of offences connected with the administration of justice.

A judge is punishable with the *pūrvasāhasadaṇḍa* for threatening, browbeating, sending out of court, or unjustly silencing, and with double of that punishment for defaming or abusing, a party to a case in his court. For not asking a question which ought to be asked (*pṛcchya*), asking one which ought not to be asked (*apṛcchya*), rejecting the answer to one which he has asked, tutoring, prompting, or reminding a witness, a judge is liable to the *madhyamasāhasadaṇḍa*.

Offences by judges which are punishable with the *uttamasāhasadaṇḍa* are, corruptly giving advice to parties, settling wrong issues, delay in the settlement of issues, wrong devices to postpone cases, wasting time so as to tire parties out and force them to leave the court, and taking up again cases disposed of.

Offences by court clerks.

A court clerk, for not taking down what has been said,

writing down what has not been said, or altering the sense or effect of depositions, is liable to the *pūrvasāhasadaṇḍa* or to punishment in proportion to his guilt.

Improper sentences. A judge or commissioner (*pradeṣṭṛ*) who imposes an improper fine is liable to a fine of twice the amount or of eight times the sum by which the fine imposed by him exceeds or falls short of the proper sum. A judge or commissioner unjustly inflicting corporal punishment is liable to the same punishment or to pay twice the amount of fine ordinarily exacted in lieu thereof. These provisions show that the *pradeṣṭṛ* exercised judicial as well as revenue and police functions.

Offences by jailors. We have, then, a number of clauses dealing with offences by persons in charge of prisons (*bandhanāgāra*) and *cārakas*, which, from the context, would appear to have been some kind of places of detention. Mr. Shamasastry translates the word by 'lock-up'.

The first of these clauses appears to relate to improper releases from a lock-up attached to a court (*dharmasthīya cāraka*), but the meaning is doubtful, and the text perhaps corrupt.

It is laid down that one who releases from a *cāraka* a man against whom an action has been brought (*abhiyukta*) shall be made to pay the amount of the claim against him and also the *madhyama sāhasadaṇḍa.* He who (improperly) releases a prisoner from a jail (*bandhanāgāra*) shall be condemned to death and forfeit all his property.

Other offences by a superintendent of a jail (*bandhanāgārādhyakṣa*) are made punishable with fines as follows: confining in a lock-up without stating the reason,[1] 24 *paṇas*; ill-treating a prisoner, 48 *paṇas*; depriving a prisoner of food and water, 96 *paṇas*; causing excessive hardships to, or extorting a bribe from, a prisoner, the *madhyamasā hasadaṇḍa*; putting a prisoner to death, 1,000 *paṇas*; outraging a female prisoner of servile condition, the *pūrvasāhasadaṇḍa*; outraging the wife of a criminal, the *madhya*

[1] Translation doubtful.

masāhasadaṇḍa; outraging an *ārya* female prisoner, the *uttamasāhasadaṇḍa.*

These punishments are strangely graduated, and the text is perhaps incomplete or corrupt.

Punishment of mutilation.

In the chapter on Mutilation, or fine in lieu thereof (*ekāngabadhaniṣkraya*), it is difficult to discern any principle on which punishments have been apportioned, and the text is, in some places, obscure and probably corrupt. It may be that, at the date of compilation of the *Arthaśāstra*, the punishment of mutilation had fallen practically into desuetude, and we have here specified a number of offences for which that punishment was prescribed by an older and less humane code, with the fines which came later to be substituted for it. It is laid down that a person who steals or injures fowls, mongooses, cats, dogs, or pigs of less than 54 *paṇas* in value shall have the end of his nose cut off or pay a fine of 54 *paṇas*. One who steals a cart, boat, or 'small animal' shall have one foot cut off or pay a fine of 300 *paṇas*. A person using false dice or other instruments for gambling shall lose a hand or pay a fine of 400 *paṇas*.[1] An adultress shall have her nose and one ear cut off or pay a fine of 500 *paṇas*. The adulterer is punishable with a fine of 1,000 *paṇas*. Whoever steals a large domestic animal, abducts a slave, or misappropriates and sells the property of a deceased person is liable to have both feet cut off and pay a fine of 600 *paṇas*. For assaulting persons of the highest castes or a spiritual guide (*gurū*), or mounting the king's carriage, horse, or elephant the punishment is amputation of the foot and one hand or a fine of 700 *paṇas*. A śūdra who pretends to be a brahman, a person who eats the property of a deva, one who conspires against the king, or who blinds both eyes of another is liable to have both eyes blinded by application of a poisonous ointment or pay a fine of 800 *paṇas*. A person who enables a thief or adulterer to escape, falsifies a royal decree, abducts a girl or a female slave, at the same time carrying off money, commits a fraud

[1] Different punishments for cheating at play and using unauthorized dice are set forth in the chapter on gambling, v. p. 108.

in business (*kūṭavyavahārin*), or sells bad meat is liable to lose both feet and one hand or pay a fine of 900 *paṇas*.

For stealing images of devas or animals, abducting men, or taking wrongful possession of fields, houses, gold bullion or coins, precious stones, or crops the punishment is the *uttamasāhasadaṇḍa* or, in the alternative, death.

Selling of human flesh is punishable with death.

Death penalty.

The next chapter is headed *śuddhacitraśća daṇḍakalpaḥ*, meaning 'death penalty with or without torture'. The chapter does not include all the cases for which the death penalty is prescribed by the *Arthaśāstra*: at the same time it mentions a number of offences punishable otherwise. The meaning of some of the forms of death which it mentions is uncertain. The *sloka*, with which it concludes, runs as follows: 'Such painful punishments are in accordance with the *śāstras* of great sages, but it is deemed just (*dharmya*) to put to death without torture criminals who are not cruel.' This verse seems to indicate that, at the date of the *Arthaśāstra's* compilation, the more cruel forms of the death penalty were falling into desuetude.

Homicide in affray.

A curious instance of progressive attenuation of the severity of punishment is found in the case of homicide in the course of a riot or an affray, with which the chapter opens. It is laid down that he who kills a man in a riot or an affray shall be tortured to death. But where a person wounded in a fight dies within seven nights, the man who caused his death shall be put to death 'simply' (i. e. without torture); where death ensues within a fortnight the punishment is the *uttamasāhasadaṇḍa*; if within a month, a fine of 500 *paṇas* and payment of compensation.

It would seem that, according to some ancient rule, the punishment for killing a man in an affray was death accompanied by torture. This rule was later construed to mean that the death penalty with torture should be inflicted only where death had followed instantaneously from a blow given in a fight. In most cases, probably, it could be made out that the death had not been instantaneous.

Wounding.

The next clause provides for wounding with a weapon the

uttamasāhasadaṇḍa, for wounding by a person intoxicated, amputation of a hand, for murder, the death penalty. Abortion. Causing abortion by violence is punishable with the *uttama*, by drugs with the *madhyama*, by general ill-treatment or annoyance (*parikleśa*) with the *pūrvasāhasadaṇḍa*.

Offences punishable with impalement. A list of offences punishable with impalement (*śūka*) includes murder with violence, infliction of undeserved punishment, spreading of false reports, highway robbery, and theft of or wilful injury to the king's horse, elephant, or chariot.

Abetment. A person supplying a murderer or thief with food, clothing, fire, or other necessaries, or information or advice, is punishable with the *uttamasāhasadaṇḍa*. If he does so in ignorance Treason. he is to be censured. A person who aims at subverting the royal authority, forces his way into the private apartments of the palace, or incites forest tribes or other enemies against the kingdom, or creates disaffection in city or country is liable to death by the torture called *śirohastaprādīpika*. The meaning of this word is not known, but it was apparently a form of torture in which fire was applied to the head and hands. For the same offences a brahman is to be drowned.

Parricide. For slaying mother or father, or teacher (*ācārya*), or an ascetic, the punishment is death by *tvakchirahrādīpika*, meaning, apparently, application of fire to the head and skin; for insulting a parent, teacher, or ascetic, cutting out the tongue; for biting or scratching any of their limbs, amputation of the corresponding limb.

Other capital offences. For stealing a herd of cattle, death without torture; for making a breach in a reservoir containing water, drowning in the same; for damaging a dry reservoir, the *uttamasāhasadaṇḍa*; for damage to a neglected reservoir, already breached, the *madhyamasāhasadaṇḍa*.

For causing death by poison the punishment is drowning; a woman who murders a man other than her husband is to be drowned. Any woman who murders her husband, spiritual guide (*gurū*), or offspring, or is guilty of arson or poisoning, should be put to death by means of bulls (by being gored by bulls ?). Any person who sets fire to pastures, crops, threshing-floors, or timber- or elephant-forests should be burnt in the same fire. Any one who insults the king, betrays the secrets of the king's council, plots against the king, or defiles a brahman's kitchen should have his tongue cut out. Any person other than a soldier stealing arms or armour should be put to death by being shot with arrows.

Sexual crime.

A man having sexual intercourse with an immature girl is liable to have his hand cut off or pay a fine of 400 *paṇas*; if the girl dies in consequence, the punishment is death.

According to one rule, a man having sexual intercourse with a mature unmarried girl is liable to have his middle finger cut off or pay a fine of 200 *paṇas*, and to pay compensation to her father. But another rule says that a man having such intercourse with a maiden with her consent shall pay a fine of 54 *paṇas* only, and the maiden in such a case shall pay a fine of half that amount. Another rule, again, says that a man having connexion with a woman who remains unmarried for three years after attaining maturity (with her consent) commits no offence and is not liable to pay compensation to her father, if she has no jewellery on her person, because her father, by keeping her unmarried, loses authority over her. But if she have jewellery, and the seducer takes possession of it, it shall be regarded as theft.

Offences connected with marriage.

A number of offences connected with marriage are specified: one man impersonating another who has paid the bride-price (*śulka*) for a girl; obtaining a bride for one man after undertaking to get her for another; refusing to give a girl in marriage as agreed upon; substituting a different girl for the one whom it has been agreed to give in marriage. For the first of these offences the punishment is amputation of the hand or a fine of 400 *paṇas*, and making good the bride-price; the others are punishable with fine only. Mention is made of a peculiar custom by which a man who rescued a woman from the hands of thieves, or saved her from a flood, or in time of famine, or when lost in a forest, or abandoned, acquired a right to have sexual intercourse with her. But this custom had perhaps fallen into desuetude, for it is said that it should not apply to any woman who is of high caste, or who does not desire sexual intercourse, or has children.

Miscellaneous offences. In the final chapter of the book it is laid down that whoever causes a brahman to partake of forbidden food or drink shall be punished with the *uttamasāhasadaṇḍa*. For a similar offence against a *kṣatriya* the punishment is the *madhyama*, against a *Vaiśya* the *pūrvasāhasadaṇḍa*, and against a *śūdra* a fine of 54 *paṇas*. House-trespass by day is punishable with the *pūrva*, and by night with the *madhyamasāhasadaṇḍa*; trespassing with arms in another's house, by day or night, with the *uttamasāhasadaṇḍa*. But beggars, pedlars, lunatics, and intoxicated persons entering a house, and neighbours entering a house, even by force, in case of danger, are not to be punished, unless they have been specially prohibited from entering. For mounting the roof of his own house after midnight a man was liable to the *pūrva*; for mounting another's roof, to the *madhyamasāhasadaṇḍa*.

Protection of caravans. It is laid down that merchants travelling in caravans (*sārthikās*) should camp in a part of the village allotted to them, and should make known the value of their goods to a responsible local official. If any of the goods should be stolen or lost, the village head-man (*grāmasvāmin*) must make good the loss. If the theft or loss occur in a place lying between the boundaries of two villages, the local superintendent of pastures, if any (*vivītādhyakṣa*),[1] must make it good. Where there is no superintendent of pastures, the responsibility falls on a functionary called the *corarajjuka*, whose duties are not otherwise specified, but were evidently connected with the arresting of thieves. Apparently, where there was no local head-man or responsible official, the cost of recouping the trader's loss was to be distributed over the inhabitants of a neighbouring area, which might extend to five or ten villages.

Injury through negligence. Personal injury caused through defective construction of a house or cart, or by causing to fall into a pit or well, by cutting down a tree, letting loose a domestic animal, keeping

[1] p. 79.

a wild or unbroken (*adānta*) animal, or throwing sticks, clods, or stones, or discharging arrows at a carriage or elephant, is to be treated as an assault (*daṇḍaparūsya*). Apparently injury caused by the collision (*saṅghaṭṭana*) of a vehicle was regarded in the same light, but if the driver gave warning by calling out '*apehi*' ('get out of the way'), he was not liable to punishment.

There is a remarkable provision that 'a man slain by an angry elephant shall give a *kumbha* of liquor less by a *droṇa*, and also garlands and unguent, and a cloth to clean the tusks'. Presumably these offerings were to be made by his heirs. The reason given is that 'death caused by an elephant is as meritorious as the bath taken at the end of a horse-sacrifice (*aśvamedha*)'. This maxim is followed by rules to the effect that when a person, through no fault of his own, is killed by an elephant, the driver shall be punished with the *uttamasāhasadaṇḍa*, and that if injury is caused by a horned or tusked animal, through the owner's fault, he shall be liable to the *pūrvasāhasadaṇḍa*. We have here, perhaps, an example of an ancient superstition corrected by later common sense.

Witchcraft.

As regards witchcraft, the general rule is that any person who attempts to injure another thereby shall suffer the same injury himself. For attempting incest through witchcraft the punishment is death after amputation of a limb.

Adultery.

For committing adultery with a brahman woman a *kṣatriya* was liable to the *uttamasāhasadaṇḍa*, a *vaiśya* to confiscation of all his property, and a *śūdra* to be wrapped in mats and burnt alive. A brahman, *kṣatriya*, or *vaiśya* committing adultery with a woman of degraded (*śvapāka*) caste should be branded and banished, or degraded to the same caste. A *śūdra* or *śvapāka* committing adultery (apparently, with a woman of higher rank) should be put to death, and the woman with whom he commits the offence should have her ears and nose cut off.

If a man have illicit intercourse with a female ascetic (*pravrajita*), he and she are each liable to a fine of 24 *paṇas*.

The concluding verses of the penal code set forth that

'when the king punishes an innocent man, he shall dedicate to Varūṇa and throw into water a sum equivalent to thirty times the unjust punishment, to be afterwards distributed to brahmans. Thus will the king be purged of the sin of unjust punishment; for Varūṇa is the ruler of sinners among men'.

XI

THE *KAUTILĪYA ARTHAŚĀSTRA*

POLICY

After dealing with the subject of Law, the *Arthaśāstra* passes to that of Policy.

Methods of dealing with seditious persons.

First are set forth a series of devices of cynical ingenuity for compassing the destruction of seditious leaders who cannot be put down openly. In these schemes, as might be expected, spies play an important part: a few examples may suffice. The brother of a seditious high official (*mahāmātra*), after being approached by a spy, may be brought before the king, who, by transferring to him the *mahāmātra's* property, will induce him to murder the latter, after which the brother may be arrested and put to death for the crime of fratricide.

The king may dispatch a disloyal official with a weak force, to which have been attached a number of cut-throats in the king's secret service, on a dangerous mission—such as to destroy a wild tribe or hostile village, punish a refractory town, or instal a governor (*rāṣṭrapāla*) or warden of marches (*antapāla*) in a remote and wild tract. In the course of any fighting that ensues, the king's cut-throat spies may murder the seditious official, who may afterwards be reported to have been killed in the fighting.

A female mendicant may persuade a seditious chief (*rāṣṭramukhya*) that the wife, daughter, or daughter-in-law of another seditious chief has fallen in love with him. When the chief thus deluded makes over presents of jewellery to the mendicant for delivery to the lady whom he believes to be in love with him, the mendicant will show them to the other chief, to whom she will betray the secret. On a fight ensuing between the two chiefs, ruffians in the king's service may kill one of them, and the other may be arrested and punished for the crime.

Various methods of poisoning are also recommended.

Next come the chapters on 'Replenishment of the Treasury' (*kośābhisaṁharaṇa*) and 'Remuneration of government servants' (*bhṛtyabharaṇīya*) to which reference has already been made,[1] and these are followed by three chapters on the conduct of courtiers, containing a series of shrewd maxims for the behaviour by which an astute time-server may obtain and preserve the royal favour, and, having thus attained the position of chief minister, may consolidate and maintain his power.

The remainder of the *Arthaśāstra*, that is to say, about two-fifths of its total contents, is mainly concerned with Foreign Policy and War.

This part of the work is prefaced by an exposition of certain philosophic theories relating to the nature of sovereignty and what may be called the balance of power.

Elements of sovereignty.

The 'elements of sovereignty' (*prakṛtayaḥ*) are said to be seven in number, namely: the ruler (*svāmin*), the minister (*amātya*), the country (*janapada*), the fort (*durga*), the treasury (*kośa*), the army (*daṇḍa*), and the ally (*mitra*). Or the elements of sovereignty found in a single state may be reckoned as six, excluding the ally.

Two policies are contrasted: *śama*, which is defined as the enjoyment in security of the results of work, and *vyāyāma*, or effort to achieve a result. Of these words, *kṣema* and *yoga* respectively are almost equivalents.

Sixfold policy.

The source (*yoni*) of *śama* and *vyāyāma* is said to lie in the (proper) application of the sixfold policy, or six policies (*ṣāḍguṇya*): (1) *sandhi*, equivalent to *paṇabandha*, or agreement between states, with pledges or guarantees; (2) *vigraha*, war; (3) *āsana*, equivalent to *upekṣaṇa*, indifference or neutrality; (4) *yāna*, invasion or attack; (5) *saṁsraya*, equivalent to *parārpaṇa*, seeking the protection of another; (6) *dvaidhībhāva*, making peace with one and war with another. Deterioration (*kṣaya*), remaining stationary

[1] Cf. pp. 34, 36, 37, 81.

(*sthāna*), and increase or progress (*vṛddhi*) are the three possible phases or conditions of a state. Of these the human causes are policy (*naya*) and impolicy (*apanaya*), the divine, fortune (*aya*) and misfortune (*anaya*).

Policy of aggression. The spirit of the maxims on foreign policy is frankly aggressive.

'The king', it is said, 'well endowed by nature, and in respect of the elements of sovereignty, who is the abode of policy is the conqueror (*vijigīṣu*).'

The ruler of territory adjacent to that of the conqueror is the enemy. The ruler of territory adjacent to that of the enemy, and separated by it from the conqueror's territory, is the conqueror's friend or ally. Other powers taken into consideration are the enemy's ally, and the allies of the conqueror's and the enemy's allies; the *madhyama* king, whose territory is close to those of the conqueror and his enemy and who is capable of helping either of them; and the *udāsīna*, or neutral king.

The circle of states. The conqueror, his ally, and his ally's ally are said to constitute a circle of states, and, as each state has six elements of sovereignty, each circle of states comprises eighteen elements of sovereignty. Again, as the conqueror, his enemy, and the *madhyama* and *udāsīna* kings form each the centre of a circle of states, in all seventy-two elements of sovereignty, it is said, are taken into consideration. As to the application of the six kinds of policy, it is laid down that he who is inferior in strength to another should make peace with him; he who is superior in strength should make war; whoever thinks: 'No enemy can hurt me, nor can I hurt my enemy,' should observe neutrality; whoever is amply provided with means of aggression should attack his enemy; the weak should seek protection; to accomplish an object, for which he requires help, a ruler should adopt the double policy of making peace with one state and war with another. The **Diplomacy.** course of diplomatic intrigue, by which an able ruler may gradually increase his power at the expense of neighbouring states, is described with almost wearisome minuteness, and with a candour which verges on cynicism. Here again

Force.

spies and secret agents figure largely. Diplomacy, however, must be backed by force, and this part of the *Arthaśāstra* contains the maxims for recruiting professional armies, to which reference has been made above,[1] and also hints on strategy and tactics of all arms.

The object set before the model king, or *vijigīṣu*, is that of building up an empire by a combination of diplomacy and warlike prowess. 'Having thus seized the territory of his enemy,' it is said, 'the conqueror should aim at acquiring that of the *madyama*, and next that of the *udāsīna* king. This is the way to conquer the world.'

Policy for a weak state.

Unbroken success is not postulated. A weak king attacked by a powerful enemy should seek the protection of one who is stronger than his enemy. In the absence of such a protector, he should combine with a number of his equals or inferiors. Failing such a combination, he should seek protection in a fort. Failing this, he should make peace with his enemy by placing his kingdom at the latter's disposal, and, having obtained his protection, should serve his interests in every way. In making peace, he may give one of his sons as a hostage. But when, by following a wise policy as a vassal king, he has succeeded in increasing his power, he may break through his agreement, after arranging by some device for the escape of the hostage. In another passage it is said that conquerors are of three kinds—the just or virtuous conqueror (*dharmavijayin*), who is satisfied with submission and fealty; the grasping conqueror, who aims at acquiring land and money, and is himself in fear of his enemies; and the ruthless or demon-like conqueror (*asuravijayin*), who would deprive the conquered of land, treasure, sons, wives, and life itself. A weak king attacked by the first may make submission to him, and obtain his protection; the second may be bought off with money; the third may be appeased by surrender of territory and treasure. Or, failing to make peace with a powerful enemy, the weak king may resort to intrigue, and, by means of secret agents, bring about disaffection among the subjects of his enemy or his assassination.

Three kinds of conquerors.

[1] Cf. p. 26.

For dealing with conquered country, a wise policy of conciliation is enjoined.

Treatment of conquered country.

'Having acquired a new territory,' it is said, 'the conqueror should, by the good qualities of his administration, overshadow the defects and surpass twofold the good qualities of the enemy whom he has expelled. By justice and virtue, industry and kindness, by remission of taxes and bestowal of gifts and honours, he should please and benefit the people of the country. He must faithfully keep his promises to those who have taken his side; otherwise he would forfeit the confidence of his own subjects as well as that of foreigners. He should study the character and adopt the dress, language, and customs of his new subjects. He should observe the religious festivals and ceremonies of the country. His secret agents should contrive to impress on the leading men of districts, villages, castes, and corporations the vices and defects of the late government, and the high esteem and favour with which they are regarded by the conqueror, and his devotion to their interests. He should be liberal in gifts and in remission of taxes, and attentive to the public security. On religious institutions, as well as on the learned, the eloquent, the virtuous, and the brave, he should bestow liberally lands and other property and remissions of taxation. He should release prisoners, and show favour to the poor, to orphans, and to the sick. He should prohibit the slaughter of animals for half a month during the *caturmāsya* (the four months of the rainy season), for four days at the full moon, and on the days of his own star and that of the country; also all slaughter of female and young animals, as well as castration. He should do away with abuses which are injurious to the army or the treasury, and establish righteous customs.'

Allusion to Northern Empire.

There is a chapter headed, 'The knowledge of power, place, time, strength, and weakness' (*śaktideśakālabalābalajnānam*), in which the following passage occurs: 'The place is the earth (*deśaḥpṛthivī*). There the northern region, extending from the Himalayas to the ocean, is the dominion of no mean ruler (*atiryakcakravartikṣetram*).' This may be read as an allusion to Candragupta's empire, for, as we have seen,[1] it covered the whole of Northern India, extending westward to the coast of the Arabian Sea, and

[1] Cf. pp. 23–7.

there is no record of an empire so extensive having existed in India before his time. It is possible, too, that the grandiloquent description 'extending from the Himalayas to the Sea' applied to the conquests or dominions of various kings, which is found in many later inscriptions, may be derived from the tradition of the Maurya empire, and, perhaps, from this passage of the *Kauṭilīya Arthaśāstra*. On the whole, however, the polity contemplated in this treatise is evidently that of a small state, ruled by an ordinary raja, and this is consistent with the probability that the empire comprised a number of vassal kingdoms. Reference has been made above [1] to another passage, which supports the traditional rule of policy that a conqueror should maintain a kingdom which submitted to him, if possible, under a member of its ancient royal family.

Prescriptions for poisons, &c.

The *Arthaśāstra* concludes with a series of prescriptions for poisons and poisonous fumes and concoctions, by which the complexion or the colour of the hair may be changed, blindness, dumbness, leprosy, and other diseases caused, or supernatural powers acquired, such as the power of fasting, of performing long journeys without fatigue, of touching or holding fire without being burnt, seeing in the dark, or becoming invisible, and *mantras* or spells, by the repetition of which whole villages may be thrown into deep sleep and doors caused to open. The following are a few examples.

'The powder prepared from the roots of *dhāmārgava* (*luffa foetida*) mixed with the powder of the flower of *bhallātaka* (*semecarpus anacardium*) causes, when administered, death in the course of a month.'

'The smoke caused by burning the powder of *śatakardama* (?) *uccidinga* (?) *karavira* (*nerium odorum*), *katutumbi* (a kind of bitter gourd), and fish, together with the straw of *madana* (?) *kodrava* (*paspalum scrobiculatum*), *hastikarna*, or *palasa*, destroys animal life as far as it is carried by the wind.'

'Whoever has anointed his legs with the oil extracted from paste prepared from the roots of *paribhadraka* (*erythrina indica*), *pratibala*, *vañjula* (a kind of rattan), *vajra* (*euphorbia*), and *banana*, mixed with the serum of the flesh of a frog, can walk over fire. Having fasted for three nights, on the day

[1] Cf. p. 31.

of the star Puṣya, place in the skull of a man who has been slain with a weapon, or impaled, soil and barley-seed, and irrigate them with milk of goats and sheep. Wearing a garland made of the sprouts of the barley, one may walk invisible to others.'

'The slough of a snake filled with powdered bones and marrow of a cow sacrificed during the funeral rites of a brahman will make cattle invisible.'

'Procure three white spines of a porcupine and, after fasting for seven nights, make libations of honey and clarified butter on a fire kindled from 108 pieces of *khadira* (*mimosa catechu*) wood, while repeating a *mantra* (given in the text). Then bury one of the spines at the entrance of a village or house while chanting the same *mantra*, and every being therein will fall asleep.'

Kauṭilya's *Arthaśāstra* reveals a mentality combining cold and calculating sagacity with almost childlike credulity. Summary.

The picture which the work presents is that of a paternal government, tempered by respect for religion and custom, and, probably, limited also by the power and privileges of guilds and corporations. Though the government was not democratic, it is likely that the life of the guilds and various other associations may have afforded occasion for such democratic processes as elections, debates, and decisions by majority vote. The State employed a very large number of officials and aimed at a close control over its subjects in many of their activities, regulating trade, commerce, and industry, levying taxes on sales, imports, and exports, as well as internal transit dues, fixing prices, maintaining communications by land and water, as well as irrigation works, registering births and deaths, and movements of travellers, and enforcing numerous regulations in the interests of public safety and convenience in town and country. In villages the care of the sick and infirm by government is enjoined, and among the buildings prescribed to be erected in fortified cities is the hospital (*bhaiṣajyagṛha*). Collecting a large proportion of its revenue in kind, the State itself engaged in manufactures and commerce.

We find no mention of schools. Probably the State did not concern itself with education, although the Aśoka edicts show that the knowledge of reading was widely diffused. It may have been imparted in monastic schools.[1] On the whole, it may be claimed for the *Arthaśāstra* that its general spirit is enlightened and humane, and though in some places it advocates methods and expedients flagrantly repugnant to our ideas of public morality, the general objects held in view are the maintenance of law and order, the punishment of the wicked, and the protection of the peaceable citizen. On these grounds the extensive employment of spies and secret agents may be defended, although the system must have been liable to abuse. Trade must have been severely hampered by the regulations and duties imposed on it, and by the attempts to fix prices. The system of land revenue assessment—a moderate fixed share of the produce, with additional temporary cesses to meet emergent requirements of the State—seems to have been elastic, and should not have been oppressive if the injunction to levy the additional cesses only where the harvest had been good were observed ; but here, also, there was probably room for abuse.

About the penal code, as already observed, there is a good deal of obscurity, but it seems likely that the cruel punishments mentioned in the *Arthaśāstra*, such as mutilation and death with torture, were becoming obsolete at the date of this work. Provisions making serious offences punishable with fine recall the eric fines of the Brehon Law. As already noticed, persons condemned to pay fines might be required to work off the amounts as slaves, and the system may have been economical.

The society for which these laws and institutions were designed evidently comprised, like the population of India at the present day, widely different scales of civilization, and this is clearly recognized, for example, in the sections relating to marriage, where eight customary kinds or classes of marriage are mentioned, of which four are regarded as superior, but the general rule is laid down that any form of marriage is permissible which is approved by custom in the class to which the parties belong. Similarly, as regards

[1] Vincent Smith, *Asoka, the Buddhist Emperor of India*, pp. 138–9.

succession to property, it is provided that the division of an inheritance shall be made in accordance with the custom of the district, caste, *saṅgha*, or village. There is clear evidence of the existence of a multitude of castes and the traditional theory of four original castes, and others derived from unions between members of different castes, which had actually occurred, though prohibited in principle. We find also the broad racial distinction between *ārya* and *mleccha*. *Śūdras*, evidently, were *ārya* by race, and there is nothing to indicate that they were regarded as a conquered race reduced to servitude. The duties of a *Śūdra* are said to be not only attendance on the twice-born, but also *vārtā*, which is explained as including agriculture, cattle-keeping, and trade, and *kārūkuśīlavakarma*, or the occupations of artisan, musician, &c. The occupations included under the head of *vārtā* were prescribed for *Vaiśyas* also, along with study, the performance of sacrifices, and the giving of gifts.

While it is clear that slavery existed, and must have been attended with some of the abuses inseparable from the institution, we find provisions of law designed to protect slaves, and especially female slaves, from ill-treatment. While it is clear, too, that persons of any caste might, in certain circumstances, be reduced to slavery, we may suppose that the general precept that 'no *ārya* should be a slave' reflected public sentiment, and it is, perhaps, safe to infer that people other than *mlecchas* were not often found in the condition of permanent slavery.

XII

MAURYA INSTITUTIONS

GREEK EVIDENCE

Greek and Latin sources.

When proceeding to consider the evidence contained in the works of Greek and Latin authors which bears on social and political conditions in India during the Maurya period, it is important to have a clear idea of its limitations. It is known that accounts of India were written by a number of Greeks or Macedonians who visited the country during that period: Megasthenes, already mentioned, who was sent as ambassador from Seleukos to the court of Candragupta Maurya; Patrokles, admiral of Seleuko's fleet; Deimachos, ambassador from Seleukos to Candragupta's successor, called by the Greeks Amitrochades or Amitrochates, and by Indian authorities Bindusāra; Dionysios, ambassador from Ptolemy Philadelphos of Egypt to Bindusāra or Aśoka—it is not certain which; Timosthenes, Ptolemy's admiral. None of these accounts has survived in its original form. What we have are descriptions of India by Greek and Latin authors who wrote centuries later, and who never visited India themselves, but probably derived most of their information, directly or indirectly, from the earlier accounts of the Greek writers just mentioned and those of Alexander's companions, and, in some instances, have quoted one or other of them as authority for statements which they make. It seems that, towards the close of Aśoka's reign, intercourse by land between the Hellenic world and India became interrupted, perhaps owing to the rise of the Parthian power, and even when, in later times, direct maritime trade became established between India and the Roman Empire, Greek and Latin writers on India continued to rely on the traditional authority of the distinguished men who visited the country in Alexander's train and during the century following his invasion.

It has been remarked by E. R. Bevan[1] that 'for many centuries the India known to the West was India as portrayed by the historians of Alexander's expedition, and of Megasthenes'.

Thus, in dealing with Greek and Latin sources of information about the Maurya period, we have to allow for probable inaccuracies, both in the original authorities and in the later works based on them, which have come down to us, and in this connexion it is well to bear in mind another observation of Mr. Bevan: 'In the case of the ancient Greeks, scientific curiosity was constantly being interfered with and thwarted by another interest, which was strong in them —the love of literary form, the delight in logical expression.'

Megasthenes.

The chief original authority quoted by name in extant documents whose evidence it is necessary to consider is Megasthenes, and of him we know that he was the representative of Seleukos at the court of Sibyrtios, satrap of Arachosia (Kandahar), and that he was sent on several occasions as ambassador to Sandrokottos at Palimbothra, to which place he travelled by a royal road. How long he stayed in India is uncertain, but, according to his own account, the only parts of the country actually visited by him were Pāṭaliputra and the regions through which he passed on his journeys to and from that city, and what he knew of the lower part of the country traversed by the Ganges was by hearsay.

Indian castes.

It will be convenient, first, to quote corresponding passages from the works of Diodorus, Strabo, Pliny, and Arrian respectively, based on Megasthenes, which deal with divisions of the Indian population.

Diodorus.

Diodorus says, in his epitome of Megasthenes:

The philosophers.

'The whole population of India is divided into seven castes (μέρη), of which the first is formed by the collective body of the philosophers (σύστημα φιλοσόφων), which, in point of number,

[1] *Cambridge History of India*, vol. i, chap. xvi, 'India in Early Greek and Latin Literature'.

is inferior to the other classes, but in point of dignity pre-eminent over all. For the philosophers, being exempted from all public duties, are neither the masters nor the servants of others. They are, however, engaged by private persons to offer the sacrifices due in lifetime, and to celebrate the obsequies of the dead : for they are believed to be most dear to the gods, and to be most conversant with matters pertaining to Hades. In requital of such services they receive valuable gifts and privileges. To the people of India at large they also render great benefits, when, gathered together at the beginning of the year, they forewarn the assembled multitudes about droughts and wet weather, and also about propitious winds and diseases, and other topics capable of profiting the hearers. Thus the people and the sovereign learning beforehand what is to happen, always make adequate provision against a coming deficiency, and never fail to prepare beforehand what will help in time of need. The philosopher who errs in his predictions incurs no other penalty than obloquy, and he then observes silence for the rest of his life.

The husbandmen.

'The second caste (*μέρος*) consists of the husbandmen, who appear to be far more numerous than the others. Being, moreover, exempted from fighting and other public services, they devote the whole of their time to tillage; nor would an enemy coming upon a husbandman at work on his land do him any harm, for men of this class, being regarded as public benefactors, are protected from all injury. The land, thus remaining unravaged, and producing heavy crops, supplies the inhabitants with all that is requisite to make life very enjoyable. The husbandmen themselves, with their wives and children, live in the country and entirely avoid going into town. They pay a land-tribute to the king, because all India is the property of the crown, and no private person is permitted to own land. Besides the land-tribute, they pay into the royal treasury a fourth part of the produce of the soil.

Herdsmen and hunters.

'The third caste (*φῦλον*) consists of the neat-herds and shepherds (*βουκόλων καὶ ποιμένων*) and in general of all herdsmen (*νομέων*), who neither settle in towns nor in villages, but live in tents. By hunting and trapping they clear the country of various birds and wild beasts. As they apply themselves eagerly and assiduously to this pursuit, they free India from the pests with which it abounds—all sorts of wild beasts and birds, which devour the seeds sown by the husbandmen.

'The fourth caste (μέρος) consists of the artisans (τεχνιτῶν). Of these some are armourers, while others make the implements which husbandmen and others find useful in their different callings. This class is not only exempted from paying taxes, but even receives maintenance from the royal exchequer.

The artisans.

'The fifth caste is the military (πέμπτον δὲ τὸ στρατιωτικόν). It is well organized and equipped for war, holds the second place in point of numbers, and gives itself up to idleness and amusement in the times of peace. The entire force—men-at-arms, war-horses, war-elephants, and all—are maintained at the king's expense.

The soldiers.

'The sixth caste (ἕκτον) consists of the overseers (ἐφόρων). It is their province to inquire into and superintend all that goes on in India, and make report to the king, or, where the state is without a king (ἀβασίλευτος), to the magistrates.

The overseers.

'The seventh caste (μέρος) consists of the councillors and assessors—of those who deliberate on public affairs. It is the smallest class, looking to number, but the most respected, on account of the high character and the wisdom of its members; for from their ranks the advisers of the king are taken, and the treasurers of the state, and the arbiters, who settle disputes. The generals of the army also, and the chief magistrates, usually belong to this class. Such, then, are about the parts into which the body politic in India is divided. No one is allowed to marry out of his own caste (οὐκ ἔξεστι δὲ γαμεῖν ἐξ ἄλλου γένους), or to exercise any calling or art except his own: for instance, a soldier cannot become a husbandman or an artisan a philosopher.' [1]

The councillors.

Strabo says, in his description of India:

Indian castes—Strabo.

'According to him (Megasthenes) the population of India is divided into seven parts (μέρη). The philosophers are first in rank, but form the smallest class in point of number. Their services are employed privately by persons who wish to offer sacrifices or perform other sacred rites, and also publicly by the kings, at what is called the Great Synod, wherein, at the beginning of the new year, all the philosophers are gathered together before the king at the gates, where any philosopher who may have committed any useful suggestion to writing, or observed any means for improving the crops or the cattle, or for promoting the public interests, declares it publicly. If any one is detected giving false information therein, the law condemns him to be silent

The philosophers.

[1] ii. 40, 41.

for the rest of his life, but he who gives sound advice is exempted from paying any taxes or contribution.

The husbandmen.

'The second caste (δεύτερον δὲ μέρος) consists of the husbandmen, who form the bulk of the population and are in disposition most mild and gentle. They are exempted from military service, and cultivate the lands undisturbed by fear. They never go to town, either to take part in its tumults or for any other purpose. It therefore not infrequently happens that, at the same time, and in the same part of the country, men may be seen drawn up in array of battle, and fighting at the risk of their lives, while other men close at hand are ploughing and digging in perfect security, having their soldiers to protect them. The whole of the land is the property of the king, and the husbandmen till it on condition of receiving one-fourth of the produce.

Herdsmen and hunters.

'The third caste (τρίτον) consists of herdsmen and hunters, who alone are allowed to hunt, and to keep cattle, and to sell draught animals, and let them out to hire. In return for clearing the land of wild beasts and fowls, who devour the seeds sown in the fields, they receive an allowance of grain from the king. They lead a wandering life and live under tents. . . .[1]

Traders.

'The fourth class (τέταρτον μέρος), after herdsmen and hunters, consists of those who work as traders, of those who vend wares, and of those who are employed in bodily labour. Some of them pay tribute and render to the state certain prescribed services. But the armour-makers and shipbuilders receive wages and their victuals from the king, for whom alone they work. The general in command of the army supplies the soldiers with weapons, and the admiral of the fleet (ναύαρχος) lets out ships on hire for the transport both of passengers and merchandise.

Fighting men.

'The fifth class (πέμπτον) consists of fighting men, who, when not engaged in active service, pass their time in idleness and drinking. They are maintained at the king's expense, and hence they are always ready, when occasion calls, to take the field; for they carry nothing of their own with them but their own bodies.

Overseers.

'The sixth class (ἕκτον) consists of the overseers (ἔφοροι), to whom is consigned the duty of watching all that goes on and making reports secretly to the king. Some are entrusted with the inspection of the city, and others with that of the army. The former employ as their coadjutors the courtesans of the city, and the latter the courtesans of the camp. The

[1] xv. i. 39–41.

ablest and most trustworthy men are appointed to fill these offices.

Councillors.

'The seventh class (ἕβδομον) consists of the councillors and assessors of the king. To them belong the highest posts of government, the tribunals of justice, and the general administration of public affairs. No one is allowed to marry out of his own caste (οὐκ ἔστι δ' οὔτε γαμεῖν ἐξ ἄλλου γένους), or to exchange one profession or trade for another, or to follow more than one business. An exception is made in favour of the philosopher, who, for his virtue, is allowed this privilege. . . .[1]

Strabo's further notice of the philosophers.

'Speaking of the philosophers, he (Megasthenes) says that such of them as live on the mountains are worshippers of Dionysos, showing as proofs that he had come among them, the wild vine, which grows in their country only, and the ivy and the laurel and the myrtle and the box-tree, and other evergreens, none of which are found beyond the Euphrates, except a few in parks, which it requires great care to preserve. They observe also certain customs, which are bacchanalian. Thus, they dress in muslin, wear the turban, use perfumes, array themselves in garments dyed of bright colours, and their kings, when they appear in public, are preceded by the music of drums and gongs. But the philosophers who live on the plains worship Herakles. . . . Megasthenes makes a different division of the philosophers, saying that they are of two kinds; one of which he calls the Brachmanes, and the other the Sarmanes.[2] The Brachmanes are most esteemed, for they are more consistent in their opinions. From the time of their conception in the womb, they are under the guardian care of learned men, who go to the mother, and, under the pretence of using some incantations for the welfare of herself and her unborn babe, in reality give her prudent hints and counsels. The women, who listen most willingly, are thought to be the most fortunate in their children. After their birth, the children are under the care of one person after another, and, as they advance in age, each succeeding master is more accomplished than his predecessor. The philosophers have their abode in a grove in front of the city, within a moderate-sized enclosure. They live in simple style, and lie on beds of rushes or skins. They abstain from animal food and sexual pleasures, and spend their time in listening to serious discourse, and in imparting their knowledge

[1] xv. i. 46–9.

[2] The word Garmanes, which appears in existing texts, is generally held to be a copyist's error for Sarmanes.

to such as will listen to them. The hearer is not allowed to speak, or even to cough, and much less to spit, and, if he offends in any of these ways, he is cast out from their society that very day, as being a man who is wanting in self-restraint. After living in this manner for seven-and-thirty years, each individual retires to his own property, where he lives for the rest of his days in ease and security. They then array themselves in fine muslin and wear a few trinkets of gold on their fingers and in their ears. They eat flesh, but not of animals employed in labour. They abstain from hot and highly-seasoned food. They marry as many wives as they please with a view to have numerous children, for, by having many wives, greater advantages are enjoyed, and since they have no slaves, they have more need to have children around them to attend to their wants. The Brachmanes do not communicate a knowledge of philosophy to their wives, lest they should divulge any of the forbidden mysteries to the profane, if they became depraved, or lest they should desert them if they became good philosophers : for no one who despises pleasure and pain as well as life and death wishes to be in subjection to another, but this is characteristic of a good man, and of a good woman. Death is with them a very frequent subject of discourse. They regard this life as, so to speak, a time when the child within the womb becomes mature ; and death as a birth into a real and happy life for the votaries of philosophy. On this account, they undergo much discipline as a preparation for death. They consider nothing that befalls man to be either good or bad, to suppose otherwise being a dreamlike illusion—else how could some be affected with sorrow and others with pleasure by the very same things, and how could the same things affect the same individuals at different times with the opposite emotions ?

'Their ideas about physical phenomena, the same author tells us, are very crude, for they are better in their actions than in their reasonings, inasmuch as their belief is, in great measure, based upon fables, yet, on many points, their opinions coincide with those of the Greeks, for, like them, they say that the world had a beginning, and is liable to destruction, and is in shape spherical, and that the deity who made it, and who governs it, is diffused through all its parts. They hold that various first principles operate in the universe, and that water was the principle employed in the making of the world. In addition to the four elements, there is a fifth agency, from which the heaven and the stars were produced. The earth is placed in the centre of the universe. Concerning generation, and the nature of the soul, and many other subjects, they express views like those maintained by the Greeks. They wrap up their doctrines about immortality and future judgement, and kindred topics in allegories after the manner of Plato. Such are his statements regarding the Brachmanes. Of the Saramanes he tells us that those who are held in most honour are called the Hylobioi. They live in the woods, where they subsist on leaves of trees and wild fruits, and wear garments made from the bark of trees. They abstain from sexual intercourse and from wine. They communicate with the kings, who consult them by messengers regarding the causes of things, and who, through them, worship and supplicate the deity. Next in honour to the Hylobioi are the physicians, since they are engaged in the study of the nature of man. They are simple in their habits, but do not live in the fields. Their food consists of rice and barley meal, which they can always get for the mere asking or receive from those who entertain them as guests in their houses. By their knowledge of pharmacy they can make marriages fruitful, and determine the sex of the offspring. They effect cures rather by regulating diet than by the use of medicine. The remedies most esteemed are ointments and plasters. All others they consider to be, in a great measure, pernicious in their nature. This class and the other class practise fortitude, both by undergoing active toil, and by the endurance of pain, so that they remain for a whole day motionless in one fixed attitude. Besides these, there are diviners and sorcerers, and adepts in the rites and customs relating to the dead, who go about begging, both in villages and towns. Even such of them as are of superior culture and refinement, inculcate such superstitions regarding Hades as they consider favourable to piety and holiness of life. Women pursue philosophy with some of them, but abstain from sexual intercourse. . . .' [1]

'The Indians worship Zeus Ombrios (i.e. the Rainy), the river Ganges, and the indigenous deities of the country.'[2]

'The Pramnai are philosophers opposed to the Brachmanes, and are contentious and proud of argument. They ridicule the Brachmanes, who study physiology and astronomy, as fools and impostors. Some of them are called the Pramnai of the mountains, others the Gymnetai, and others again the Pramnai of the city or the Pramnai of the country. Those of the mountains wear deer-skins and carry wallets

[1] xv. i. 58–60. [2] xv. i. 69.

filled with roots and drugs, professing to cure diseases by means of incantations, charms, and amulets. The Gymnetai, in accordance with their name, are naked, and live generally in the open air practising endurance, as I have already mentioned, for seven-and-thirty years. Women live in their society without sexual commerce. The Pramnai of the city live in towns, and wear muslin robes, while those of the country clothe themselves with skins of fawns or antelopes.' [1]

Pliny. Pliny refers to the classes of the Indian population as follows :

'For among the more civilized Indian communities life is spent in a great variety of separate occupations. Some till the soil, some are soldiers, some traders ; the noblest and richest take part in the direction of state affairs, administering justice, and sit in council with the kings. A fifth class (*genus*) devotes itself to the philosophy prevalent in the country, which almost assumes the form of a religion, and the members always put an end to their life by a voluntary death on a burning funeral pile. In addition to these classes there is one (*unum super haec est*), half-wild, which is constantly engaged in a task of immense labour, beyond the power of words to describe—that of hunting and taming elephants.' [2]

Indian castes—Arrian. Arrian, professing to base his account on Megasthenes, says :

The Sophists. 'But further in India the whole people is divided into about seven castes (γένεα). Among these are the Sophists (σοφισταί), who are not so numerous as the others, but hold the supreme place of dignity and honour ; for they are under no necessity of doing any bodily labour at all or of contributing from the produce of their labour anything to the common stock, nor indeed is any duty absolutely binding on them, except to perform the sacrifice offered to the gods on behalf of the State. If any one, again, has a private sacrifice to offer, one of the sophists shows him the proper mode, as if he could not otherwise make an acceptable offering to the gods. To them also the knowledge of divination among the Indians is exclusively restricted, and none but a sophist is allowed to practise that art. They predict about such matters as the seasons of the year, and any calamity which may befall the State. These sages go naked, living during winter in the open

[1] xv. i. 70–1.

[2] vi. 22.

air, to enjoy the sunshine, and, during the summer, when the heat is too powerful, in meadows and low grounds under large trees, the shadow whereof, Nearchus[1] says, extends to five plethra in circuit, adding that even ten thousand men could be covered by the shadow of a single tree. They live upon the fruits which each season produces, and on the bark of trees—the bark being no less sweet and nutritious than the fruit of the date-palm. But the private fortunes of individuals they do not care to predict, either because divination does not concern itself with trifling matters, or because to take any trouble about such is deemed unbecoming. But if any one of them fails to predict truly, he incurs, it is said, no further penalty than being obliged to be silent for the future, and there is no power on earth to compel that man to speak, who has once been condemned to silence.

The husbandmen.

'After them, the second caste (δεύτεροι) consists of the tillers of the soil, who form the most numerous class of the population. They are neither furnished with arms, nor have any military duties to perform, but they cultivate the soil, and pay tribute to the king and the independent (αὐτόνομοι) cities.[2] In time of civil war the soldiers are not allowed to molest the husbandmen or ravage their lands: hence, while the former are fighting and killing each other as they can, the latter may be seen close at hand, tranquilly pursuing their work—perhaps ploughing or gathering in their crop, pruning the trees, or reaping the harvest.

The herdsmen.

'The third caste (τρίτον) among the Indians consist of the herdsmen, both shepherds and neat-herds, and they neither live in cities nor in villages, but they are nomadic, and live on the hills. They, too, are subject to tribute, and this they pay in cattle. They scour the country in pursuit of fowl and wild beasts.

Handicraftsmen and retailers.

'The fourth caste (τέταρτον) consists of handicraftsmen and retail dealers. They have to perform gratuitously certain public services, and to pay tribute from the products of their labour. An exception, however, is made in favour of those who fabricate the weapons of war, and, not only so, but they even draw pay from the State. In this class are included shipbuilders, and the sailors employed in the navigation of the rivers.

Warriors.

'The fifth class (πέμπτον γένος) among the Indians consists

[1] Admiral of Alexander the Great's fleet.

[2] McCrindle translates αὐτόνομοι here as 'independent', but in later passages (cf. p. 150) as 'self-governed'. The latter seems the better rendering (cf. Stein, *Megasthenes und Kauṭilya*, p. 226).

of the warriors, who are second, in point of numbers, to the husbandmen, but lead a life of supreme freedom and enjoyment. They have only military duties to perform. Others make their arms, and others supply them with horses, and they have others to attend on them in the camp, who take care of their horses, clean their arms, drive their elephants, prepare their chariots, and act as their charioteers. As long as they are required to fight, they fight, and, when peace returns, they abandon themselves to enjoyment—the pay, which they receive from the State being so liberal that they can with ease maintain themselves, and others besides.

Superintendents. 'The sixth class (*ἕκτοι*) consists of those called superintendents (*ἐπίσκοποι*). They spy out what goes on in country and town, and report everything to the king, when the people have a king, and to the magistrate, when the people are self-governed (*αὐτόνομοι*),[1] and it is against use and wont for them to give in a false report; but indeed no Indian is accused of lying.

Councillors. 'The seventh caste (*ἕβδομοι*) consists of the councillors of state, who advise the king, or the magistrate of self-governed cities,[1] in the management of public affairs. In point of numbers this is a small class, but it is distinguished by superior wisdom and justice, and hence enjoys the prerogative of choosing governors, chiefs of provinces, deputy-governors, superintendents of the treasury, generals of the army, admirals of the navy, controllers, and commissioners, who superintend agriculture.

'The custom of the country prohibits intermarriage between the castes (*γαμέειν δὲ ἐξ ἑτέρου γένεος οὐ θέμις*). For instance, the husbandmen cannot take a wife from the artisan caste, nor the artisan a wife from the husbandman caste. Custom also prohibits any one from exercising two trades, or from changing from one caste to another. One cannot, for instance, become a husbandman if he is a herdsman, or become a herdsman if he is an artisan. It is permitted that the sophist only be from any caste, for the life of a sophist is not an easy one, but the hardest of all.'[2]

Megasthenes' knowledge of caste probably superficial. While the above passages are, no doubt, based, mainly at any rate, on Megasthenes, it is evident that they do not reproduce his account exactly, and we do not know what liberties may have been taken with his text. It seems that he had gained a superficial acquaintance with the Indian

[1] Cf. p. 149, note 2. [2] *Indika*, xi, xii.

caste system in its functional and racial aspects. The words γένος, φῦλον connote race and family, and may properly be translated 'caste', but μέρος, σύστημα do not connote any idea of race. We do not know what terms may have been used by Megasthenes in this connexion. But Diodorus, Strabo, and Arrian all three refer to the general rule against intermarriage between castes, using the word γένος.

From a general knowledge of the functional character of caste, Megasthenes would naturally be led to include in one caste all persons in India following one avocation, or similar avocations, and, thus, to treat Brahman and non-Brahman priests, monks, and ascetics of different denominations as forming one class of 'philosophers' or 'sophists'. In this view he may, probably, have been supported by what appeared to him to be the popular estimation, and by current language. In several of Aśoka's edicts [1] we find the expression *brāhmaṇaśramaṇa* and *śramaṇabrāhmaṇa,* in their *prākrit* equivalents, written as a compound word referring to a class of persons, 'brāhmans and ascetics', and respect for the class enjoined. Megasthenes, however, as appears from the versions of Strabo and Arrian, noticed that certain kinds of ascetics, such as the Buddhist *śramaṇas,* were drawn from various classes of the population, and from this concluded that the 'philosophers' or 'sophists' formed an exception to the general rule that a person might not exchange one profession or caste for another. At the same time, as the second passage quoted above from Strabo shows, Megasthenes was aware of a distinction between Brahmaṇas and Śramaṇas, by him called Brachmanes and Sarmanes and regarded as subdivisions of the class of philosophers, and of the hereditary prestige enjoyed by the former. He does not seem to have been aware of the theory of four castes, which, probably, corresponded as little with actuality in his time as it does at present.

His view of Indian philosophy and religions.

Megasthenes, we may be sure, made no close or detailed study of the multitudinous Indian philosophies and religions, which we now, on later literary evidence, classify as Brah-

[1] Cf. 'Major Rock Edicts', III, IV, IX, XI; 'Pillar Edict', VII.

manical Hinduism, Buddhism, and Jainism, but which, of course, bore no such names at that time. Probably he had opportunities of conversation with Indian philosophers, priests, and ascetics, and his attention was arrested by certain outstanding features, such as the pantheistic tendency of Indian beliefs, and the practice of wrapping up philosophical doctrine in allegories—a point which has escaped some modern European observers. Megasthenes' statement that the Indian philosophers held the earth to be spherical in shape does not find support in Indian literature, which however, shows that, in ancient times, the Indians were aware of the convexity of the inhabited world, which they likened to the back of a tortoise rising from the boundless ocean.[1] The fifth element of the Indians, to which Megasthenes refers, is the ākāśa or 'ether' of Sanskrit books.

Naturally, he was led to identify Indian deities with those of Greece, as Śiva (probably) with Dionysos, Viṣṇu with Herakles, and Indra with Zeus. His interest was aroused also by certain ascetic precepts and practices. The period of thirty-seven years, which he assigns for the education of a Brachmane, corresponds to the maximum allowed by Manu [2] for the Brahmācārya stage of life, and his category of Hylobioi recalls the vanaprastha stage. Whether Strabo's description of the Pramnai is based on Megasthenes or another authority is not quite clear. The name, perhaps, corresponds to the Sanskrit *pramāṇika*, an appellation given to philosophers who ridiculed Brahmans putting their trust in vedic ceremonies.[3]

Pliny's statement that the philosophers always put an end to their life is, obviously, a generalization based on one or two instances of suicide by Indian ascetics, which came to the notice of the Greeks. It is contradicted by the following passage of Strabo :

'Megasthenes, however, says that self-destruction is not a dogma of the philosophers, but that those who commit this

[1] Cf. Kern, Translation of Bṛhat Saṃhitā, *J. R. A. S.*, n.s., vol. v, p. 81, note.

[2] Chap. iii, sec. 1.

[3] Cf. Bevan, *Cambridge History of India*, vol. i, ch. xvi ; Rapson, *Ancient India*, pp. 58–61.

act are regarded as foolhardy; that some are naturally of a severe temper and inflict wounds upon their bodies or cast themselves down a precipice, that those who are impatient of pain drown themselves, while those that are capable of enduring pain strangle themselves, and those of ardent tempers throw themselves into the fire. Kalānos[1] was a man of this stamp.'[2]

Comparison with the *Arthaśāstra*. The cultivators.

Strabo's description of the cultivators as a mild and gentle class of people, the most numerous in the population, who never go to town, or take part in its tumults, applies, with little qualification, at the present day.

From various references in the *Arthaśāstra* to plundering in time of war, Dr. Otto Stein has argued[3] the incorrectness of Megasthenes' assertion that the cultivators were immune from such devastation. It is not clear, however, that the passages of the *Arthaśāstra* in question refer to the plundering of cultivators, and there seems to be no good reason why Megasthenes' general statement on the point should not be accepted, though, no doubt, there were exceptions to the rule.

Strabo says that all land in India was the property of the king, and the husbandmen who tilled it received only one-fourth of the produce as their remuneration. Diodorus supports Strabo's statement as to the king's sole ownership of land, but says that the cultivators paid the king a rent, and one-fourth of the produce, in addition. Arrian says nothing about the ownership of land, but records that the cultivators paid tribute to the king and to the independent cities.

It is likely that, on these points, none of the three has reproduced exactly Megasthenes' account. From the *Arthaśāstra* we gather that there were crown lands, some of which were let out to cultivators, who paid one-half, one-fourth, or other shares of the produce, according to circumstances, while those who held land other than crown land paid different shares as tax, and other taxes besides. We

[1] The Indian ascetic, who was interviewed at Taxila by Onesikritos, pilot of Alexander's fleet, afterwards accompanied Alexander, and eventually committed suicide by burning.

[2] xv. 68.

[3] *Megasthenes und Kauṭilya*, pp. 126, 127, 151.

shall, perhaps, be safe in assuming that Megasthenes did not compile a full record of all the various forms of Indian land-tenures and land-taxation, or that the later authors condensed, and, in doing so, distorted his account.

The soldiers.

His description of the fifth class, soldiers, corresponds with the indications of the *Arthaśāstra*, and other evidence of immemorial Indian custom, in so far as it represents the soldiers as a professional class distinct from the general population. Here, again, Megasthenes probably failed to observe subdivisions in the class. Diodorus and Arrian represent him as saying that it was a very large class—second, in point of numbers, to the husbandmen—and the numbers of the army, if all the maula men, liable to be called out for occasional military service, were included, may well have been very great. On the other hand, the description of the warriors as receiving high pay, and leading a life of ease and enjoyment in time of peace, would apply to the standing army of *bhṛta* and *śreṇī* soldiers.

Herdsmen and hunters.

What class or classes of people may have been covered by Megasthenes' third caste of 'herdsmen and hunters' is doubtful. It may have included the forest tribes (*āṭavika*) of the *Arthaśāstra*, or the herdsmen employed under the 'superintendents of cattle' (*go'dhyakṣa*).[1]

Handicraftsmen.

The descriptions of the fourth caste may be compared with the chapters of the *Arthaśāstra* relating to the superintendents of the armoury (*ayudhāgāra*)[2] and shipping (*nau*).[3] According to Strabo's version, the admiral of the fleet (ναύαρχος) used to let out royal ships for hire for the transport of passengers and merchandise, and this is one of the duties of the *nāvadhyakṣa* as prescribed by the *Arthaśāstra*.

Overseers.

The sixth of Megasthenes' 'castes' would seem, from the description of their duties, to refer to the numerous spies, whose employment is recommended in various passages of the *Arthaśāstra*. The members of this class are called by Diodorus and Strabo ἔφοροι, and by Arrian ἐπίσκοποι. Both of these terms may be translated 'overseer'. The name

[1] Cf. p. 73. [2] Cf. p. 58. [3] Cf. p. 72.

ἔφοροι (*ephori*) was given specially to a class of magistrates found in many Dorian Greek states, who, at times, exercised very extensive powers and functions, including scrutiny of the conduct of other magistrates, and censorship of the morals of private citizens. At Athens, the inspectors who were sometimes sent to report on the administration of subject states were called ἐπίσκοποι (*episcopi*). It is possible that Megasthenes may have confounded the class of spies with the numerous *adhyakṣas* petty superintendents in different departments, whose employment is prescribed in the *Arthaśāstra*.

Councillors.

It is more difficult to reconcile with the *Arthaśāstra* his description of the seventh 'caste' of 'councillors'. He speaks of it as a small class, but the king's council of ministers (*mantrin* or *amātya*) contemplated by Kauṭilya is a body of from twelve to twenty members only.[1] As mentioned above,[2] it would appear that the title amātya, equivalent to mantrin, and meaning, properly, 'councillor' or 'minister', was given, not only to the members of the king's council, but also to a class of subordinate officials.

Self-governed cities.

It will be noticed that, in the passage quoted from Arrian above, but not in the corresponding extract from Strabo, there is mention of 'self-governed cities' (αὐτόνομοι πόλεις), meaning, apparently, independent towns or states with a republican form of government, and Diodorus refers to states 'without a king'. The evidence as to the existence of such towns or states in Ancient India has been exhaustively discussed by Dr. Otto Stein.[3] Here it may suffice to say that the *Arthaśāstra* contains no clear reference to any such political units.

At the close of an early chapter [4] on 'Protection of Princes', which deals, among other subjects, with the question of succession to the throne, occurs the verse :

kulasya vā bhavedrajyaṁ kulasaṅgho hi durjayaḥ arāja-vyasanabādhaḥ śaśvadāvasati ksitim—

which Mr. Shamasastry translates—'Sovereignty may (some-

[1] Cf. p. 34. [2] Cf. p. 35.
[3] *Megasthenes und Kauṭilya*, pp. 224–32. [4] Bk. I, ch. xvii.

times) be the property of a clan; for the corporation of clans is invincible in its nature, and, being free from the calamities of anarchy, can have a permanent existence on earth'—and regards as 'a clear proof of the existence of republican or oligarchical forms of government in ancient India'.

Possibly, the obscure epithet, *rājaśabdopajīvin*, applied elsewhere[1] to certain communities—Licchivis, Vṛjis, Mallas, &c., may have reference to such forms of government, but few will agree that the proof of their existence in Ancient India is clear. At the same time, the Greek evidence on the point is not to be lightly discarded.

[1] Cf. p. 76.

XIII

MAURYA INSTITUTIONS

GREEK EVIDENCE (*continued*)

THE GOVERNMENT AND LAWS

THE following is Strabo's account, purporting to be based on Megasthenes, of the government at Pāṭaliputra.

The agoranomi.

'Of the great officers of state (ἀρχόντων), some have charge of the market, others of the city (οἱ μέν εἰσιν ἀγορανόμοι οἱ δ' ἀστυνόμοι), others of the soldiers. Some superintend the rivers, measure the land, as is done in Egypt, and inspect the sluices, by which water is let out from the main channels into their branches, so that every one may have an equal supply of it. The same persons have charge also of the huntsmen, and are entrusted with the power of rewarding or punishing them according to their deserts. They collect the taxes and superintend the occupations connected with land, as those of the wood-cutters, the carpenters, the blacksmiths, and the miners. They construct roads, and, at every ten stadia, set up a pillar to show the by-roads and distances. Those who have charge of the city (ἀστυνόμοι) are divided into six bodies of five each. The members of the first look after everything relating to the industrial arts. Those of the second attend to the entertainment of foreigners. To these they assign lodgings, and they keep watch over their mode of life by means of those persons whom they give to them for assistants. They escort them on the way when they leave the country, or, in the event of their dying, forward their property to their relations. They take care of them when they are sick, and, if they die, bury them. The third body consists of those who inquire, when and how births and deaths occur, with a view, not only of levying a tax, but also in order that births and deaths among both high and low may not escape the cognizance of the government. The fourth class superintend trade and commerce. Its members have charge of weights and measures and see that the products in their seasons are sold by public notice. No one is allowed to deal in more than one kind of commodity, unless he pays a double

The astynomi.

tax. The fifth class supervises manufactured articles, which they sell by public notice. What is new is sold separately from what is old, and there is a fine for mixing the two together. The sixth and last class consists of those who collect the tenth of the prices of the articles sold. Fraud in the payment of this tax is punishable with death. Such are the functions which these bodies separately discharge. In their collective capacity they have charge both of their special departments, and also of matters affecting the general interest, as the keeping of public buildings in proper repair, the regulation of prices, the care of markets, harbours, and temples.

Military departments.

'Next to the city magistrates, there is a third governing body (συναρχία), which directs military affairs. This also consists of six divisions, with five members to each. One division is appointed to co-operate with the admiral of the fleet, another with the superintendant of the bullock trains, which are used for transporting engines of war, food for the soldiers, provender for the cattle, and other military requisites. They supply servants, who beat the drum, and others who carry gongs; grooms also for the horses, and mechanists and their assistants. To the sound of the gongs they send out foragers to bring in grass, and, by a system of rewards and punishments, ensure the work being done with dispatch and safety. The third division has charge of the foot-soldiers, the fourth of the horses, the fifth of the war-chariots, and the sixth of the elephants. There are royal stables for the horses and elephants, and also a royal magazine for the arms, because the soldier has to return his arms to the magazine and his horse and his elephant to the stables. They use the elephants without bridles. The chariots are drawn on the march by oxen, but the horses are led along by a halter, that their legs may not be galled and inflamed, nor their spirits damped by drawing chariots. In addition to the charioteer, there are two fighting men who sit up in the chariot beside him. The war-elephant carries four men—three who shoot arrows and the driver.'

It will be seen that, according to Strabo, Megasthenes found in India two classes of superior civil officials—the ἀγορανόμοι (*agŏranomi*) and the ἀστυνόμοι (*astynomi*)—administering the rural area and the capital city respectively, and that the work of the latter, of which Megasthenes probably saw most during his residences at Pāṭaliputra, is described in much more detail than that of the former.

The word ἀγορανόμοι is translated by McCrindle as 'officers in charge of the market', and that is its literal meaning, but the word was used for the Latin aediles, as explained in the following extracts from Smith's *Dictionary of Greek and Roman Antiquities*:

Agoranomi and aediles.

'Agoranomi (ἀγορανόμοι) were public functionaries in most of the Grecian states, whose duties corresponded, in many respects, to those of the Roman aediles, whence Greek writers on Roman affairs call the aediles by this name. . . .

'Aediles (ἀγορανόμοι) . . . They had the general superintendence of buildings, both sacred and private; under this power they provided for the support and repair of temples, curiae, &c., and took care that private buildings, which were in a ruinous state, were repaired by the owners or pulled down. The superintendence over the supply and distribution of water at Rome was, at an early period, a matter of public administration. According to Frontinus, this was the duty of the censors; but, when there were no censors, it was within the province of the aediles. The care of the streets and pavements, with the cleansing and draining of the city, belonged to the aediles, and the care of the cloacae. . . The aediles had to see that the public lands were not improperly used, and that the pasture-grounds of the state were not trespassed upon; and they had power to punish by fine any unlawful act in this respect. The fines were employed in paving roads, and in other public purposes. They had a general superintendence over buying and selling, and, as a consequence, the supervision of the markets, of things exposed for sale, such as slaves, and of weights and measures: from this part of their duty is derived the name under which the aediles are mentioned by Greek writers (ἀγορανόμοι) . . . The general superintendence of police comprehended the duty of preserving order, decency, and the inspection of the baths and houses of entertainment, of brothels, and of prostitutes.'

The ἀστυνόμοι (*astynomi*) were public officers in most of the Greek states, in charge of the cities, whose duty it was to preserve order in the streets, and keep them clean, and to see that all buildings, both public and private, were in a safe state, and not likely to cause injury by falling down.

It will be remembered [1] that, according to the *Arthaśāstra*,

[1] Cf. p. 44.

Comparison with *Artha-śāstra.*

the *Samāhartṛ* should look after the fort or city (*durga*) as well as the rural area (*rāṣṭra*), mines, irrigation works, forests, cattle, and communications, and has also police duties. The heading 'durga' includes the collection of tolls on sales of goods, the supervision of weights and measures, control of liquor-shops, gaming-houses, and courtesans, and all the duties of the *Nāgaraka*, or city-superintendent, who is subordinate to the *Samāhartṛ*. *Rāṣṭra* includes crown-lands, pastures, and market towns (*paṭṭana*). Thus it will be seen that the range of functions prescribed by the *Arthaśāstra* for the *Samāhartṛ* covers most of those which appertained to the Roman aediles, whom Strabo would call ἀγορανόμοι. He represents, however, the ἀγορανόμοι as a body of officials concerned with the rural area only, and the city as managed by an independent body of ἀστυνόμοι comprising six boards, whereas, according to the *Arthaśāstra*, there should be one *samāhartṛ*, to whom the *nāgaraka* should be subordinate. That is the organization recommended for a small state. It may be supposed that, to meet the needs of a great city, such as Pāṭaliputra, and the home provinces of a great empire, the primary organization was modified and expanded in the manner indicated by Strabo.

Agronomi.

We do not know what Greek expressions Megasthenes may have used in this connexion. It has been suggested that the name given by him to the officials in charge of rural administration was not ἀγορανόμοι but ἀγρονόμοι, a name which occurs in certain passages of Aristotle's 'Politics' and Plato's 'Laws' as that of a class exercising in rural areas functions corresponding to those which devolved on the ἀστυνόμοι in towns. Dr. Otto Stein conjectures that the office of ἀγρονόμος not being so well known as that of ἀγορανόμος, the latter may have been substituted for the former in Strabo's rendering of Megasthenes.[1]

Samāhartṛ and *Nāgaraka.*

However this may be, if we examine the duties of the ἀγορανόμοι and ἀστυνόμοι, as described by Strabo, we find that they correspond fairly closely to those assigned by the *Arthaśāstra* to the *Samāhartṛ* and *Nāgaraka.*

[1] Stein, *Megasthenes und Kauṭilya*, pp. 233–5.

According to *Kauṭilya*, the *samāhartṛ* should have general charge of the collection of all revenue, should control irrigation, the cultivation of crown lands, through the *sītādhyakṣa*, mining, a government monopoly, through the *ākarādhyakṣa* and *khaṇyadhyakṣa*, the working of metals other than gold and silver through the *Lohādhyakṣa*, and the working of gold and silver through the *suvarṇādhyakṣa*. He should also be responsible for the upkeep of roads. As regards 'industrial arts', we find that, besides metallurgy, the manufacture of cloth should be carried on by the *samāhartṛ* in government factories controlled by *sutrādhyakṣas*, and in the book entitled *Kaṇṭakaśodhanam* regulations are laid down for independent artisans of different classes, for whose control in rural areas the *samāhartṛ* is made responsible, and in the city the *nāgaraka*. Among the latter's duties is to keep an eye on strangers visiting the city. The gopas and sthānikas, directly subordinate in the rural area to commissioners (*pradeṣṭṛ*) and in the city to the *nāgaraka*, are required to keep complete registers of the population. The *samāhartṛ* and *nāgaraka* control trade and commerce through the *saṁsthādhyakṣa*, and weights and measures through the same official and the *pautavādhyakṣa*. The sale of articles by public notice is prescribed in the chapter on the *śulkādhyakṣa*, and fines for adulteration in the book on *Kaṇṭakaśodhana*. We have in the *Arthaśāstra*, as in Megasthenes' account, an *ad valorem* tax on sales, the *śulka*. Megasthenes gives its rate as ten per cent., while the *Arthaśāstra* has various rates, ranging from four to twenty per cent. The duties assigned by Strabo to the *astynomi*, in their collective capacity, viz. the repair of public buildings, the regulation of prices, and the care of markets, harbours, and temples, are among those for which the *Arthaśāstra* makes the *samāhartṛ* and *nāgaraka* responsible.

Riverain surveys.

In his brief notice of the duties of the ἀγορανόμοι Strabo states, first, that they 'superintend the rivers and measure the land as is done in Egypt'.

The *Arthaśāstra*, in its opening summary of the duties

of the *samāhartṛ*,[1] mentions, among his subordinates, the *nadīpāla* or ' superintendent of rivers ', but what his duties were does not clearly appear.

The system of land measurement in Egypt is referred to in another passage of Strabo [2] :

' This exact and minute subdivision is necessitated by the constant disturbance of boundaries caused by the Nile in its inundations, in which it adds (to some) and takes away (from others), alters shapes, and destroys the other signs by which the property of one can be distinguished from that of another, so that it (the land) has to be remeasured repeatedly.

Those familiar with land-revenue administration in the lower Ganges valley will not need to be reminded that, owing to alluvion and diluvion, frequent re-survey of land is required, both for fiscal purposes and for the settlement of boundary disputes. Of such operations in the neighbourhood of Pāṭaliputra Megasthenes may have seen something, and it may be that, in associating supervision of the rivers with measurement of the land ' as is done in Egypt ', he referred to the supervision and inspection of river-beds and alluvial deposits for revenue purposes. Here again it may be that Strabo has distorted Megasthenes' account.

Irrigation.

Next, according to Strabo, the same officials ' inspect the sluices, by which water is let out from the main channels into their branches ', τὰς κλειστὰς διώρυχας ἀφ' ὧν εἰς τὰς ὀχετείας ταμιεύεται τὸ ὕδωρ. In the *Arthaśāstra* we find frequent reference to irrigation works by the general description *setubandha*, which, apparently, would cover any tank or dam for holding water and also large or small canals or channels conveying water to the fields. Sluices appear to be specially mentioned in one place only,[3] if Mr. Shamasastry's translation is correct, but whether the word *pāra* has that meaning is perhaps open to doubt.[4] We find nothing about inspection of the sluices ' so that every one may have an equal supply ' of water. The *Arthaśāstra*, however, indicates that there were various kinds of waterworks, some the property of the king,

[1] Cf. p. 44. [2] xvii, p. 787. [3] Cf. p. 103.
[4] Cf. Stein, *Megasthenes und Kauṭilya*, pp. 25, 26.

some of private individuals, and *setu*, which must be taken to mean management or supervision of irrigation, is included in the summary of the *samāhartṛ's* duties.[1] It seems reasonable to suppose that in India in the Maurya period, as now, there were irrigation works of many varieties, great and small, public and private; that some of them were provided with sluices of more or less simple construction; and that the public, if not the private, works were subject to regulation with the object of securing an equitable distribution of water.

Boards of Five.

In Strabo's account of the Boards of Five by which the city government and military affairs were controlled at Pāṭaliputra, we may perhaps recognize the Indian custom of referring to any small body or group of persons, irrespective of number, as a *pancāyat* or body of five.

The admiral

Of the six military boards, according to him, the first is appointed to co-operate with the admiral of the fleet (τὴν μὲν μετὰ τοῦ ναυάρχου τάττουσι). In the *Arthaśāstra* we find mention of a superintendent of ships (*nāvadhyakṣa*) and of royal ships (*rājānāvas*),[2] but not of warships. The *nāvadhyakṣa* is subordinate to the *samāhartṛ*, that is to say, belongs to a purely civil department, and receives, it would seem, a salary of 1,000 *paṇas* a year only. There is no historical record of fighting with or from ships or boats, on the rivers, or around the coasts of India during the Maurya period. Nevertheless, it is not unreasonable to suppose that, in Megasthenes' time, there were warships, and that the same department was concerned with them as with the royal ships which were used for peaceful traffic, just as, according to the *Arthaśāstra*, the same *adhyakṣas* would be concerned with royal horses, elephants, and chariots used for war and peace. The duties assigned by the *Arthaśāstra* to the *nāvadhyakṣa* may have come, by Megasthenes' time, to be entrusted at Pāṭaliputra to a board. It is also possible that, as in the case of the senapati, the same title, *nāvadhyakṣa*, may have been given to a class of subordinate officers and to the admiral of the whole fleet. Another possible supposition is that there was not actually any war-fleet, but that Megasthenes, hearing

[1] Cf. p. 44.

[2] Cf. p. 72.

of the title *nāvadhyakṣa*, was led, from similarity of sound, to identify it with ναύαρχος.

Strength of army. As to the strength of Candragupta's standing army, the statement of Pliny, based on Megasthenes, that it comprised 600,000 infantry, 30,000 cavalry, and 9,000 elephants, has been quoted above.[1] The number of chariots has not been given by Pliny. The number maintained by the king of the Prasii, according to reports which reached Alexander, is given by Diodorus and Quintus Curtius as 2,000, and by Plutarch as 8,000.[2] Plutarch gives the total strength of Candragupta's army as 600,000. Arrian, in his *Indika*,[3] gives some information about the arms used by Indian soldiers. Each horseman, he says, carried two lances and a buckler. The infantry carried the broadsword as their principal weapon, and, as additional arms, either javelins or bows and arrows. The arrow was discharged with the aid of pressure from the left foot on the end of the bow resting on the ground, and with such force that neither shield nor breastplate could withstand it.

Weapons.

Slavery. Strabo [4] quotes Megasthenes as saying that none of the Indians employed slaves, but points out that, according to Onesikritos,[5] this custom was peculiar to the country—probably part of Sind—ruled by a chief named Mousikanos, and slavery did exist in other parts of India. Arrian,[6] however, probably relying on Megasthenes, states that 'all Indians are free, and not one of them is a slave'. The *Kauṭilīya Arthaśāstra*, as we have seen, distinctly recognizes the institution of slavery, for which it provides elaborate regulations, and Aśoka's edicts [7] mention slaves (*dāsa*), whom they distinguish from hired servants (*bhātaka*), enjoining kind treatment of both. It is possible that Megasthenes may have been misled by a statement of Onesikritos that slavery did not exist among the people ruled by Mousikanos, and taken it as applying to the whole of India. Or it may be that slavery in India being of mild character

[1] Cf. p. 5.
[2] Cf. pp. 1–3.
[3] Ch. 16.
[4] xv. i. 54.
[5] Pilot of Alexander's fleet.
[6] *Indika*, x.
[7] R. E. IX, XI, XIII; P. E. VII.

and limited extent as compared with that which prevailed in the Hellenic world, he did not become aware of its existence. Perhaps he had heard of the principle, laid down in the *Arthaśāstra*, that no *Ārya* should be kept in the condition of slavery—*na tvevāryasya dāsabhāvah.* This, if literally applied, would have exempted from permanent slavery the great bulk of the population, *śudras* being regarded as *Āryas*, although the *Arthaśāstra* admits of *Āryas* being reduced temporarily to servitude.

With regard to marriage among the Indians, Strabo says: Marriage.

> 'They marry many wives, whom they buy from their parents for a yoke of oxen.'

From this it may perhaps be inferred that the '*ārṣa*' form of marriage, mentioned in the *Arthaśāstra* as one of the superior (*dharmya*) forms, came prominently to the notice of Megasthenes. The *Arthaśāstra* allows unlimited polygamy, subject to the condition that wives previously married shall be compensated.

The punishment of criminals by mutilation appears to have been noticed by Megasthenes. Strabo says: Mutilation.

> 'A person convicted of bearing false witness suffers a mutilation of his extremities. He who maims another not only suffers in return the loss of the like limb, but his hand also is cut off. If he causes a workman to lose his hand or his eye, he is put to death.'

In the *Arthaśāstra*, as we have seen, a chapter is devoted to penal mutilations and fines in lieu thereof.

XIV

MAURYA INSTITUTIONS

GREEK EVIDENCE (*continued*)

Manners and Customs

Character of the people.

Some further observations of Greek and Latin writers regarding the character, manners, and customs of the Indians require notice. Speaking of the Indian population in general, Strabo says:

'The Indians all live frugally, especially when in camp. They care not to congregate in large unruly masses, and they consequently observe good order. Theft is a thing of very rare occurrence. Megasthenes, who was in the camp of Sandrokottos, which consisted of 400,000 men, says that he found that the thefts reported on any one day did not exceed the value of 200 drachmai, and this among a people who have no written laws, but are ignorant of writing, and conduct all matters by memory. They lead nevertheless happy lives, being simple in their manners and frugal. They never drink wine except at sacrifices. Their beverage is prepared from rice instead of barley, and their food is principally a rice pottage. The simplicity of their laws and their contracts is proved by the fact that they seldom go to law. They have no suits about pledges or deposits, nor do they require either seals or witnesses, but make their deposits and confide in each other. Their houses and property they generally leave unguarded. These things show their moderation and good sense.'[1]

Arrian's remark that no Indian was accused of lying has been quoted above.[2] In this there is, doubtless, exaggeration, and the provisions of the *Arthaśāstra* regarding contracts and legal procedure do not suggest that the Indians universally trusted one another or that litigation was unknown among them. Still, it is fair to record the tradi-

[1] xv. i. 53. [2] p. 150.

tional reputation which they enjoyed in the ancient Greek and Roman world for gentleness, honesty, simplicity, and truthfulness. Aelian,[1] in his *Varia Historia*, says :

'The Indians neither put out money at usury nor know how to borrow. It is contrary to established usage for an Indian either to do or suffer wrong, and, therefore, they neither make contracts nor require securities.'

Stobaeus in his *Seria* gives the following extract from an author named Nikolaos Damaskenos : [2]

'Among the Indians, one who is unable to recover a loan or a deposit has no remedy at law. All the creditor can do is to blame himself for trusting a rogue.'

These statements probably rest on the evidence of Megasthenes or other Greeks who visited India during the Maurya period. It may be inferred that, in regard to the virtues above mentioned, the Indians with whom they came into contact compared favourably with the general standards of the Hellenic world at that time, and no one acquainted with the peasantry of India, who form some 80 per cent. of the population, will deny them the same qualities now.

Writing.

The statement made by Strabo, on the authority of Megasthenes, that the Indians had no written laws, being ignorant of writing, and conducted all matters by memory, is thus explained by Bühler : [3]

'In another often discussed passage, Megasthenes says that the Indians decided judicial cases according to unwritten laws, and adds, in explanation, that they knew no *γράμματα*, and settled everything *ἀπὸ μνήμης*. . . . Megasthenes took the term *smṛti* used by his informants in the sense of *μνήμη*,

[1] Claudius Aelianus, born at Praeneste, the modern Palestrina, near Rome, flourished about the middle of the second century A.D. He wrote, in Greek, the two works Ποικίλη Ἱστορία, *Varia Historia*, a miscellaneous history (here quoted), and Περὶ Ζώων ἰδιότητος, *De Animalium Natura*, 'on the peculiarities of animals', referred to below.

[2] Iohannes Stobaeus, author of a collection of extracts from the works of Greek writers, many of which are now lost. When or where Stobaeus himself lived is not known for certain. He was, apparently, a native of Stobi in Macedonia. Of Nikolaos little is known except that he was a native of Damascus and lived in the time of the Emperor Augustus, at whose request he wrote a universal history.

[3] Indian Palaeography, English version, *Ind. Ant.* 1904, app., p. 6 ; cf. *supra*, p. 32.

" memory ", while they meant it in the sense of " the sacred tradition, concerning law ", or " the law-books ", which, according to Indian principles, can only be explained orally by one who knows the Dharma.'

In a later passage [1] Strabo quotes Nearchus as saying that the Indians wrote letters on pieces of closely woven linen, while Quintus Curtius records [2] that the tender bark of trees was used by them for writing on. The practice of writing on strips of cotton cloth survived until very recently in Southern India, and ancient manuscripts on birch bark (*bhūrja-betula utilis*) have been found in Kashmir and Orissa.[3]

In the chapter of the *Arthaśāstra* on Forest Produce,[4] under the head of ' Leaves ' (*patra*), two varieties of palm—*tāḷi* (*Corypha taliera*) and *tāla* (*Borassus flabelliformis*)—and *bhūrja* (birch) are mentioned. Probably the two kinds of palm-leaves are mentioned as important forest products on account of their use as writing materials, and the entry *bhūrja* has reference not to leaves, but to bark, included under this head because birch-bark, when used for writing on, was cut in strips of the same size and shape as the palm-leaf strips used for the same purpose.[5] In different places [6] the word *patra* is used in the sense of letter or writ, and in one [7] more particularly for the material on which royal writs or decrees (*śāsana*) were made out. In Buddhist tradition the writing materials which occur most often are the leaves of *tāḍatāla* and *tādī-tālī*, and no doubt they were what was commonly used at Pāṭaliputra.

It seems unlikely that Megasthenes can have stated that the Indians were ignorant of writing. Possibly he observed that law-books were not referred to in the courts, maxims of law being committed to memory, and Strabo may have misunderstood him on the point.

Intoxicating liquor. With regard to the use of intoxicating liquor in India, Strabo's words are : *οἶνον τε γὰρ οὐ πίνειν ἀλλ' ἐν θυσίαις μόνον, πίνειν δ' ἀπ' ὀρύζης ἀντὶ κριθίνων συντιθέντας.*

[1] Strabo, xv. i. 67.
[2] *Hist. Alex.* viii. 9.
[3] Bühler, loc. cit., pp. 92, 93.
[4] Cf. p. 58.
[5] Bühler, loc. cit., p. 94.
[6] Bk. I, chs. xv, xix.
[7] Bk. II, ch. x.

The Greek word οἶνος covered fermented juice of the grape, and also fermented liquor of other kinds. Herodotus [1] mentions οἶνος ἐκ κριθῶν—barley-wine, a kind of beer. Grape-wine is mentioned in the chapter of the *Arthaśāstra* on the Superintendent of Liquor (*surādhyakṣa*), where it is said that 'the juice of grapes (*mṛdvīkāraso*) is called *madhu*, and is known by the names of the countries from which it comes as *kāpiśāyana* and *hārahūraka*'. *Kāpiśāyana* would mean wine from Kāpiśa, i.e. Northern Afghanistan, which was either included in or adjacent to Candragupta's empire. *Hārahūraka* would be wine from the country of the Harahauras, a people mentioned in the *Bṛhat Saṁhita* [2] as inhabiting a region to the west or perhaps north-west of Bhāratavarṣa. Jayaswal has suggested [3] that Harahura = Arachosia, i.e. Kandahar. The *Arthaśāstra* mentions also a liquor made from rice named *ṁedaka*. At the present day, as is well known, rice-beer, as well as distilled spirit made from rice, is largely drunk in various parts of India.

In stating that the Indians drank wine at sacrifices, Megasthenes may have referred to the use of alcoholic liquor in certain ceremonials, which subsists to this day. Or it may be that the only drinking which came to his notice was that which occurred in connexion with certain religious festivals. The *Arthaśāstra* mentions the issue of special liquor licences on such occasions.[4] It is likely enough that in Megasthenes' time, as at present, while drinking was practised by certain classes of the population, and permitted subject to state regulation, abstinence from alcohol was the general rule.

Strabo's statement that rice was the principal food of the Indians corresponds with what would have come to Megasthenes' notice at Pāṭaliputra. Rice.

Speaking of the climate and agricultural products of the land, Strabo says: Other crops.

'By the vapours which ascend from so many rivers, and

[1] ii. 77.

[2] Cf. Fleet, *Ind. Ant.*, vol. xxii, 1893, pp. 169 ff.

[3] *J.B.O.R.S.*, vol. ii, p. 79, note.

[4] Cf. p. 66.

by the Etesian winds, India, as Eratosthenes[1] states, is watered by the summer rains, and the level country is inundated. During the rainy season flax and millet, as well as sesamum, rice, and bosmoron are sown, and in the winter season, wheat, barley, pulse, and other esculents, with which we are unacquainted.'[2]

The 'flax' here referred to was probably jute. The meaning of 'bosmoron' is uncertain, but it may have been some kind of millet.

Luxuries. Strabo thus describes the habits of the wealthier Indians:

'Their favourite mode of exercising the body is by friction in various ways, but especially by passing smooth ebony rollers over the surface of the body. . . . In contrast to the simplicity they observe in other matters, they love finery and ornament. They wear dresses worked in gold and adorned with precious stones, and also flowered robes made of fine muslin. Attendants follow them with umbrellas; for they hold beauty in high esteem, and resort to any device which helps to improve their looks.'[3]

Of massage there are numerous mentions in the *Artha-śāstra*, as in the Indian dramas and epics. On the habits of the people in respect of clothes and personal adornment the *Arthaśāstra* does not throw much direct light, but the catalogues found in the chapters on the Treasury and Collection of Tolls suggest luxurious standards in the wealthy classes.

Horses and elephants. Strabo has been represented as stating, on the authority of Megasthenes, that no private person in India was allowed to keep a horse or elephant, the possession of either being regarded as a royal privilege. Strabo's words are: *ἵππον δὲ καὶ ἐλέφαντα τρέφειν οὐκ ἔξεστιν ἰδιώτῃ· βασιλικὸν δ᾽ ἑκάτερον νενόμισται τὸ κτῆμα. . . .*

Among the meanings of *τρέφειν* are 'to breed', 'to bring up'.

Arrian states that the animals used for riding by the generality of Indians were camels, horses, and asses, and by

[1] President of the Alexandrian library from 240 to 196 B.C., and said to have been the first to raise Geography to the rank of a science. In his notices of India he is believed to have utilized the writings of Patrokles.

[2] xv. i. 13.

[3] xv. i. 41.

rich men elephants. 'For', he adds, 'among the Indians, the elephant is a royal mount, next in honour as a conveyance is a four-horsed carriage; to drive one horse is undignified.'[1]

Probably Megasthenes recorded that the king held a monopoly, not of the use of elephants and horses, but of the capture of elephants and breeding of horses, and perhaps of the importation of horses from foreign countries. This would be natural, in view of the great importance of the supply of elephants and horses for military purposes.

We have seen that the *Arthaśāstra* lays great stress on the value of elephant forests as part of the royal domain, gives elaborate instructions for the hunting of elephants and their training for purposes of peace and war, and makes the killing of an elephant a capital offence. In the chapter on the Superintendent of Horses, which contains similar instructions for training, there is a classification of horses in the royal stables, of which the first heading is *paṇyāgārikam*, translated by Shamasastry as 'those that are kept in salehouse for sale'. It may be that of the elephants and horses trained in the State establishments, those left over after providing for military and other State requirements were offered for sale to private persons.

To this day there is a tradition in India that the elephant is a 'royal beast'; the right of capturing elephants is reserved by the State; and the killing of a wild elephant is not allowed by law, except in the case of dangerous animals, specially notified as such, for the destruction of which a reward is offered. Up till very recently the Government elephant-catching (*kheddah*) establishments were maintained, primarily, to provide an annual supply of elephants for the army, the surplus being sold to the public. Government horse-breeding establishments have worked on similar lines.

Chariot races.

Aelian thus describes chariot races, with teams of oxen and horses, as practised at Pāṭaliputra:

'The Indians make much ado about the oxen that run

[1] *Indika*, xvii.

fast; and both the king himself and many of the greatest nobles take contending views of their swiftness, and make bets in gold and silver, and think it no disgrace to stake their money on these animals. They yoke them to chariots, and incur hazard on the chance of victory. The horses that are yoked to the car run in the middle with an ox on either side, and one of these wheels sharp round the turning-post and must run thirty stadia. The oxen run at a pace equal to that of the horses, and you could not decide which was the faster, the ox or the horse. And if the king has laid a wager on his own oxen with any one, he becomes so excited over the contest that he follows in his chariot to instigate the driver to speed faster. The driver again pricks the horses with the goad till the blood streams, but he keeps his hand off the oxen, for they run without needing the goad. And to such a pitch does the emulation in the match between the oxen rise, that not only do the rich and the owners of the oxen lay heavy bets upon them, but even the spectators, just as Idomeneus the Cretan and the Locrian Ajax are represented in Homer betting against each other.'[1]

In the *Arthaśāstra* we find mention, in the chapter dealing with the Superintendent of Cattle, of (a ccording to one reading) a class of oxen which 'equal horses in speed', and betting of all kinds is placed, as we have seen, under the supervision of the *dyūtādhyakṣa*.

Buildings. Arrian has left on record[2] the interesting observation that, in India, those cities which were situated on the banks of rivers or the sea-coast were built of wood, because brick buildings could not long resist the effects of rainfall and inundation, while those on high and dry sites were built of bricks and lime. The inference suggests itself that, in Megasthenes' time, the city of Pāṭaliputra, near the confluence of the Son and Ganges, must have been built chiefly if not entirely of wood. It will also occur to those familiar with Indian conditions that, on the alluvial banks of the great rivers, at a time when timber was easily available, buildings would be constructed of wood rather than masonry, not on account of the effects of rain and inundation, but for two other good reasons: (*a*) the lack of firm foundation and probability of sinkage, and (*b*) the risk of erosion and

[1] *De Anim.* xv. xxiv.

[2] *Indika*, x.

undermining through change of a river's course. In the deltaic country of Bengal the rapid diluviation of river banks is a common experience, and when a site is thus undermined and washed away, the hopeless ruin of every masonry structure on it necessarily results. Diluviation.

Such diluviation, however, does not happen quite suddenly. Gradual encroachment gives a warning—it may be of weeks, months, or years—and, in the case of structures of wood or other transportable material, much may be saved by timely removal. For masonry buildings the doom is total and irretrievable if, as is commonly the case, the river's encroachment cannot be staved off. For this reason, in the villages and small towns of the Bengal delta masonry buildings are comparatively rare, and houses and shops are made of wood or bamboo and matting, with roofs of thatch or, nowadays, of corrugated iron sheets. Still, the need of more substantial structures, the risk of fire, and the cost of building-timber when it has to be brought from distant forests, are considerations in view of which, after a time, brick buildings come to be erected, especially on sites which have not been diluviated for many years, and are therefore regarded as safe. The oscillations of the great rivers obeying no known laws, a particular site may survive for years or even for centuries, and in such cases people will erect masonry buildings, taking the risk of diluviation, which is thought to be small.

In the case of important towns protective measures against erosion are adopted with more or less success, but even then great buildings are menaced with sinkage, and the difficulty of securing the foundations of such edifices as the High Court and the Victoria Memorial at Calcutta is well known. Sinkage.

The result of excavations on the site of the ancient city of Pāṭaliputra goes to show that it was built on alluvial deposits of the Ganges and Son, and mainly of wood. Of the structures under excavation at Kumrahar, Dr. Spooner writes[1]: Excavations at Kumrahar.

'These, as far as can be judged, were wholly built of wood.

[1] *J.R.A.S.*, Jan. 1915, 'The Zorastrian Period of Indian History', pp. 73–5.

Possibly portions were made of brick, but stone was used sparingly, for certain features only . . . at Kumrahar, what we see is the first use of dressed stone for building purposes, where stone is still subordinated to wood, and largely restricted to columnar use, and use in decorative adjuncts to the structure. . . . Such foundations as have hitherto been met with in this city are of wood. . . .'

Elsewhere in the same article, referring to the location of 'the columnar rows of a vast pillared hall' at Kumrahar, he says [1]:

'It has proved, however, a work of unusual difficulty to determine the extent of the building, owing to the singular fact that the massive and imperishable portions of the structure have wholly disappeared, apparently by sinkage. The wooden parts, the roof, the floor, &c., have been burnt or have decayed, as the case may be, and all that is left at present to tell the story of the place is the *disjecta membra* of its ruin and the singular stratigraphical indications of the soil.'

Among the 'stratigraphical indications' here referred to are a layer of ashes, showing that the wooden palace had been destroyed by fire, and chemical discoloration of the soil resulting from the decay of the timber baulks which formed its foundations. Others are thus explained:

'When we find, for example, that heaps of pillar fragments lie in rows at regular intervals across the site; that underneath these heaps of stone descending tubular holes occur, filled from above; that these holes are always round in plan, of fixed diameter, and regularly spaced, we see as clearly that rows of columns originally stood at these particular points, as though we actually had the pillars in position.' [2]

Here it is inferred that the lower portions of the columns, which, being underground, had escaped destruction by fire or other means, eventually, on the decay of the timber foundations on which they stood, sank through the soft soil, leaving tubular holes. Most probably much of the ancient site of Pāṭaliputra has been washed away by the Ganges and Son at one time or another. Indeed, one would expect

[1] *J. R. A. S.*, Jan. 1915, 'The Zorastrian Period of Indian History', p. 64.

[2] Ibid., p. 65.

the whole site to have been diluviated and re-formed more than once in the course of so many centuries; but apparently, by chance or perhaps owing to protective works, the site of the palace referred to in the above extracts has remained undisturbed by the action of the rivers. Probably in Megasthenes' time good building-timber was available in plenty at Pāṭaliputra, as sāl forests may then have occupied extensive tracts not far from the city, which are now denuded.

Pāṭaliputra fort.

Arrian goes on to quote Megasthenes as stating that the city of Pāṭaliputra was eighty stadia in length and fifteen in breadth, and was surrounded by a ditch six plethra in width and thirty yards (*pechea*) in depth, and that its wall had five hundred and seventy towers and sixty-four gates. Strabo's description, according to which the wall was of wood and pierced with loopholes, has been quoted above.[1] In the course of excavations on the site of Pāṭaliputra portions of wooden palisade, which, it is thought, may have formed part of the ancient wooden walls of the city, have been found at depths of ten to fifteen feet below the surface, and the difficulties of masonry construction on the site would account for the wall being of wood. Dr. Otto Stein has noted,[2] as a discrepancy between Megasthenes and Kauṭilya, that in the elaborate instructions for fortification which the *Arthaśāstra* contains, there is no mention of a wooden wall, but the point does not seem very important. The *Arthaśāstra* lays down that the fort should be surrounded with a rampart (*vapra*), on the top of which there should be a parapet-wall (*prākāra*) of brick. It may be taken that the author of the treatise recommended this as the best type of construction for a fort on a high and firm site, and did not think it necessary to mention the modifications, such as substitution of a wooden palisade for the brick parapet, which might be introduced in less favourable situations.

[1] Cf. p. 3.

[2] *Megasthenes und Kauṭilya*, pp. 34, 299.

XV

MAURYA INSTITUTIONS

GREEK EVIDENCE (*continued*)

The Court

Strabo.

Strabo thus describes the customs of the Pāṭaliputra court :

'The care of the king's person is entrusted to women, who also are bought from their parents. The bodyguards and the rest of the soldiery are posted outside the gates. A woman who kills a king when drunk is rewarded by becoming the wife of his successor. The sons succeed the father. Moreover, the king does not sleep in the day-time, and at night he is compelled, as a precaution against attack, to change his couch from hour to hour. Of the occasions on which he goes out, in peace time (τῶν τε μὴ κατὰ πόλεμον ἐξόδων), one is for the purpose of hearing cases (ἐπὶ τὰς κρίσεις), which occupy him throughout the day, even at the time appointed for massage. A second is for the performance of sacrifice. The third is when he goes to hunt in a kind of bacchic procession, surrounded by women, who form a circle outside the spearmen. A rope is stretched to mark the road, and it is death for any one to go past it among the women. Drummers and bell-ringers lead the way. In his hunting enclosures, the king shoots with a bow from an elevated place, two or three armed women standing beside him. When hunting in a place not enclosed, he shoots from an elephant. Some of the women are in chariots, some on horseback, some on elephants, fully armed as in war.[1]

'When the king washes his hair, they celebrate a great festival and send him great presents, each person seeking to outrival his neighbour in displaying his wealth. . . . In the processions at their festivals, many elephants adorned with gold and silver are in the train, as well as four-horsed chariots and yokes of oxen. Then comes a great host of attendants in their holiday attire, with vessels of gold, such as large basins

[1] xv. i. 55.

and goblets, six feet in breadth, tables, chairs of state, drinking-cups and lavers all made of Indian copper, and set many of them with precious stones—emeralds, beryls, and Indian garnets—garments embroidered and interwoven with gold, wild beasts—such as buffaloes, leopards, tame lions—and a multitude of birds of variegated plumage and fine song. Kleitarchos [1] mentions four-wheeled carriages carrying trees of the large-leaved sort, from which were suspended in cages different kinds of tame birds, among which he speaks of the orion [2] as that which had the sweetest note, and of another called the Katreus,[3] which was the most beautiful in appearance and had the most variegated plumage.' [4]

The following is Aelian's description, probably based on Megasthenes, of the palace at Pāṭaliputra: Aelian.

'In the Indian royal palace, where the greatest of all the kings of the country resides, besides much else which is calculated to excite admiration, and which neither Memnonian Susa with all its costly splendour, nor Ekbatana with all its magnificence, can vie (for, methinks, only the well-known vanity of the Persians could prompt such a comparison), there are other wonders besides, which I cannot undertake to describe in this treatise. In the parks tame peacocks are kept, and pheasants which have been domesticated, and among cultivated plants there are some to which the king's servants attend with special care, for there are shady groves and pasture-grounds planted with trees, and branches of trees which the art of the woodsman has deftly interwoven. . . . Within the palace grounds there are also artificial ponds of great beauty, in which they keep fish of enormous size but quite tame. No one has permission to fish for these except the king's sons while yet in their boyhood. These youngsters amuse themselves without the least risk of being drowned while fishing in the unruffled sheet of water and learning how to sail their boats.' [5]

Among the royal amusements, Aelian mentions the spectacle of fights between men (possibly wrestling matches), and between elephants and other animals.[6]

1 Author of a history of Alexander, whose contemporary he was.

2 Species not identified.

3 Perhaps monal pheasant (cf. McCrindle, *Ancient India as described in Classical Literature*, p. 76, note 1).

4 xv. i. 69.

5 *De Anim.* XIII, XVIII.

6 Ibid., XV. XV.

Quintus Curtius.

Quintus Curtius, in his *History of Alexander the Great*, gives another account of Indian courts :

'The luxury of their kings,' he says, 'or as they call it, their magnificence, is carried to a vicious excess without a parallel in the world. When the king condescends to show himself in public his attendants carry in their hands silver censors and perfume with incense all the road by which it is his pleasure to be conveyed. He lolls in a golden palanquin, garnished with pearls which dangle all round it, and he is robed in fine muslin embroidered with purple and gold. Behind his palanquin follow men-at-arms, and his body-guards, of whom some carry boughs of trees on which birds are perched trained to interrupt business with their cries. The palace is adorned with gilded pillars clasped all round with a vine embossed in gold, while silver images of those birds which most charm the eye diversify the workmanship. The palace is open to all comers even when the king is having his hair combed and dressed. It is then that he gives audience to ambassadors, and administers justice to his subjects. His slippers being after this taken off, his feet are rubbed with scented ointments. His principal exercise is hunting; amid the vows and songs of his courtesans he shoots the game enclosed within the royal park. The arrow, which are two cubits long, are discharged with more effort than effect, for, though the force of these missiles depends on their lightness, they are loaded with an obnoxious weight. He rides on horseback when making short journeys, but when bound on a distant expedition he rides in a chariot mounted on elephants, and, huge as these animals are, their bodies are covered completely over with trappings of gold. That no form of shameless profligacy may be wanting, he is accompanied by a long train of courtesans carried in golden palanquins, and this troop holds a separate place in the procession from the queen's retinue, and is as sumptuously appointed. His food is prepared by women, who also serve him with wine, which is much used by all the Indians. When the king falls into a drunken sleep his courtesans carry him away to his bedchamber, invoking the gods of the night in their native hymns.' [1]

It is not clear whether Quintus Curtius is here describing the habits of the Imperial Maurya Court or of some of the minor Indian potentates; probably the latter would be

[1] Bk. VIII, ch. ix.

disposed to imitate the Imperial state as far as their resources allowed. As to the general luxury and magnificence of the Indian court, the concordant testimony of Strabo, Aelian, and Quintus Curtius finds support in the indications which the *Arthaśāstra* affords. In saying that wine is 'much used by all the Indians', Quintus Curtius is in conflict with Strabo, as has been seen. That the Maurya princes drank wine is likely enough, for it would be quite in accord with Indian traditions for the royal family to allow themselves an indulgence which was eschewed by the more respectable part of their subjects. But the charge of habitual drunkenness which Quintus brings against Indian kings can hardly have been true of the ambitious and successful Candragupta. Possibly it may have applied to his successor, Bindusāra, or Amitrochates, of whom Athenaeus tells the story that he begged Antiochos Soter to send him some figs and raisin wine, and also to buy and send him a professor. Antiochos replied, sending the figs and wine, but explaining that it was not lawful for Greeks to sell a professor.[1] Strabo's statement that 'a woman who kills a king when drunk is rewarded by becoming the wife of his successor' no doubt has reference to some tradition of such a case having occurred.

On the whole, Strabo's description of the court represents the sovereign as leading a strenuous life, though surrounded with pomp and luxury; not sleeping in the day-time—the absence of the siesta struck Megasthenes, accustomed to other Asiatic courts—and fully occupied with public affairs when not engaged in war, the chase, or religious observances.

Prescriptions of the *Arthaśāstra*. The king's duty.

This account corresponds with the prescriptions of the *Arthaśāstra*, which, in an early chapter,[2] lays down that the secret of success for kings lies in self-control (*indriyajaya*). 'The king', it says, 'who has not his organs of sense under his control, though possessed of the four quarters of the earth, perishes soon,' and gives historical examples in proof. Further on it is laid down that the king should gratify his

[1] ix. 394.

[2] Bk. I, ch. vi.

desires without offending the principles of righteousness and economy.[1]

The king's daily routine.

In the chapter [2] which prescribes the king's daily routine of life (*rājapraṇidhi*) the virtue especially inculcated is *utthāna*—energy, watchfulness, literally ' standing up '. The opening sentence says that ' if the king be energetic, his servants will be equally energetic ' (*rājānamuttiṣṭamāna-muttiṣṭante bhṛtyāḥ*). It is laid down that he ' shall divide the day and the night each into eight watches of one hour and a half '. Of these, only three—the third, fourth, and fifth watches of the night, or four and a half hours altogether —are allowed for sleep. In the sixth watch he is to be awakened by the sound of trumpets and ' recall to his mind the injunctions of sciences as well as the day's duties '; during the seventh he shall sit considering administrative measures and send out spies, and during the eighth he shall receive benedictions from his chief priests, and having seen his physician, chief cook, and astrologer, and having saluted a cow with its calf, and a bull, by walking round them, he shall proceed to the *upasthāna*. This word is translated by Shamasastry ' court ', but, from the context, ' office ' or ' hall of audience ' would seem a better rendering.

In the first watch of the day, and apparently in the *upasthāna*, the king should attend to the arrangements for the security of his person and receive accounts of income and expenditure. In the second he should attend to the affairs of the people of the city as well as of the country; in the third, bathe, dine, and study; in the fourth, receive gold and attend to the appointment of superintendents (*adhyakṣa*); in the fifth, issue written orders to his ministers and receive the reports of spies; the sixth he should devote to recreation or deliberation; in the seventh, inspect his troops; and in the eighth, discuss military operations with the commander-in-chief. In the first watch of the night he should receive secret emissaries, and in the second, bathe, sup, and read before retiring to rest.

This programme is given evidently as a ' counsel of per-

[1] Bk. I, ch. vii. [2] Bk. I, ch. xix.

fection', and it is added that the king may alter the division of night and day, and discharge his duties in accordance with his capacity.

We may well suppose, however, that Candragupta, the founder of a great empire and dynasty, set a high standard of duty.

The *upasthāna.*

Noticing divergences between Megasthenes and Kauṭilya, Dr. Otto Stein points out [1] that the *Arthaśāstra* does not attribute to the king any functions as a judge of first instance or of appeal, but contemplates a separate establishment of judges; also that the Greek expression ἔξοδος implies going out of the palace, whereas, according to the *Arthaśāstra,* the *upasthāna* is part of the palace. But the hearing of subjects' petitions in the *upasthāna,* as prescribed in the *Arthaśāstra,* might not readily be distinguished by Megasthenes from a judicial function, and we may suppose that the *upasthāna,* though within the palace precincts, was a separate building at some little distance from the king's private apartments, and that he went to it in some form of processional state. The *Arthaśāstra* represents the king as transacting in the *upasthāna* other official business besides the hearing of petitions, and as devoting to the latter duty less time than, according to Strabo, His Majesty occupied in hearing cases. It does not, however, purport to lay down the routine of the king's daily duties quite rigidly, and it may be that on occasion he gave up the greater part of a day to the hearing of a specially important case, and that Megasthenes generalized from what he observed in one or two instances.

Accessibility.

The *Arthaśāstra* lays down that in the *upasthāna* the king 'shall never cause petitioners to wait at the door, for when a king makes himself inaccessible he brings about, through his officers, disaffection among his subjects and the triumph of his enemies'. Quintus Curtius, who gives such a generally unfavourable picture of Indian rulers, notices, as we have seen, their accessibility, and their practice of administering

[1] *Megasthenes und Kauṭilya*, pp. 79, 80.

justice and transacting other business while their toilet was being made.

Precautions for the king's safety.

In two points Strabo's account of the royal household at Pāṭaliputra finds striking confirmation in the *Arthaśāstra*, namely, the attendance on the king of a body-guard of armed women, and the personal services rendered to him by female slaves, both being connected with a feature alluded to by Strabo in one sentence, but strongly emphasized in the *Arthaśāstra*—the danger of assassination to which the king was exposed.

Female guards and attendants.

The *Arthaśāstra* enjoins [1] that the king, on rising from his bed, shall be received first by troops of women armed with bows—evidently his immediate body-guard—also that female slaves shall bathe and massage the king, make his bed, wash his clothes, and adorn him with garlands. Both of these prescriptions are found in the chapter on 'Precautions for the king's safety' (*Ātmarakṣitakam*), and it may be inferred that, as guards and personal attendants on the king, women were thought more trustworthy than men. As to the recruitment of the female guards, and the race or class to which they belonged, the *Arthaśāstra* is silent. It is not certain whether they were slaves.

The author of the *Arthaśāstra* insists strongly that self-preservation is the first duty of kings, and in the opening sentence of an early chapter [2] lays down that, 'having secured his own personal safety first from his wives and his sons, the king will be in a position to maintain the security of his kingdom against internal and external enemies'.

The king's wives.

About the king's wives he gives very little information, and, in his chapter [3] on the part of the palace reserved for them, is chiefly concerned with regulations for the king's safety, quoting instances of kings in past times who were assassinated by their queens. From the minister's point of view, seemingly, the queen was necessary for ensuring the succession to the throne, but always a trouble and danger. She is always to be watched by aged men and women, 'in the guise of mothers and fathers', and eunuchs, and to have

[1] Bk. I, ch. xxi. [2] Bk. I, ch. xvii. [3] Bk. I, ch. xx.

no communication with wandering ascetics or mountebanks or female slaves, other than those attached to the harem, nor with free women from outside, except such as attend on her in confinement. Everything that goes into or issues from the harem is to be carefully inspected and sealed before being allowed to pass.

The king's sons.

Similarly, the injunctions [1] of the *Arthaśāstra* with regard to the king's sons are largely directed towards securing his personal safety, 'for princes, like crabs, devour their begetter'. Suggestions of different authors for dealing with princes are rejected by Kauṭilya. He does not approve of putting temptations in their way, 'for to acquaint the innocent with sin (*abuddhabodhanam*) is a great crime'.

Education of princes.

Young men are impressionable, and accept as *śāstra* whatever they are taught. Therefore the young prince should be taught righteousness and deterred from vice through scenes got up for the purpose, in which various characters are enacted by secret agents. According to how they respond to the education they receive, princes are classified as intelligent and capable, indolent or perverse. The instructions for treatment of princes according to the aptitudes they display are somewhat obscure. It is laid down that a prince possessed of good qualities should be appointed commander-in-chief or installed as heir-apparent, and that even an only son who is undisciplined should not be allowed to come to the throne.

Succession to the throne.

Elsewhere a verse seems to prescribe that the king's eldest son should succeed to the throne, except when it involves danger. Apparently, the rule was that the eldest son should be made heir-apparent unless disqualified by character: if the eldest son was disqualified, another son possessing the necessary qualifications should succeed, or, failing any qualified son, a qualified grandson. A prince excluded from inheritance should endeavour, by faithful service, to regain his father's favour. If he fails to do so, he may take refuge with another king or seek an independent livelihood. He may gain adherents and amass wealth by unscrupulous

[1] Bk. I, ch. xvii.

means, such as stealing the goods of religious sects, rich widows, or merchants, or property of gods (*devadravya*) other than endowments of learned brahmans, and then conspire to oust the king by violence from his throne.

On the other hand, suggestions are given as to how the king should treat a son whom he has excluded from succession. If the prince has been finally cut off (*tyakta*), the king may have him killed by a secret emissary. Otherwise he may be conciliated through his mother or other agents and induced to come to court, where he may be encouraged with promises of succession and at the same time kept under guard. Or an unruly prince may be banished.[1]

Other precautions.

The *Arthaśāstra* does not mention the king's changing his bed during the night to avoid assassination, and it is unlikely that this can have been a usual precaution, though it may have been resorted to on some occasions, of which Megasthenes heard. Various rules are given by Kauṭilya for the employment of trustworthy persons about the king, guards to be provided on different occasions, special precautions to be taken in regard to his food, medicine, clothing, perfumes and garlands, carriages, riding-animals, and boats. In order to practise shooting at moving as well as stationary marks the king should hunt, but only in forests which have been cleared of robbers, enemies, and snakes.[2] Strabo's reference to royal hunting enclosures is supported, as we have seen, by a passage of the *Arthaśāstra* prescribing the reservation for the king of a game-forest surrounded by a ditch.

[1] Bk. I, ch. xviii.

[2] Bk. I, ch. xx.

XVI

BINDUSĀRA. AŚOKA

THE ROCK INSCRIPTIONS

Of Candragupta's son and successor, Bindusāra, called by Strabo Amitrochades and by Athenaeus Amitrochates, we know little. He has been credited with conquests in the south of India by Vincent Smith,[1] with some hesitation, and also by Jayaswal,[2] chiefly on the authority of Tāranātha.[3] It is not clear, however, from Schiefner's rendering of Tāranātha, whether the conquests effected through the magical power of the brahman minister, Cāṇakya, to which he refers, took place in the reign of Candragupta or in that of Bindusāra. From Strabo [4] we learn that Seleukos was represented at Bindusāra's court by Deimachos, and, from the anecdote of Athenaeus quoted above, that Bindusāra corresponded with Seleukos's successor, Antiochos Soter. **Bindusāra.**

The third sovereign of the Maurya line, Aśokavardhana, commonly called Aśoka, is celebrated in Buddhist literature as patron and propagator of Buddhism, and detailed narratives of his career are found in the Pāli chronicles of Ceylon, as well as in many Buddhist books of Indian, Nepalese, Tibetan, and Chinese origin. He is mentioned also in the Purāṇas and in Jaina literature. Unfortunately the Buddhist accounts of Aśoka, for the most part, cannot be relied on, exhibiting as they do the defects which may be expected in works composed with a view to edification rather than historical accuracy, as well as discrepancies attributable to local jealousies and rivalry among the sects by which Buddhism has been divided. **Aśoka.** From the historical point of view, the most important documents relating to Aśoka's reign are the well-known inscriptions on rocks and columns **His inscriptions.**

[1] *Early History of India*, pp. 148, 149.
[2] *J.B.O.R.S.*, vol. ii, pp. 79 ff. [3] Cf. p. 24. [4] II. i. 9.

in different parts of India, which are attributed to him—the only inscriptions of the Maurya period that have been found.[1] They have been for many years the subject of exhaustive study by eminent scholars, and a brief account of them only will be attempted here, for the information of the general reader.

They have been found on conspicuous rock-faces at fourteen, and on monolith columns of sandstone at ten different places in India, as well as on the walls of three caves cut in solid rock for the use of ascetics. Aśoka's name appears in one of these documents only, a short rock-inscription found in 1915 at Maski in the Raichur district of the dominions of H.H. the Nizam of Hyderābād. Before that, however, the correctness of the tradition attributing to Aśoka the other inscriptions, purporting to have been made by order of Piyadasi (*Priyadarsi*—' of friendly mien '), had been supported from numerous references in Buddhist literature and internal evidence. Two of the inscriptions are engraved in the Kharoṣṭhi character, an ancient script similar to the Aramaic, which was written from right to left, and is believed to have been introduced in the Panjab during the period of Persian dominion, four or five centuries before Christ. The remainder are in the Brāhmī character, written from left to right, from which the Devanāgari or Sanskrit alphabet and the modern alphabets of Northern and Western India have been evolved. For fuller accounts of the Kharoṣṭhi and Brāhmī scripts, the most ancient forms of writing found in India, the reader is referred to Bühler's ' Indian Palaeography '.[2]

Languages of the inscriptions. The inscriptions are in various local dialects akin to Sanskrit and Pāli, and were evidently intended to be read by the general public. Portions of them have become effaced, as might be expected, by the natural wear of centuries, and the gaps thus occurring have been supplied by collating different versions of the same proclamation or ' edict ', and in part by conjecture. Several of the inscrip-

[1] Except brief inscriptions on *stūpa* railings, &c., referred to in ch. xix below.

[2] *Ind. Ant.*, vol. xxxiii, 1904, App., pp. 18–44.

tions contain words or passages in the interpretation of which difficulty has arisen, and on these questions new light is being thrown by the investigations of students, and new theories are put forward from time to time, but the points which still remain open to discussion are not of great importance from the historical point of view. The versions here given do not pretend to critical accuracy, nor does a detailed statement of the authorities on which they rest seem called for, but it is believed that they convey approximately the purport of the documents, so far as it has been ascertained. For a fuller account and bibliography of the inscriptions the reader is referred to Vincent Smith's work, *Aśoka, the Buddhist Emperor of India.* With the exception of the three dedicatory notices on caves, to be described later, they are proclamations in the nature of homilies, issued by Aśoka with a view to the moral improvement of his subjects, to which, in the literature of the subject, the somewhat inappropriate name of 'edicts' has been given.

Sites of the Major Rock Edicts.

Of the fourteen rock-inscriptions, seven contain versions of the whole or part of what are called, in the literature of the subject, the 'fourteen Major Rock Edicts', and are found at the following places:

1. Shābāzgardi, in the Yuzufzai country, 40 miles north-east of Peshawar, North-west Frontier Province.
2. Mansehra, in the Hazāra district of the Panjab.
3. Kālsi, among the foot-hills of the Himalayas, 15 miles west of the hill-station of Masuri.
4. Sōpara, in the Thāna district, Bombay Presidency, near the sea-coast, about 35 miles north of Bombay.
5. Girnar, near Junagaḍh in Kathiawar, on the rock already referred to, which bears also later inscriptions relating to the artificial lake or reservoir called Sudarśana.
6. Dhauli, 7 miles south of Bhuvaneśvar in the Purí district of Orissa.[1]
7. Jaugaḍha, or Jogadh, an ancient walled town in the Ganjam district of the Madras Presidency.[2]

[1] p. 194. [2] p. 194.

Characters of the inscriptions.

Of these seven inscriptions, the first two are in the Kharoṣṭhi character and the others in Brāhmī.

The Major Rock Edicts.

A summary of the text of the fourteen 'Major Rock Edicts' is given below.

I. No animal must be slain for sacrifice here. Formerly, on the occasion of a royal banquet, thousands of living creatures were slaughtered. Now three animals only—two peacocks and a deer—are slaughtered daily for the royal household, and before long even this will cease.

II. Everywhere in the dominions (*vijite* [1]) of King Piyadasi, as well as among neighbouring (*aṁta*) nations and princes, such as the Coḍas, the Pāndiyas, the Satyaputras, the Keralaputras, Tambapanni, the Yona king called Aṁtiyoke, and those who are vassal kings of that Aṁtiyoke, King Piyadasi, beloved of the devas (*devānām piya*), has provided for the treatment of diseases [2] of men and animals, and has caused wells to be dug and trees planted for the enjoyment of men and animals.

III. In the thirteenth year after my coronation I ordered that everywhere in my dominions (*vijite*) my yutas, rajukas, and pradeśikas should go forth on tour (*anusamyāna* [3]) every five years for the preaching of the Sacred Law (*dhammanusathi*), as well as for other business. They should preach obedience to parents, and liberality towards friends, acquaintances, and relatives, brahmans and śramaṇas. The pariṣad also will issue orders to the yutas according to the letter as well as according to the spirit.

IV. For many centuries the slaughter and cruel treatment of living beings, and unbecoming behaviour (*asampratipati*) towards relations, brahmans, and śramanas increased. But now, in consequence of the fulfilment of the Sacred Law (*dhammacarana*) by King Piyadasi (*devānāmpiya*), the drum of the Sacred Law (*dhammaghoṣa* [4]) has taken the place of

[1] Bühler's translation. An alternative is suggested below, p. 205.

[2] Lit. 'made healing arrangements (*cikīcha*)'.

[3] The meaning of this word is doubtful. Smith (*Aśoka*, p. 164), following Jayaswal (*J.B.O.R.S.* iv. 37), interprets it as referring to periodical transfers of officials.

[4] An expression found in Buddhist literature.

the war-drum and edifying shows have been exhibited to the people.

V. In the fourteenth year from my coronation I appointed overseers of the Sacred Law (*dhammamahāmātā*). They are occupied with the observance of the Sacred Law (*dhammadhistāna*) among all religious sects (*pāṣaṇda*), with the growth of the Sacred Law, and with the welfare and happiness of my dhammayuta,[1] as also among Yonas, Kāmbojas, Gandhāras, Rāstikas, Pitinikas, and all other nations on my western frontier (*aparānta*). They are busy among servants and masters, among brahmans, the wealthy, the helpless and the aged, in the control of their subordinates, and in the revision of capital sentences and sentences of imprisonment. At Pāṭaliputra, and in outlying towns (Pāṭaliputesu ca bahiresu ca nagaresu), they supervise the female establishments of my brothers and sisters, and throughout my dominions (*vijita*) they are concerned with the maintenance of the Sacred Law and with pious gifts (*dhammadāna*).

VI. Formerly the dispatch of business and the receipt of reports (*prativedana*) did not take place properly. Now I have ordained that the reporters (*prativedaka*) may report to me the concerns of the people (*atham* (*artham*) *janasa prativedatu*) at all places—while I am at meals, or in my private apartments, in my carriage, or in my pleasure-garden. Everywhere I dispatch public business. Moreover, if with respect to anything which I order by word of mouth, or which as an urgent matter (*ācāyika, atiyayika*) is entrusted to the mahāmātas,[2] a dispute or deliberation arises in the pariṣad, I have given orders that it shall be brought forthwith to my cognizance in any place and at any time; for I am never satisfied with my exertions (*uthānasi*[*ā*]), and with the dispatch of business. For I consider the welfare of all people to be something for which I must work. But the root of that is exertion (*usṭānam, uthānam*[*e*]). There

[1] Cf. Smith, *Aśoka*, p. 166.

[2] Perhaps officials concerned with the promotion of morality and religion, subordinate to the *dhammamahāmātas* (cf. Harit Krishna Deb, *Aśoka's Dhammalipis* (Calcutta, May 1919), and *J.A.S.B.*, n.s. 1920, vol. xvi, no. 8).

is no more important work than to secure the welfare of all. And the purpose of every effort that I make is that I may discharge my debt to creatures, that I may make some happy here (*idha, ia, hida*—i. e. in this world), and they may gain heaven—svagam, spagam, spagram (*svargam*)—in the next (*paratra*).

VII. King Piyadasi devānāmpiya desires that adherents of creeds (*pāṣaṇḍa*) of all kinds may dwell everywhere, for they all seek after self-control and purity of mind.

VIII. Formerly the devānāmpiya used to go forth on pleasure tours (*vihārayātrā*), in which the chase and similar amusements were pursued. Now, in the eleventh year from the coronation of King Piyadasi, he went in search of true knowledge, and hence, in place of such pleasure-tours, he has instituted religious tours (*dhammayātā*), which are devoted to inspection of the country and the people, visits and gifts to holy men, and preaching and discussion of the Sacred Law.

IX. It is customary to perform various auspicious rites (*maṅgala*) on the occasion of misfortunes, at marriages of sons and daughters, at the birth of sons, at the time of starting on a journey. At such times women, in particular, observe trivial and useless rites. Now auspicious rites ought, indeed, to be performed. But rites of this description produce no results. The following, which is the rite of the Sacred Law (*dhammamaṅgala*), produces truly great results. It includes kindness towards slaves and servants (*dāsabhātaka*), reverence towards venerable persons, self-control in relations with living creatures, liberality towards brahmans and śramaṇas. These and other similar virtuous actions are called the auspicious rites of the Sacred Law. Every worldly auspicious rite is of doubtful efficiency. It may or may not accomplish its object in this world. But the auspicious rite of the Sacred Law is effective without reference to time (*akālika*). If it does not secure the desired object here, it yet produces endless merit in the next world (*paratra*). But, if it does secure the desired object, both are gained—the desired object is gained here and endless merit is produced also in the next world.

X. King Piyadasi does not think that glory and fame bring much profit, except that he desires glory and fame with the view that, at present and in the future, the people may practise obedience to the Sacred Law. All the king's efforts are made with reference to the results for a future life—that all may be free from the danger of sin. This is difficult to accomplish, whether for the low or the great, except by the greatest exertion and by renouncing everything.

XI. King Piyadasi devānāmpiya speaks thus: There is no such almsgiving (*dāna*) as the almsgiving of the Sacred Law (*dhammadāna*). This includes the good treatment of slaves and servants, obedience towards parents, liberality towards friends, acquaintances, relatives, śramaṇas, and brahmans, and abstaining from sacrificial slaughter (*anarambha*) of all living creatures.

XII. King Piyadasi devānāmpiya honours men of all creeds (*sarva-pāṣaṇḍa*), both ascetics (*pravrajita*) and householders (*gṛhastha*), by gifts and marks of honour of various kinds, but thinks gifts and honours of less importance than the object that an increase of essential good (*sāra*) may take place among men of all creeds. This may be produced in various ways, but chiefly by control of speech (*vācagupti*). A man should not extol his own religion and find fault with others unnecessarily: when he does so of necessity, he should be moderate in his language. And he should honour other creeds for their good points. Thus a man exalts his own creed and benefits others; by taking the opposite course he injures both his own creed and the others.

For he who extols his own creed and condemns all others, thinking thereby to benefit his own creed, injures it, on the contrary, exceedingly. Hence, self-restraint in this matter is commendable, so that men may hear the Sacred Law one from the other, and take pleasure in the hearing. For it is the desire of devānāmpiya that men of all creeds shall hear much and possess holy doctrines. And to the adherents of all religions it must be said: 'The devānāmpiya thinks less of gifts and honours than of the object that a large increase of essential good may take place among men of all creeds. For this end are working the overseers of the Sacred Law (*dhammamahāmātā*), the superintendents (*mahāmātā*) of women, the Vācabhūmikas,[1] and other bodies (*nikāyā*). And this is the result: the exaltation of one's own creed, and the promotion of the interests of the Sacred Law.'

XIII. In the ninth year from his coronation King Piyadasi devānāmpiya conquered Kaliṅga. One hundred and fifty thousand persons were carried away thence, one hundred thousand were slain, and many times as many died. Since then, as the result of that conquest, the devānāmpiya has become jealous in the protection of the Sacred Law, and in his love for it and the teaching of it. That has come from the repentance of the devānāmpiya on account of his conquest of Kaliṅga. For the conquest of a country results in its people being slain or dying of disease or being carried off. That is very painful and regrettable to the devānāmpiya. But what appears still more regrettable to him is this. In such a country there dwell brahmans and śramaṇas, religious men of different creeds, and householders (*grahatha, gihitha*), men of strict principle, who practise the virtues of obedience towards the first-born, towards parents, and towards venerable persons, and becoming behaviour towards friends, acquaintances, companions, relations, slaves, and servants, and such men suffer injuries or death, or forcible separation from their beloved ones. Others, who themselves escape unharmed, grieve in sympathy with afflicted friends and relatives. Even the hundredth or thousandth part of those men who were slain or otherwise died, or were carried off during the conquest of Kaliṅga, now appears to the devānāmpiya matter of deepest regret, and, even if a man should do him an injury, he holds that all that can be borne should be borne. Even on the people of the forests (*aṭavi*) in his dominions (*vijita*) he has compassion, and would spare, though having power to destroy them, if they refrain from doing evil; for he desires for all beings peace and security, self-restraint, equity, and happiness. But this

[1] Meaning doubtful. Apparently a class of officials.

conquest he holds to be the greatest, namely, the conquest through the Sacred Law (*dhammavijaya*), which he has made both here and over all his neighbours, even as far as six hundred yojanas, where the King of the Yonas called Aṁtiyoka dwells, and, beyond this Aṁtiyoka, where the four kings dwell, viz. he called Turamaya, he called Aṁtikine, he called Maka, and he called Alikasudra ; in the south, where the Coḍas and Paṁdas dwell, as far as the Tambapāṇini : here, too, within the empire ; among the Visas, Vajras, Yonas, Kāmbojas, in Nabhaka of the Nabhitis, among the Bhojas, the Pitinikas, the Aṁdhras, the Pulindas —everywhere they follow his preaching of the Sacred Law (*dhammanusatthi*). Even those to whom his messengers (*dūta*) do not go follow the Sacred Law as soon as they have heard his orders issued in accordance with it, and his preaching of it, and they will follow it in future. And the conquest which has been made thereby everywhere yields a feeling of joy, but it is indeed something small. The devānāmpiya esteems as precious only that which refers to the next world. And this religious edict (*dhammalipi*) has been written in order that my sons and grandsons may not think a new conquest desirable, in order that, on the occasion of any conquest that has to be made by the sword (lit. by arrows), they may find pleasure in mildness and gentleness, and that they may deem a conquest through the Sacred Law alone a real conquest. Such a conquest is of this world and the next (*hidalokika paralokika*). Let all their joy (*nirati*) be the joy of exertion (*śramarati*), for that yields bliss in this world and the next.

XIV. This religious edict (*dhammalipi*) has been written by order of King Piyadasi devānāmpiya in full, or abridged. For not everything is suitable in every place. For my empire (*vijitam*) is large, and much has been written, and I shall write more. Certain sentences have been repeated because of their sweet import. The edict has been made in order that people may act accordingly. But it may be that something has been written incompletely, through a mistake of the writer or for some other reason.

The Kaliṅga Edicts. In the rock inscriptions at Dhauli and Jaugaḍha, in Kaliṅga, the two edicts known as the 'Kaliṅga local edicts' are substituted for Nos. XI, XII, and XIII of the above series.

The Dhauli version of the first of these two special edicts, as rendered by Senart,[1] begins: 'The officers of Tosali in charge of the administration of the city are to be commanded as follows' (*tosaliyam mahamata nagalaviyohalaka vataviyam*). The Jaugaḍha version has, for 'tosaliyam', 'samapayam'. The edict warns the officials against subjecting the people of the cities to arbitrary imprisonment or torture, and, generally, against the vices of envy, readiness to be discouraged, harshness, impatience, want of application, idleness, and a 'sense of weariness'. It also directs the mahāmātas to make tours (*anysaṁyāni*) every five years, and the princes (*Kuṃārā*) of Ujjayinī and Takṣaśila every three years.[2]

The Dhauli version of the Second Kaliṅga edict is addressed to the prince and officers (*Kumāla mahāmātāca*) of Tosali, and directs that the independent (*avijita*) frontier peoples (*aṁta*) be assured of the king's benevolence, and led to observe the Sacred Law (*dhamma*), and thus secure for themselves happiness in this world and in the next. The other version of this edict addresses the mahāmātas of Samāpa.

Sites of the Minor Rock Edicts. The remaining places at which rock-inscriptions of Aśoka have been found are:

1. Maski, in Lingsugur taluk, Raichur district, of the dominions of H.H. the Nizam of Hyderābād.

2, 3, and 4. Siddapura and two adjacent villages, Jatinga-Rāmeśvara and Brahmagiri, about 45 miles south-east of Maski, in the Chitaldroog district of Mysore.

5. Sasseram (Sahasram), in the Shahabad district of South Bihar.

6. Rupnāth, near Jabalpur, Central Provinces.

7. Bairat, in the Jaipur State, Rājputāna.

[1] Senart, translated by Grierson, *Ind. Ant.*, vol. xix, 1890, pp. 82–102.

[2] According to an alternative interpretation, the mahāmātas of Tosali and Samāpā are to be transferred every five years, and those of Ujjayinī and Takṣasila every three years (Smith, *Aśoka*, pp. 195, 196; cf. *supra*, p. 188, note 3).

The First Minor Rock Edicts.

At each of these places is found inscribed a version of what is known as the First Minor Rock Edict of Aśoka. This document, though not of great length, has been much discussed by scholars, its interpretation presenting special difficulties. Here it may suffice to say that the edict refers to the fact of Aśoka having been a lay disciple (*upāsaka*) for two and a half years, and having subsequently approached or joined the saṅgha, which is interpreted as meaning that he became a professed monk. The Maski version purports to have been made by order of 'devānāmpiya Aśoka', being, as already mentioned, the only extant inscription in which the name of Aśoka is mentioned, and the Siddapura version reads as a communication addressed from Suvaṇṇagiri to certain officials (*mahāmātā*) in Isila by a prince (*āyaputa*, *āryaputra*) and his mahāmātras. Isila is understood to have been the ancient name of Siddapura: where Suvaṇṇagiri was is uncertain, but it would appear to have been the head-quarters of a viceroy of Aśoka, who was also a royal prince. The Sahasram and Rupnāth versions contain directions to have 'these things' engraved on mountains and stone pillars.

The Second Minor Rock Edict.

The Second Minor Rock Edict is a short one appended to the three versions of the First at Siddapura and adjacent villages in Mysore. It has been thus translated by Vincent Smith:

> 'Thus saith His Majesty:
>
> 'Father and mother must be hearkened to; similarly, respect for living creatures must be firmly established; truth must be spoken. These are the virtues of the Law of Piety which must be practised. Similarly, the teacher must be reverenced by the pupil, and proper courtesy must be shown to relations.
>
> 'This is the ancient nature of things—this leads to length of days, and according to this men must act.'

The Bhabrū Edict.

The inscription known as the Bhabrū Edict is on a boulder which was found at the top of a hill at Bairat in Jaipur State near another hill, at the base of which the version of the First Minor Rock Edict, known as the Bairat inscription, appears, and removed thence to Calcutta. It begins thus:

'King Piyadasi of Magadha greets the Saṅgha and wishes it prosperity and good health. Ye know, Reverend sirs, how great are my respect and goodwill to the Buddha, the Law, and the Saṅgha (*budhasi, dhammasi, saṅghasi*). Whatever has been said by the Blessed Buddha (*bhagavati budhena*), all that has been well said.'

What follows has been interpreted as recommending, in particular, seven texts or passages of Buddhist scripture, five of which have been identified in the Nikāya portion of the Pāli Buddhist Canon.

The cave inscriptions. Remains of three short inscriptions attributed to Aśoka are also found on the polished walls of three caves excavated in the hard (quartzite gneiss) rock of the Barabar hills, near Gaya in Bihar. They show that the caves were granted by King Piyadasi to the Ajīvikas, two in the thirteenth and the third in the twentieth year from his consecration.

XVII

AŚOKA (*continued*)

THE PILLAR INSCRIPTIONS

Of the Pillar Inscriptions of Aśoka the most important are the well-known series of seven edicts, of which a rendering is given below : The Seven Pillar Edicts.

I. King Piyadasi devānāmpiya speaks thus. In the twenty-seventh year from my coronation I ordered this religious edict (*dhammalipi*) to be written. Happiness in this world and in the next is difficult to gain except by the greatest love of the Sacred Law (*dhammakāmatā*), circumspection (*palikhā*), obedience (*sususā*), fear (*bhaya*), and energy (*usāha*). But, through my instructions, the longing for and love of the Sacred Law have increased day by day, and will increase still more. And my officials (*pulisā*), high and low, as well as those of middle rank, can lead the fickle back to their duty. So also the wardens of the marches (*aṁtamahāmātā*). It is their duty to protect (*pālana*), to govern (*vidhāna*), to make happy (*sukhāyana*), and to guard (*guptī*), in accordance with the Sacred Law (*dhamma*).

II. King Piyadasi devānāmpiya speaks thus. The practice of the Sacred Law is meritorious. It includes freedom from sin, good works, compassion, liberality, truthfulness, and purity. On bipeds and quadrupeds, on birds and aquatic animals I have conferred many benefits, even the boon of life, and in other ways I have done much good. In order that other men may do likewise I have caused this religious edict to be written. He who will act thus will perform a deed of merit.

III. King Piyadasi devānāmpiya speaks thus. Man sees his good deeds, saying : This good deed I have done. He does not see his evil deeds or say : This evil deed I have done ; this is what is called sin. But difficult indeed is this self-examination. Nevertheless, each one should mark the following. Such feelings as rage, cruelty, anger, pride, and jealousy are called sinful: even through these shall I bring about my fall. This conduct conduces to my welfare in this world, that to my welfare in the next.

IV. In the twenty-seventh year from my coronation I ordered this religious edict to be written. My Lajukas (*rajukas*) are established among the people—among many hundred thousand souls. I have made them independent in awarding both honours and punishments in order that they may do their work tranquilly and fearlessly: that they may give welfare and happiness to the people of the country (*janasa jānapadasa*), and may confer benefits on them. They will know what gives happiness and pain, and they will exhort the peoples of the country in accordance with the principles of the Sacred Law, so that they may gain happiness in this world and in the next. My Lajukas being eager to serve me, my other servants (*pulisāni*) also, who know my will, will render service and exhort the people, and thus the Lajukas will strive to gain my favour. For as a man, after making over his child to a clever nurse, says to himself: 'The clever nurse strives to bring up my child well'—even so I have acted with my Lajukas for the welfare and happiness of the people of the provinces, so that, being fearless and tranquil, they may do their work without perplexity. For this reason I have made my Lajukas independent in awarding honours and punishments. For equity in official business and in the award of punishments is desirable.

I have also promised a respite of three days to prisoners condemned to death, after sentence. Their relatives may secure a remission of their sentences, or, with this object, will give alms or fast. My object is that such condemned prisoners may achieve bliss in the next world, and that the practice of self-denial and charity may extend among the people.

V. In the twenty-seventh year from my coronation I forbade the slaughter of the following creatures: parrots, starlings, ruddy sheldrakes (*cakravāka*, *anas casarca*), wild ducks, bats, terrapins, boneless fish, tortoises, porcupines, bulls set free, rhinoceroses, grey doves, village pigeons, and all quadrupeds which are not used and are not eaten.[1] She-goats, ewes, and sows which are with young or in milk, and their young up to the age of six months, must not be slaughtered. Caponing of cocks is forbidden. Husks containing living creatures must not be burned. Forests must not be burned mischievously, or so as to cause injury to living creatures, nor must any live animal be given to another animal to devour. At the full moon of the three *cāturmāsyas* (four-monthly celebrations), and at the conjunction of the full moon with the constellation Tiṣya, fish shall not be killed or sold during three days, viz. the fourteenth and fifteenth days of the moon becoming full, and the first day following. Nor shall fish be killed or sold on any fast (*uposatha*) day. On the same days, no other animal found in the elephant preserves (*nāgavanasi*) or in the fishermen's preserves (*kevatabhogasi*) must be killed. On the eighth, fourteenth, and fifteenth days of each lunar half-month, on the Tiṣya and Punarvasu days, and on the full-moon days of the three seasons (*cāturmāsya*), bulls, he-goats, rams, boars, or other animals shall not be castrated. On the Tiṣya and Punarvasu days, on the full-moon days of the *cāturmāsyas*, and on the first days of the fortnights succeeding them, the branding of horses and oxen is forbidden. Up to the twenty-sixth anniversary of my coronation I have decreed twenty-five times the liberation of prisoners.

VI. In the thirteenth year from my coronation I ordered religious edicts to be written for the welfare and happiness of the people, so that, abandoning evil conduct, they might make progress in the practice of the Sacred Law. Thus do I give my attention, not only to my own relatives, but to all others near and far, so that I may lead some of them to happiness. In like manner I direct my attention to all

[1] Some names of species, the meaning of which is doubtful, are omitted.

bodies corporate (*nikāya*). I have also honoured men of all creeds with various honours. But what I consider most essential is the voluntary approach of one sect to another. In the twenty-seventh year from my coronation I ordered this religious edict to be written.

VII. King Piyadasi devānāmpiya speaks thus. Kings who lived in ages past conceived the wish that mankind should make progress in the observance of the Sacred Law, but this did not take place as was fitting. Reflecting on this, I considered by what means mankind might grow a befitting growth of the Sacred Law—by what means I might raise up some of them to do so. I decided to order sermons on the Sacred Law (*dhammasāvanāni*) to be preached and instructions on the Sacred Law (*dhammānusāthi*) to be given. My missioners and my servants (*pulisā*), who are set over many men, will spread instruction. Even the Lajukas, who are set over many hundred thousand souls, have been ordered by me to instruct my loyal subjects in various ways. With the same object I have erected pillars of the Sacred Law (*dhammathambāni*) and have appointed superintendents of the Sacred Law (*dhammamahāmātā*). I have planted banyan-trees on the high roads to give shade to man and beast. I have planted mango orchards, and ordered wells to be dug at every half-kos, and rest-houses and watering-places to be established. But such benefits are of small account and have been conferred on the people by former kings as well as by myself. I, however, have done all this in order to render men obedient to the Sacred Law. My superintendents of the Sacred Law (*dhammamahāmātā*) also are occupied with various spiritual matters affecting both ascetics (*pavajitā*) and householders, and with men of all creeds. I have arranged that they shall be occupied with the affairs of the Saṅgha, with the Ajīvika brahmans, with the Niganthas, and numerous other creeds. As various officials have been appointed for various requirements of different classes of men, so my superintendents of the Sacred Law are occupied with the spiritual requirements of men of all creeds. Both these and many other high officials are occupied with the distribution of my own charities, and those of the queens and of all my female establishments. They point out various objects of charity. I have arranged that they shall be occupied with the distribution of the charities of my sons and the other princes, and thereby promote that conduct in conformity with the Sacred Law through which compassion, liberality, truthfulness, purity, gentleness, and holiness may increase among men. King Piyadasi devānāmpiya speaks thus. The virtuous actions which I have performed have been imitated and will be imitated in the future by other men, who thereby have advanced and will advance in obedience towards parents and venerable men, in reverence for the aged, in proper conduct towards brahmans and śramaṇas, towards the poor and wretched, and towards slaves and servants. Such progress in morality has been secured by two means—rules and meditation, and, of these two, rules are of less importance, and more is accomplished by meditation. I have ordered that creatures of various species shall be exempt from slaughter, and have prescribed other rules. But through deep meditation more progress in the observance of the Sacred Law has been achieved among men, so that they do not injure created beings or slaughter living creatures.

These orders have been issued with the purpose that they may endure as long as my descendants reign—as long as the sun and moon endure. By obeying them happiness is secured in this world and in the next. I have caused this religious edict to be written in the twenty-eighth year from my coronation. It is to be engraved wherever stone columns or tablets are found, so that it may last a long time.

Sites of the Pillar Edicts. The Topra Pillar.

The complete series of the above seven edicts is found engraved on one column only, now standing in the Kotila or citadel of the Emperor Firoz Shah Tughlak, to the south of the modern city of Delhi, about five hundred yards from the Delhi gate, to which situation it was removed by Firoz Shah's orders towards the end of the fourteenth century from Topra in the district of Ambala, where it originally stood.

The Mirat Pillar. On another column, which stands on the ridge to the north of Delhi, the first five edicts are found. This column was similarly removed by Firoz Shah from its original site at Mirat and erected in the grounds of his country palace called the Khushk-i-Shikar, which stood beyond the walls of the city of Firozabad, founded by and named after him.

The Kauśāmbi Pillar. Three other columns bear the first six edicts of the series, the seventh being found on the Topra column alone. Of these columns one stands now at Allahabad, but appears, from another inscription of Aśoka which it bears, to have been erected originally at Kauśāmbi, a town often mentioned in Indian literature, the site of which has been much discussed, but seems to be identified with most probability as the place now bearing the name of Kosam, on the left bank of the Jumna about thirty miles above Allahabad.

Three Champāran Pillars. The other two columns on which the same six edicts are inscribed stand at two places in the Champāran district of Bihar, both called locally Lauriya, but distinguished in archaeological reports as Lauriyā Arārāj or Radhia, and Lauriyā Nandangaḍh or Mathia, respectively,[1] and a third pillar in the same district, at Rāmpurva, bears edicts I, II, III, and IV of the series. It is supposed that the columns erected at the three places mentioned in Champāran, with another (bearing no inscription) at Bākhira, the site of the ancient Vaisali, in the district of Muzaffarpur, mark the route of a pilgrimage which, according to Buddhist tradition, Aśoka undertook from Pāṭaliputra to visit the Buddhist holy places in the Nepal tarai.

Besides the seven principal edicts enumerated above, the following inscriptions of Aśoka on pillars have been found :

The Sārnāth Edict. 1. The inscription on a broken column at Sārnāth near Benares, of which the lower portion only still stands on its original site in the ' deer-park ', and four broken pieces, with

[1] These confusing names are fully explained in Cunningham's 'Inscriptions of Aśoka' (*Corpus Inscriptionum Indicarum*, vol. i, 1877, pp. 39–42). The two villages are named after the pillars, which are called locally ' laur ' (*phallus*). Araraj is the name of a temple near the site of one pillar, and Nandangaḍh of a ruined fort near the other. Radhia and Mathia are names of other neighbouring villages.

the 'lion capital', are preserved in the Sārnāth museum. This inscription originally consisted of eleven lines, but the first three have disappeared, with the exception of the first two syllables of the first and second lines and part of the third, which were recovered on three of the detached fragments. The remainder of the inscription is in good preservation. As conjecturally restored, it is a warning against divisions in the Saṅgha, and directs that any monk or nun who breaks up the Saṅgha shall wear the white clothing of a layman instead of the monk's yellow robe, and shall not reside in any monastery—in other words, they are to be unfrocked and expelled from the Order. The edict concludes: 'Thus should this command be brought to notice in the order of monks (*bhikhu-saṅghasi*), and in the order of nuns (*bhikhuni saṅghasi*). Thus saith the devānāmpiya. One such writing (*lipi*) accessible to you has been posted in the *saṁsarani*.[1] And even such a writing (*lipi*) ye must inscribe for the lay disciples (*upāsaka*). And the lay disciples also should come on the fast (*uposatha*) days, in order to make themselves acquainted with this decree (*śāsanam*). On every fast day regularly shall each superintendent (*mahāmāta*) attend the *uposatha* service, so that they may become thoroughly acquainted with this order, and to learn it. And, as far as your jurisdiction extends, in all town and districts ye shall cause sentence of expulsion to be carried out according to the letter thereof.'

The Sānchi Pillar Edict.

2. A much defaced inscription recovered on broken pieces of a column which stood near the great *stūpa* at Sānchi in the native state of Bhopal. From what remains it appears to be directed, like the Sārnāth edict, against divisions in the Saṅgha, prescribing that any monk or nun who breaks up the Saṅgha shall be expelled from the Order, and using the same formula, viz. that the offender shall wear white clothing, and not reside in a monastery.

The Kauśāmbi Edict.

3. The brief inscription, also much defaced, on the column at Allahabad, which is addressed to the 'Kosambiya mahā-

[1] Meaning doubtful—perhaps 'cloister' (cf. F. W. Thomas in *J. R. A. S.* 1915, p. 112).

māta ', and known as the Kausāmbi edict, is of similar purport.

The Queen's Edict.

4. A third inscription on the same column, known as ' the queen's edict ', refers to charitable donations of the second queen (*dutiyaye deviye*), whose name is given as ' Karuvaki ', mother of Tīvara.

The Rummindei Pillar Inscription.

5. A pillar standing at Rummindei in the Nepal tarai, identified as the site of the Lumbini garden, where, according to tradition, Gautama Buddha was born, bears the following inscription :

' Devānāmpiya Piyadasi, the king, when he had been consecrated twenty years, having come in person, did reverence, and, because the Sākya sage (Sākyamuni) was born here, a stone *vigadabhīca* [1] was made and a pillar erected. Also, because the venerable one (*bhagavān*) was born here, the village of Lummini was made free of the bali cess (*ubalika*) and granted the eighth shere (*aṭhabhagiya*).'

The Nigliva Pillar Inscription.

6. At Nigliva, another place in the Tarai about thirteen miles north-west from Rummindei, a broken pillar has been found, apparently removed from its original site and now lying on the bank of an artificial reservoir, which bears a partly defaced inscription, setting forth that Devānāmpiya Piyadasi, when he had been consecrated fourteen years, enlarged for the second time the *stūpa* of Buddha konakamana (*kanakamuni*), one of the three Buddhas who preceded Gautama. A few other words of the same inscription which can be traced show that it recorded also the year of Piyadasi's reign in which he ' came in person and did reverence ', but the words stating when and where this occurred have become effaced.

[1] Meaning doubtful—perhaps 'stone bearing a horse' (cf. Smith, *Aśoka*, p. 222).

XVIII

AŚOKA (*continued*)

EVIDENCE OF THE INSCRIPTIONS

THE evidence afforded by Aśoka's inscriptions may conveniently be considered under the heads of (*a*) the extent and organization of his empire, (*b*) the system of administration, (*c*) religious and moral propaganda.

The first has been noticed briefly in Chapter II above. In the passage quoted there from Chapter XXI, vol. i, of the *Cambridge History of India*, Professor Rapson refers to 'the King's dominions', adopting Bühler's translation of the expression *vijita*, which occurs in Major Rock Edicts II, III, XIII, and XIV, but the word means, literally, 'conquered', and may have been used to distinguish the territories which were added by conquest to the 'home provinces' of the Maurya state. The inscriptions in which it occurs are all found in outlying provinces. In the Bhābrū religious edict, engraved on a rock in Rājputāna, the title assumed by Aśoka is 'King of Magadha', showing that Magadha was the state to which the Imperial dynasty properly belonged. The King's dominions.

In Bengal proper, as already mentioned, no record of Maurya rule has been found, but the Greek evidence would lead one to suppose that most, if not all, of what is now Bengal was regarded as part of the home provinces in Aśoka's time.

The first of the two local edicts incised on the Dhauli rock is addressed to 'the officers (*mahāmāta*) of Tosali', and the second to 'the prince and the officers (*kumāla mahāmātāca*) of Tosali'. We must conclude that there was a royal prince charged, as viceroy, with the administration of Kaliṅga, whose head-quarters were at a place called Tosali, like those at Tokṣasīla and Ujjayini. Now Ptolemy Tosali.

mentions a town, Tosalei, beyond the Ganges, in long. 150°, lat. 23° 20′, that is, in Eastern Bengal, which he calls a 'metropolis', indicating that it was a seat of government of some kind. It does not seem extravagant to suppose that there may have been, under Aśoka, a viceroy with head-quarters somewhere east of the Ganges who was responsible for the administration of Orissa, as have been, in modern times, governors stationed at Dacca, Murshidabad, and Calcutta. On the other hand, it has been held by eminent authorities that Tosali was the name of a city at or close to Dhauli itself. This was the view taken by Kittoe [1] in 1838, and accepted by Vivien de Saint-Martin [1] and McCrindle,[2] and lately by Haraprasād Sāstri.[3] In support of it reference has been made to passages of the *Brahmānda Purāṇa* and other works, in which the names Tosala and Kosala are associated, and it is suggested that Tosala may have been an equivalent for Kosala, signifying not the Kosala of the Rāmāyana (Oudh and Benares), but the country known as Southern Kosala or Mahākosala. The name Southern Kosala, as appears from later records, was applied, properly, to the upper basin of the Mahānadi (the *Brahmānda Purāṇa* places it 'behind the Vindhya mountains'), but it may have been used, like so many names of countries in India, also in an extended sense, embracing Dhauli and the adjacent part of Kaliṅga.

Nevertheless, it seems unlikely that Ptolemy would have made the mistake of placing Tosalei, the metropolis, east of the Ganges delta, if it was really so far to the west of it as Dhauli. It is true that the errors in his data have had the effect of shifting his longitudes for many places considerably

[1] *J.A.S.B.*, vol. vii, pp. 435 ff.

[2] *Mémoires*, vol. vi, pt. I, p. 201.

[3] McCrindle, *Ptolemy*, pp. 230–1. McCrindle's statement that 'the name of Tosale is among those that are marked as having been added to our actual Greek texts by the old Latin translators' is apparently based on Vivien de Saint-Martin (loc. cit.), but, in his foot-note at p. 197, vol. vi, pt. I of the *Mémoires*, the latter merely says: 'Les noms marqués d'un astérisque paraissent être des additions des premiers interprètes latins, dont la source n'est pas connue. Plusieurs de ces additions peuvent être tirées de manuscrits grecs antérieurs à ceux que nous possédons.'

[4] *J.B.O.R.S.*, vol. vi, 1920, pp. 34–9; cf. also Kern in *J.R.A.S.*, vol. xii (n.s.), pp. 384, 385.

to the east, but this would apply to the longitudes which he gives for the mouths of the Ganges and places on that river such as Palimbothra, Tamalites, and Oreophanta, as well as to Tosalei. As we have said, in Ptolemy's time the lower course of the Ganges must have been tolerably familiar to Greek sailors and merchants, and they would be likely to give him correct information as to which side of the river Tosali was on.

It has been surmised by Lassen [1] and Burnouf that there may have been two cities of that name, and by the former that Ptolemy's Tosalei may have been somewhere in the neighbourhood of Dacca.

The situation of Tosali, mentioned in the Dhauli local edicts, must be regarded as uncertain. If we suppose that there was a viceroy responsible for the administration of Kaliṅga, with head-quarters in Eastern Bengal, we must infer that his jurisdiction included also the whole or part of Lower Bengal. As we have seen, Ptolemy mentioned a 'royal town', Gange, somewhere in the Ganges delta. Gange. What meanings exactly he attached to the terms 'metropolis' and 'basileion' respectively we do not know, but we may suppose Gange to have been the capital of a feudatory chief ruling the whole or part of the Ganges delta, in relation to whom the sovereign power of Magadha was represented by the prince-viceroy at Tosali.

Lower Bengal.

In any case, it is most likely that the social conditions and the administration of Bengal proper during the Maurya period approximated to those obtaining in the neighbouring country of Magadha, with which we find, at the dawn of history, the peoples of the Ganges delta in close political association. The mention in the *Arthaśāstra* of commercial products of Vaṅga and Puṇḍra [2] would indicate that Lower Bengal was commercially important at that time, and go to confirm Greek notices of Gange as a considerable place of trade. Again, the directions in the same work for the control of river traffic [3] seem designed for a country in which

[1] *Ind. Alt.*, vol. ii, p. 256; vol. iii, p. 158.
[2] Cf. p. 51.
[3] Cf. p. 72.

water communications were of capital importance. Strabo's reference to the system of land surveys,[1] and Arrian's mention of towns on the banks of rivers being built of wood instead of brick, which, as explained above,[2] would be specially applicable to deltaic Bengal, may not have been based solely on the observations of Megasthenes.

The *pariṣad.*

In the third of the Major Rock Edicts there is a reference to orders issued by the pariṣad to subordinate officials (*yutas*), and in the sixth to discussion in the pariṣad of urgent or important (*acayika, atiyayika*) matters entrusted to the mahāmātas. The injunction in the *Arthaśāstra* to consult the mantripariṣad with regard to important work (*ātāyike karye*) will be remembered. It might be inferred that the pariṣad mentioned in Aśoka's edicts is the mantripariṣad of the *Arthaśāstra*, but Mr. Harit Krishna Deb has pointed out that the two edicts in question being religious edicts (*dhammalipi*), the mahāmātas, to whom they refer, must be taken to be dhammamahāmātas, and the pariṣad a council of advisers on religious subjects distinct from the mantripariṣad.[3] The point is perhaps doubtful. In the seventh century, as we find from I Tsing's *Record of the Buddhist Religion as practised in India and the Malay Archipelago*, the term *pariṣad* was applied to different degrees of religious men and women.[4]

The *mahāmātras.*

The designation *mahāmāta* is found, without specification of functions, in the twelfth Major Rock Edict, the first Minor Rock Edict, the second Kaliṅga Edict, and also in the Kauśāmbi and Sarnāth Edicts. This word occurs also several times in the *Arthaśāstra*, and has been tendered by Mr. Shamasastry in his translation [5] as 'minister'. The *Arthaśāstra*, also, does not show what the duties of the mahāmātras were, but indicates that they were high officials. The term *aṁtamahāmātra* in the first Pillar Edict probably corresponds to *aṁtapāla* of the *Arthaśāstra*, and means 'warden of the marches', *aṁta* being the word used for tribes and peoples on the frontiers of the empire.

[1] Cf. pp. 157, 161–2.
[2] Cf. pp. 172–3.
[3] *J.A.S.B.*, vol. xvi (n.s.), 1920, No. 8.
[4] v. i.
[5] pp. 18, 26, 64, 71, 270, 297, 298, 299.

The office of the dhammamahāmātas was created by Aśoka, as we learn from his fifth Major Rock Edict,[1] in the fourteenth year from his coronation, and some of their duties are specified in the same edict, as well as in R. E. XII and P. E. VII. It appears that the general object of their appointment was to promote morality and religion, and they were concerned especially with the religious affairs of the Buddhist order as well as of other sects. It was part of their duty to encourage gifts for religious and charitable objects and supervise their distribution, and also to promote toleration and good feeling between different sects. In the twelfth of the Major Rock Edicts there is mention of mahāmātras for women, but what their functions were does not appear.

Rajukas.

In three of the edicts (R. E. III, P. E. IV, VII) there is mention of a class of officials called *rajuka* or *lajuka*. They would appear to have been important, since P. E. VII refers to them as being 'set over many hundred thousand souls'. What their functions were is not certain. It has been suggested by Bühler [2] that the designation, which occurs in Pāli literature, is a contraction of *rajjugrāhaka,* meaning literally 'rope-holder', and was applied to land-surveyors and, in a secondary sense, to high land-revenue officials, who may have been entrusted also with other important civil functions on account of the connexion of their duties with the measurement of land. Vincent Smith rejected this interpretation, holding the word *rājuka* to be etymologically connected with *rāja.*[3] In the *Kauṭilīya Arthaśāstra* the only *rajjukas* mentioned are the *corarajjukas,* who would seem to have been subordinate police officers.

Pradeśikas.

The *pradeśikas* mentioned in the third of the Major Rock Edicts were perhaps the same as the *pradeṣṭṛs* of the *Arthaśāstra,*[4] namely, district revenue commissioners, exercising also judicial and police functions.

Yuktas.

The designation *yuta* (*yukta*) in the same edict seems to be a general one covering subordinate officials of different

[1] Cf. *supra*, p. 189.
[2] *Z. M. D. G.*, vol. xvii, p. 466.
[3] Smith, *Aśoka*, p. 203.
[4] *K. A.*, p. 65.

departments. In the *Arthaśāstra* we have the terms *yukta* and *upayukta* with similar meaning; also *yuktakarma* for an official act, and *ayukta* for ' non-official '.

Pulisa.

It is not certain whether *pulisa*, literally ' men ', which occurs three times in the Pillar Edicts,[1] is the name of a particular class of officials or a term for officials generally.

Anusaṁyāna.

If the expression *anusaṁyāna* in the third Major Rock Edict and first Kaliṅga Edict is correctly interpreted as referring to periodical transfers of officers, the orders prescribing them may be based on an injunction of the *Arthaśāstra.*[2]

Bali.

The Rummiṇdei inscription sets forth that the village has been made *ubalika*, no doubt meaning free of the *bali* or religious cess, which is often referred to in the *Arthaśāstra*, and also *aṭhabhāgiya.*

Bhāgā.

In the *Arthaśāstra*, *bhāgā* is the word used for the share of the produce payable to the king as land-revenue, and *aṭhabhāgiya* (*aṣṭabhāgiya*) in this inscription probably means that the village was granted a remission of one-eighth of the produce, perhaps representing half the share which would ordinarily have been payable.

Precepts of the *Arthaśāstra* followed. Energy. Accessibility.

It will have been noticed that in the sixth Major Rock Edict Aśoka lays claim to the quality of energy, chiefly praised by the *Arthaśāstra* in a ruler, using the same expression, *utthāna*, and enlarges on his accessibility to the *prativedakas*, whose duty it was to make reports to him on public affairs. No doubt, as ruler of a great empire, he was unable to receive all petitioners in person. We have already referred [3] to the injunction of the *Arthaśāstra* requiring the king to enforce proper treatment of slaves and relatives, which is so strongly insisted on in Major Rock Edicts III, IX, XI, and XIII, and Pillar Edict VII.

Proper treatment of slaves and relatives.

Medical relief.

By the provisions for medical relief mentioned in Major Rock Edict II, Aśoka carried out another precept [4] of the *Arthaśāstra*. The same treatise lays down, in its chapter on the city superintendent, that on certain auspicious occa-

[1] P. E. I, III, VII.
[2] Cf. p. 194.
[3] *Supra*, p. 99.
[4] Cf. *supra*, p. 41.

sions there should be a release of prisoners from jail (*mokṣo bandhanasya*). In Pillar Edict V Aśoka takes credit for having decreed *bandhanamokṣa* twenty-five times. **Release of prisoners.**

The thirteenth Major Rock Edict mentions 'inhabitants of the forests' (*aṭavi*) within the empire. They may be the same people as the aṭavikas so often referred to in the *Arthaśāstra*. From the tenour of the edict it would appear that they were regarded as beyond the pale of dhamma. Yet they were not to be destroyed, but spared, if they refrained from doing evil. **Forest tribes.**

In the fifth Pillar Edict there is mention of the elephant-forests (*nāgavana*), to which the *Arthaśāstra* attaches such importance. **Elephant forests.**

Generally in his 'edicts' Aśoka appears as professing to model his conduct on the *Arthaśāstra*, though of course he may have had in mind not Kauṭilya's work but some other treatise or treatises containing similar precepts. In permitting, however, by his Major Rock Edict VII, adherents of various creeds (*pāṣaṇḍa*) to dwell where they pleased, he perhaps consciously departed from a rule in the chapter of the *Arthaśāstra* on town-planning, which assigns to 'heretics' (*pāṣaṇḍa*) and *caṇḍālas* a special quarter beyond the cremation ground.[1]

Buddhist tradition representing Aśoka as the saint-king, to whose missionary zeal the spread of Buddhism throughout India, and beyond its boundaries, was mainly due, finds some support in his edicts, in which the chief purpose discernible is the inculcation of dhamma (*dharma*). For this word no exact equivalent exists in European languages, but it connotes religion, piety, and morality. Derived from the root *dhṛ*, 'to hold', it signifies the rule and standard of conduct which should afford support and guidance through life to every man, and stands for a conception which may be described as fundamental and universally accepted among the peoples of India. Some of the edicts [2] recognize expressly the observance of dhamma by men of different creeds, and **Dhamma.**

[1] *K. A.*, p. 62.
[2] Cf. R. E. V, VII, XII, XIII; P. E. VII.

show that Aśoka was disposed not only to tolerate the various religions found in his empire, but in the interests of dhamma actively to encourage, supervise, and regulate their practice. At the same time there are passages which indicate clearly that he himself became, if he was not from the first, an adherent of the religion founded by Gautama Buddha. We must be on our guard against hastily attributing to Aśoka and the Buddhists of his time beliefs and practices set forth in Buddhist writings which may be of a much later date, for in regard to much of the Buddhist, as of other Indian literature, there is uncertainty as to the times and places to which different works belong.

The *Saṅgha*. In some of the edicts [1] we find mention of the *saṅgha*—a word which, at a later date certainly, and perhaps already in Aśoka's time, was used in two senses—for the general monastic order, which was the chief institution of Buddhism as an organized religion, and for the community of a particular monastery. In Kauṭilya's *Arthaśāstra*, as we have seen, there is frequent reference to *saṅghas*, which were guilds or corporations formed for various purposes—religious, industrial, commercial, military, &c., and perhaps from some such general use of the word *saṅgha* it came to be applied to the Order founded by Gautama. For detailed and, at the same time, exactly dated descriptions of the Buddhist monastic organization in India we must have recourse to the accounts of Chinese pilgrims who visited the country centuries after Aśoka's time. Such a description is furnished, for the seventh century of our era, in the *Record of the Buddhist Religion as practised in India and the Malay Archipelago*, by I Tsing, and from incidental references in Fa Hian's *Fo-kwo-ki* (Buddhist Country Records) we may gather that, in its general features, the Buddhist monastic system of India was the same in the early part of the fifth century as I Tsing found it in the seventh. According to I Tsing,[2] *saṅgha* is the correct designation of the members of a religious house who are priests (*pravrajya*, i. e. 'homeless').

[1] Minor Rock Edict I; P. E. VII; and the Sārnāth, Sānchi, and Kausāmbi Edicts.

[2] *Takakusu*, pp. 187–9.

A layman desiring to enter the religious state applied to an elder monk (*sthavira bhikṣu*) of a monastery, who examined him, particularly as to his motive, and, if found suitable, introduced him to the *saṅgha*. On being accepted by them, he received the tonsure and the five precepts—' do not kill, steal, tell a lie, commit adultery, or drink intoxicating liquor '—from his introducer, who became his *upādhyāya* or teacher, and was then called an *upāsaka*. After being instructed in ten more precepts, he went through a form of initiation, and was called a *sramanera* or novice, and after further instruction he received full ordination (*upasampada*) and became a *bhikṣu*. For the ordination of nuns (*bhikṣuṇi*) a similar course was prescribed, beginning with the grade of *upāsikā*, but including an additional grade—that of *śikṣamānā*—between those of *sramanerī* and *bhikṣuṇi*. The different degrees of Buddhist religious men and women were called *pariṣads*, which were reckoned, sometimes as five in number, viz. (1) *bhikṣu*, (2) *bhikṣuṇi*, (3) *śikṣamānā*, (4) *sramanera*, and (5) *sramanerī*, sometimes as seven, including (6) *upāsaka* and (7) *upāsikā*. In Aśoka's Sārnāth Edict we find ' *bhikhu saṅgha* ' for ' order of monks ', and ' *bhikhuni saṅgha* ' for ' order of nuns ', and we have *upāsaka* in the same edict, as well as in the first Minor Rock Edict, where it is said that Aśoka himself was an *upāsaka* for two and a half years. In the translations of these edicts the word *upāsaka* has been rendered as ' lay disciple ', but from I Tsing's account it is seen that, in the seventh century, the *upāsaka* was not a mere lay believer, nor, like the Franciscan and Dominican lay tertiaries, a person living in the world and at the same time connected with the order by the observance of certain ascetic rules, but a postulant or candidate for orders in a particular monastery. It will also be seen that in I Tsing's time, according to one opinion, the *upāsaka* did, and according to another he did not, form part of the *saṅgha*. It is likely enough that the word *upāsaka* had not exactly the same meaning in I Tsing's time that it had in Aśoka's. There is room for doubt as to the interpretation of the first Minor Rock Edict, but it seems to

Upāsaka.

Bhikṣu and *Bhikṣuṇi.*

Pariṣad.

imply that Aśoka attained some monastic grade above that of *upāsaka*. Whether he reached full ordination as a monk is uncertain, but this may have been allowed by some special dispensation. At any rate, it is clear that he took a lively and active interest in the affairs of different monasteries, as well as of the monastic order in general. One is tempted to wonder whether his immixtion in ecclesiastical matters was always welcome, and the comparison with Justinian suggests itself.

Uposatha.

In Pillar Edict V, and in the Sārnāth Edict, we find reference to *uposatha* (*upavasatha*) days. These, as appears from Buddhist sources, were weekly fast days on which Buddhist laymen visited a priest and took the *upavasatha* vows, that is, promised to observe during the day the ' eight precepts ' (*śīlas*), of which the first five were those administered to the *upāsaka* on taking the tonsure, and the remaining three—(6) not to take pleasure in music or the use of garlands or perfumes, (7) not to use a high or wide couch, and (8) not to take food at forbidden hours. The *uposatha* days would be good occasions for promulgating the king's orders, as directed in the Sārnāth Edict.

Doctrine of the Edicts.

The doctrine of Aśoka's Major Rock and Pillar Edicts cannot be called distinctively Buddhist, but is of the simplest kind, including belief in *devas*—a word which we translate, for want of a better equivalent in English, as ' gods ', but means, literally, ' bright beings ', and might be rendered by ' pure spirits '—as well as in life after death, and ' another world ', in which good actions in this life will be rewarded and bad punished. There is certainly no trace of atheism or disbelief in a personal soul. Nor is there any indication of the metaphysical theories of *karma* and ' rebirth ', although it is very likely that they may have been popular in Aśoka's time as they are now. Evidently Aśoka was anxious to promote toleration and do away with sectarian strife, and for this reason avoided distinctive doctrine in his general edicts. The chief virtue inculcated is that of charity and kindness to all living creatures.

Respect for

The doctrine of respect for animal life is not of course

peculiar to Buddhism, but has always been a prominent feature of every Indian religion. There seems to be no necessity for connecting it with the theory of 'rebirth', though each may find support in the other. Respect for animal life is perhaps sufficiently accounted for by an instinctive sympathy, which is universal in mankind, and in Europe takes the form of 'kindness to animals'. The difficulty of reconciling this sentiment with the imperious need for animal food has led to many controversies and illogical compromises; for it is clearly illogical to respect the life of one species of animal and not of another, or to profess kindness to animals and kill certain animals for food. Differences of opinion on this great question have been the chief cause of religious conflict in tolerant India, and to this day the most serious religious riots between Hindus and Muhammadans arise out of the slaughter of cows by the latter in sacrifice and for food. Perhaps we may see in animal sacrifice itself an evidence of respect for animal life—a recognition that the taking of life is an act of solemn import, only permissible when it has the sanction of religion.

animal life.

This question is of such importance in Indian history that it will not be out of place here to quote Watters's explanation[1] of the expression 'three pure meats' or 'foods' which is found in Buddhist literature.

Three pure foods.

'The explanation of the *san-ching* or "three pure kinds of flesh" is briefly as follows. In the time of Buddha there was in Vaisali a wealthy general, Siha, who was a convert to Buddhism. He became a liberal supporter of the Brethren, and kept them constantly supplied with good flesh food. When it was noised abroad that the bhikshus were in the habit of eating such food specially provided for them, the Tirthikas made the practice a matter of angry reproach. Then the abstemious ascetic Brethren, learning this, reported the circumstances to the Master, who thereupon called the Brethren together. When they were assembled, he announced to them the law that they were not to eat the flesh of any animal which they had seen put to death for them, or about which they had been told that it had been killed for them, or about which they had reason to

[1] *Yuan Chwang*, i, pp. 54–7.

suspect that it had been slain for them. But he permitted to the Brethren as " pure " (that is, lawful) food the flesh of animals, the slaughter of which had not been seen by the bhikshus, not heard of by them, and not suspected by them to have been on their account. . . . The animal food now permitted to the bhikshus came to be known as the " three pures " or " three pure kinds of flesh ", and it was tersely described as "unseen, unheard, unsuspected". . . . Then two more kinds of animal food were declared lawful for the Brethren, viz. the flesh of animals which had died a natural death, and that of animals which had been killed by a bird of prey or other savage creature, so there came to be five classes or descriptions of flesh which the professed Buddhist was at liberty to use as food. Then the " unseen, unheard, unsuspected " came to be treated as one class, and this together with the " natural death ", and " bird killed " made a san-ching.'

Hīnayāna and Mahāyāna.

Generally speaking, laxity in regard to the use of flesh as food was associated with the Hīnayāna system, and what was in Mahāyāna literature called 'gradual teaching', and contrasted with the 'instantaneous teaching' of Mahāyānism. The expressions 'gradual teaching' and 'instantaneous teaching' are thus explained by Watters:

'The Buddha suited his sermons and precepts to the moral and spiritual attainments and requirements of his audience. Those who were low in the scale he led on gradually by the setting forth of simple truths, by parable and lesson, and by mild restrictions as to life and conduct. At a later period of his ministry he taught higher truths, and inculcated a stricter purity and more thorough self-denial. Thus, in the matter of flesh-food, he sanctioned the use of it as an ordinary article of food by his own example and implied permission. Afterwards, when he found that some of his disciples gave offence by begging for beef and mutton, and asking to have animals killed for them, and eating as daily food flesh which should only be taken in exceptional circumstances, he introduced restrictions and prohibitions. But the " instantaneous teaching ", which took no note of circumstances and environments, revealed sublime spiritual truths to be comprehended and accepted at once by higher minds, taught for these a morality absolute and universal, and instituted rules for his professed disciples to be of eternal, unchanging obligation. . . . The "gradual teaching" is practically co-extensive with the Hīnayāna system, and the Buddha describes his teaching and *vinaya* as *gradual*, growing and developing like the mango fruit according to some scriptures. The " instantaneous teaching " is the Mahāyāna system as found in those scriptures of the Buddhists which are outside of the Hinayānist Tripiṭaka. . . . Our pilgrim being an adherent of the Mahāyānist system, refused to admit the validity of the " three-fold pure " flesh-food indulgence, which the excellent Hinayānist Brethren of Yenk'i followed. The Buddhist scriptures, to which Yuan Chuang adhered, prohibit absolutely the use of flesh of any kind as food by " the sons of Buddha ". This prohibition is based on the grounds of universal compassion and the doctrine of *Karma*. Mahāyānism teaches that the eating of an animal's flesh retards the spiritual growth of the Brother who eats it, and entails evil consequences in future existences. Some Mahāyānists were strict in abstaining not only from all kinds of flesh food, but also from milk and its products. . . . There have also, however, been Mahāyānists who allowed the use of animal food of certain kinds, and we find wild geese, calves, and deer called *san-ching-shih*, or " three pure (lawful) articles of food ".'

Many centuries later, as we shall see, a Mahāyānist attempt to prevent animal sacrifice and excommunicate fishermen led to a revolution in Bengal.

Whether, in Aśoka's time, the development of Buddhism, on the whole, favoured strictness or laxity as regards respect for animal life is perhaps open to doubt.

Restrictions on slaughter of animals.

The restrictions which his edicts impose on the slaughter of animals are cautious and moderate, following in their general lines, though not exactly, the rules of the *Arthaśāstra*. The first Major Rock Edict merely prohibits the slaughter of animals for sacrifice at certain places, and mentions the example set in the royal establishment. The fifth Pillar Edict refers to a general prohibition against the slaughter of four-footed animals, 'which are not used and are not eaten'. This amounts to saying that such animals shall not be killed uselessly or wantonly. The edict mentions also protection granted to certain animals specifically, but these do not include any of the bovine species, except bulls set free (for breeding). Other domestic animals the slaughter of which is prohibited are she-goats, ewes, and sows which are with young or in milk, and their young up to the age of six months. Besides these, the animals protected, so far as they have been identified, are wild species. There is a prohibition against fishing, or the killing of any animal in an elephant-forest, on certain days of the year. Caponing of cocks is prohibited absolutely, and castration of other animals on certain days. The *Arthaśāstra*, as we have seen in its chapter on the superintendent of slaughter-houses,[1] prohibits the slaughter of calves, bulls, and milch-cows, but not of other cows or oxen. The other animals of which the same chapter prohibits molestation or slaughter appear to be all wild species, among them the brahmany duck, wild goose, and parrot protected by Aśoka. The chapter on the superintendent of cattle [2] mentions beasts fit for slaughter, and sale of beef by cow-herds. The chapter on the treatment of a conquered country [3] lays down that the ruler should prohibit all slaughter of animals for a fortnight during the rainy season and for four days at each full moon—also that he should prohibit (restrict ?) slaughter of females and young animals, and castration.

Pāṣaṇḍas.

While the *Kauṭilīya Arthaśāstra* is not a Buddhist composition, there does not seem to be sufficient ground for regarding it as 'brahmanical' in the sense of 'anti-buddhist'. The passage in which it is laid down that *pāṣaṇḍas* should live beyond the cremation ground has been quoted. In another part of the *Arthaśāstra* where it occurs, the word *pāṣaṇḍa* is explained by the commentator, Bhaṭṭasvāmin, as meaning 'Buddhist mendicants',[4] but this interpretation seems doubtful. In Aśoka's edicts the word is taken to mean an adherent of any creed or sect. Probably the passage of the *Arthaśāstra* in question has been reproduced from some older work, in which the term *pāṣaṇḍa* was applied to members of some sect regarded by the author as heretics, who should be excommunicated.

Preaching of Dhamma

In the thirteenth Major Rock Edict Aśoka takes credit

[1] Cf. p. 67.
[2] Cf. p. 73.
[3] Cf. p. 135.
[4] *K. A.*, p. 181.

for the 'conquest of the Sacred Law' (*dhammavijaya*) effected during his reign both within and beyond the limits of his empire. Among the regions beyond his frontier to which this conquest has extended, he mentions, first, the territories of the Yona (Greek) king Aṁtiyoka, and, next and beyond them, those of the four kings Turamaya, Aṁtikine, Maka, and Alikasudra. These names correspond, as shown below, with those of Hellenic rulers, who are known to have been contemporaries of Aśoka. beyond the frontier. North.

Aṁtiyoka (also mentioned in R. E. II) = Antiochos Theos, King of Syria and Western Asia (261–246 B.C.), grandson of Seleukos Nikator, and successor of Antiochos Soter.

Turamaya = Ptolemy Philadelphos of Egypt (285–247 B.C.).

Aṁtikine = Antigonos Gonatos of Macedonia (277–239 B.C.).

Maka = Magas of Cyrene, half-brother of Ptolemy Philadelphos (285–258 B.C.).

Alikasudra = King of Epirus (272–258 B.C.).

As to the precise nature and effects of this 'conquest' we are left in the dark: it is unfortunate that Greek records are silent on the subject. From the edict we gather that the 'conquest' was made through envoys (*dūta*). They were sent to the various countries to preach, not Buddhism, but 'dhamma', and, in Aśoka's view, as we know, 'dhamma' was compatible with adherence to various creeds. We may infer that the envoys were politely received.

The other countries beyond the frontiers of the empire South. to which, according to the thirteenth Major Rock Edict, the dhammavijaya extended, are described as 'in the south where the Coḍas and Pāṁdas dwell, as far as the Tambapānini'. In the second Major Rock Edict we find 'the Coḍas, the Pāndiyas, the Satyaputras, the Keralaputras, Tambapanni'.

Coḍa or Cola was, in ancient times, the name of a people inhabiting a tract of country along the eastern coast of the Indian peninsula called Coḍa or Colamandala, a name which in the form Coromandel is familiar to students of the history of British India. We must infer that the Coḍa country mentioned in Aśoka's edicts lay south of Kaliṅga. Pāṇḍya is the Sanskrit form of the name Pāndiya or Pāṁda applied to a people inhabiting what are now the Madura and Tinnevelli districts. It is now accepted that Tambapanni and Tambapānini (Tāmraparṇī) in Major Rock Edicts II and XIII represent not Ceylon but the Tāmraparni River, which flows through Tinnevelli district, and near the mouth of which there was, in ancient times, a famous pearl-fishery.[1]

As we have seen,[2] the *Arthaśāstra* mentions a class of pearls called *tāmraparṇika*. The Keralaputras were the people of Malabar. The Satyaputras, not mentioned elsewhere, were evidently another people of Southern India.

Among border peoples.

The remaining peoples mentioned in the thirteenth Major Rock Edict are border peoples subject to the emperor's control. The countries occupied by some of them are indicated by Professor Rapson in the passage in Chapter xxi, vol. i, of the *Cambridge History of India*, an extract of which has been given,[3] but it should be said here that while the Yonas and Kāmbojas, grouped in Major Rock Edict V with the Gāndhāras, are located approximately without hesitation—the name Yona here being applied, doubtless, to Greek settlements on the north-west frontier of India—authorities are not agreed as to the location of the Bhojas, Pitinikas (Petunikas, Petenikas), and Aṁdhras (Andhraś), and that of the Nabhakas and Pulindas has not been settled. In the fifth Major Rock Edict the Pitinikas are associated with the Rāṣṭikas and other peoples on the western frontier of the empire.

No mention of Kashmir or Nepal Valley,

The inscriptions of Aśoka which have so far been discovered do not support the traditions current in Kashmir and the Nepal Valley of the inclusion of those countries in his empire, though they prove that it embraced a part of what is now the Nepal Tarai, bordering on North Bihar and Oudh. Nor do the inscriptions confirm the Buddhist legend of the dispatch of missionaries during his reign, after the

[1] Cf. Smith, *Aśoka*, pp. 162, 168 ; also McCrindle, *Ptolemy*, p. 57.
[2] Cf. p. 49. [3] Cf. p. 23.

'Third Council', to preach Buddhism in Kashmir, the Himalayan mountain region, Burma, and Ceylon. It is not even proved historically that Aśoka sent forth missionaries to preach Buddhism at all, since Buddhism and dhamma were not the same thing. At the same time, it is likely that many if not all of the dhammamāhāmātas and dhammayutas employed by him, and the envoys whom he sent to preach dhamma in foreign countries, were of the Buddhist persuasion, to which he himself belonged, and that he may have given the first impulse to the missionary enterprise which, in course of time, carried that religion throughout Asia. Outside Buddhism, the only religious denominations specifically referred to in Aśoka's inscriptions are the Niganthas (Nirgranthas), mentioned in the seventh Pillar Edict, and the Ajīvikas, named in the same edict and in two of his cave inscriptions. According to Jaina literature, Nirgranthas and Ājīvikas were different Jaina sects.

or of Burma or Ceylon.

Impulse to Buddhist missionary enterprise.

Nirgranthas and Ājīvikas.

In the enumeration of countries in the Major Rock Edicts II, V, and XIII we do not find mention of any part of what is now Bengal. At this we need not be surprised, seeing that in these edicts Aśoka is proclaiming the wide extent of the provisions made by him for the material benefit of all living creatures and for the promotion of dhamma, and, with this object in view, he naturally mentions places on the frontiers of the empire, and not the countries immediately adjoining Magadha. Obviously, no inference as to the prevalence of Buddhism in Bengal under Aśoka can be drawn from the fact that Fa Hian found twenty-four Buddhist saṅghārāmas at Tāmralipti at the beginning of the fifth century A.D., or from the legends current in the seventh, which attributed to Aśoka *stūpas* found by Yuan Chwang at various places. We may accept it as proved that, from a very early date, intercourse was carried on between Pāṭaliputra and Ceylon, through Tāmralipti, by sea, but there is no reliable evidence of Buddhism having spread to Ceylon in Aśoka's time. It is, however, very likely that the Buddhist religion did gain a footing early in the countries adjoining Magadha on the east and south-east, where, as

Bengal proper.

later history shows, the cult of Gautama took very firm root and survived longer than elsewhere in India.

Kāmarupa. The edicts do not mention Kāmarupa among the border countries, and it is curious to find Yuan Chwang recording, in the seventh century, that the people of Kāmarupa did not believe in Buddhism, and that no Buddhist monastery had ever been erected there. We may perhaps infer that Aśoka did not send missionaries or envoys to preach dhamma in Kāmarupa, but it should be borne in mind that the edicts do not mention either Kashmir (unless included in Kāmboja) or Nepal.

XIX

ART OF THE MAURYA PERIOD. CONCLUSION

We have now considered the literary evidence bearing on the civilization of the Maurya period as contained in the *Kauṭilīya Arthaśāstra*, the works of Greek and Latin writers on India, and Aśoka's inscriptions. It remains to notice the evidence furnished by such products of the arts of the period as survive. We are here again confronted with the difficulty of fixing dates. The existing monuments, which may be ascribed approximately to the Maurya age, are not very numerous, but they are of exceptional interest, and suggest many problems.

Pillars.

Of the great monolithic pillars attributed to Aśoka, ten which bear his inscriptions, and one without inscription, which stands at Bākhira,[1] have already been mentioned. At Rāmpūrva, in the Champāran district of North Bihar, besides the inscribed pillar referred to above,[2] there is another of the same type, but without inscription. At Patna some fragments of a similar column have been found buried underground, and near Benares there is the stump of another, which was destroyed by local Muhammadans in the course of a riot which took place in 1809.

Pillar capitals.

Of these pillars only those at Bākhira and Lauriya Nandangarh are practically perfect, with 'bell-shaped' capitals, each surmounted by the sculptured figure of a seated lion. The others are more or less mutilated and without their capitals, but in the case of four the remains of capitals, more or less damaged, have been found near the sites of the pillars.

The Sārnāth lion-capital

The first of these capitals—that of the Sārnāth pillar—is thus described in the catalogue of the Museum of Archaeology at Sārnāth, where it is preserved.

'Capital of Aśoka column (ht. 7 ft.; width across the

[1] Cf. p. 202. [2] Cf. p. 202.

abacus 2 ft. 10 in.). The lower portion, 2 ft. in height, has, as usual, the shape of a bell decorated with conventional petals in Persepolitan style. They are sixteen in number. The necking above the bell is circular in horizontal section and has a torus moulding with plain surface. The middle portion, which is fashioned into a circular abacus resembling a common drum 1 ft. 1½ in. high, is decorated with four wheels, of twenty-four spokes each, in high relief. The ends of the axles are left rough, from which it may be surmised that they were originally covered with caps, probably of precious metal. This is proved by the existence of three fine holes pierced into the rim of each axle, into which metal pins were evidently inserted to keep the cap in position. The spaces between the wheels are occupied by the figures of an elephant, a bull, a horse, and a lion, following each other from right to left in the direction of the *pradakshina*. Three of these animals are represented as walking, the horse as running at full gallop. These figures are all more or less damaged, but they are wonderfully life-like, and their pose graceful.

'The abacus is surmounted with figures of four life-sized lions placed back to back, so that only the fore-parts are shown. They are each 3 ft. 9 in. high. Two of them are in perfect preservation. The heads of the other two were found detached, and have been refixed. The upper paw of one and the lower paw of the other were not recovered. In place of eye-balls some sort of precious stones were originally inserted into the sockets, as is clearly shown by the existence of very fine holes in the upper and lower lids, which received thin iron pins to keep the jewels in position. One such pin still remains in the upper lid of the left eye of one of the lions.

'The capital was carved out of a single block of sandstone, but is now broken across just above the bell. It was originally surmounted by a wheel (*chakra*), the symbol of the Buddhist Law, supported on a short stone shaft. The latter was not discovered, but its thickness can be estimated from the mortice hole, 8 in. in diameter, drilled into the stone between the lions' heads. Of the wheel itself, four small fragments were found. The ends of thirteen spokes remain on these pieces. Their total number was presumably thirty-two.... The material of which the capital is made is a black-spotted, buff-coloured sandstone from Chunār, but of a much finer grain than the Chunār stone used in the construction of houses in Benares and its neighbourhood.'

Portions of the capital of the Sānchi pillar, which have

been recovered, show that it was of similar type, surmounted by a group of four seated lions carrying a stone 'wheel of the law'. The two stone figures of animals—a lion and a bull respectively—which crowned the two Rāmpūrva pillars have been recovered near their sites, and tradition has it that the Allahabad (Kausambi) pillar once carried a stone lion.

Dimensions of pillars.

The shafts of these pillars are all of circular horizontal section, tapering very gradually. Their dimensions vary. The height of the Topra pillar's mutilated shaft is 37 ft. above the platform in Firoz Shah's 'Kotila' at Delhi, on which it stands; its circumference at base 9⅓ ft., and at top 6½ ft.

The total height of the Bākhirā pillar above the level of the water, in which its base is now submerged, is 44 ft. 2 in. (shaft 32 ft., capital 12 ft. 2 in.), the diameter of its shaft being 49·8 in. at water-level and 38·7 in. at the top. The shaft of the Lauriya-Nandangaḍh pillar has a height above ground level of 32 ft. 9½ in., a diameter of 35½ in. at base, and of 22¼ in. at top. The total height of its lion-capital is 6 ft. 10 in. The total height of the Sārnāth pillar, including its capital (7 ft.), is estimated at about 50 ft., that of the Sānchī pillar at 42 ft. All the pillars are of fine-grained sandstone, and have, in common with other sculptures attributed to the Maurya period, a special, brilliant polish, said to be similar to that which is found on examples of ancient Persian stonework at Persepolis and elsewhere.

Material of pillars.

The monoliths in question are believed to have been quarried in the neighbourhood of Chunar in the district of Mirzapur. Quarries yielding the same kind of sandstone are worked there to this day, and no other place is known where the huge blocks required for the purpose could have been obtained. When it is considered that the weight of each of the monoliths is estimated at about 50 tons, it will be apparent that their transport to and erection at such distant sites as Topra near Umballa, Sānchī in Bhopal, and the Nepalese Tarai, were no mean engineering feats.

An idea of the labour and organization involved may be

Removal of Topra pillar.

formed from the following account by the chronicler, Shams-i-Sirāj 'Afif,[1] of the Topra pillar's removal to Delhi:

'After thinking over the best means of lowering the column, orders were issued commanding the attendance of all the people dwelling in the neighbourhood within and without the Doab, and all soldiers, both horse and foot. They were ordered to bring all implements and materials suitable for the work. Directions were issued for bringing parcels of the cotton of the Simbal (silk cotton tree). Quantities of this silk cotton were placed round the column, and when the earth at its base was removed, it fell gently over on the bed prepared for it. The cotton was then removed by degrees, and after some days the pillar lay safe upon the ground. When the foundations of the pillar were examined, a large square stone was found as a base, which also was taken out. The pillar was then encased from top to bottom in reeds and raw skins, so that no damage might accrue to it. A carriage with forty-two wheels was constructed, and ropes were attached to each wheel. Thousands of men hauled at every rope, and after great labour and difficulty the pillar was raised on to the carriage. A strong rope was fastened to each wheel, and two hundred men pulled at each of these ropes. By the simultaneous exertions of so many thousand men the carriage was moved, and was brought to the banks of the Jumna. Here the Sultan came to meet it. A number of large boats had been collected, some of which could carry 5,000 and 7,000 maunds of grain, and the least of them 2,000 maunds. The column was very ingeniously transferred to these boats, and was then conducted to Firozabad, where it was landed and conveyed into the Kushk with infinite labour and skill.

'At this time the author of this book was twelve years of age and a pupil of the respected Mir Khan. When the pillar was brought to the palace, a building was commenced for its reception near the Jam'a Masjid, and the most skilful architects and workmen were employed. It was constructed of stone and mortar, and consisted of several stages. When a stage was finished the column was raised on to it, another stage was then built, and the pillar was again raised, and so on in succession until it reached the intended height. On arriving at this stage, other contrivances had to be devised to place it in an erect position. Ropes of great thickness were obtained, and windlasses were placed on

[1] Cf. Elliot, *Hist. India*, iii. 350–3.

each of the six stages of the base. The ends of the ropes were fastened to the top of the pillar, and the other end passed over the windlasses, which were firmly secured with many fastenings. The wheels were then turned, and the column was raised about half a *gaz*. Logs of wood and bags of cotton were then placed under it, to prevent it sinking again. In this way, by degrees, and in the course of several days, the column was raised to the perpendicular. Large beams were then placed round it as supports, until quite a cage of scaffolding was formed. It was thus secured in an upright position, straight as an arrow, without the slightest deviation from the perpendicular. The square stone, before spoken of, was placed under the pillar.'

Date of pillars.

The fact that ten of the pillars bear inscriptions of Aśoka is proof that they were erected not later than his reign: it does not prove that none of them was erected earlier. The Rummindei pillar is the only one the inscription on which shows that it was set up by Aśoka's order. In the seventh of his Pillar Edicts, after recording that he has erected 'pillars of the Sacred Law' (*dhammathambāni*), he directs that the edict is to be engraved wherever stone pillars or tablets are found. In the Sahasram and Rupnāth versions of the first Minor Rock Edict there is a direction to have 'these things' engraved 'wherever there are stone pillars here'. It may be inferred that pillars similar to those bearing Aśoka's edicts had been erected in India before his time, but he was the first to use such monuments for the propagation of dhamma.

On the other hand, the wide distribution of similar columns, and an estimate of the power, resources, and organization needed for the purpose, especially on the supposition that all were quarried in the one district not far from Pāṭaliputra, suggest that their erection must have been the work of rulers over an extensive territory. We may therefore safely ascribe these monuments to the period covered by the reigns of the first three Maurya emperors, Candragupta, Bindusāra, and Aśoka. This would be consistent with the evidences of Persian influence in the style of the pillars—the bell-shaped capitals surmounted by animal figures—features which they have in common with isolated

Persian influence.

columns found at different places formerly included in the dominions of the Achaemenian rulers of Persia. For it is known that, about five centuries before Christ, Darius, son of Hystaspes, conquered and annexed to his dominions the valley of the Indus, which formed thereafter the Achaemenid province of India, so that for about two centuries before the foundation of the Maurya dynasty the ruling chiefs of Northern India had been brought into contact with the great Persian empire, and it was natural that they should be influenced by its prestige and example.

The Sānchi great *stūpa.*

The fragments of a pillar bearing one of Aśoka's inscriptions, found near the great *stūpa* which stands on the levelled summit of a hill near Sānchī or Sānchī-Kanakeda, twenty miles north-east of the capital of Bhopal State, help towards assigning dates to the successive stages of that monument. *Stūpa*, it should here be explained, is the name given in Buddhist literature to structures erected over relics, or as memorials on holy sites, the type of which is thus described by Grünwedel: [1]

> 'A *stūpa* consists of a circular or square base supporting a dome (garbha), on which stands a square block or neck (gala) representing a box to hold a relic, crowned by a capital consisting of a number of flat tiles. Above this is the umbrella or spire (chuḍamani—Burmese hti)—single or with several roofs, usually three, over one another.'

In some cases the *stūpa* was surrounded by a stone railing (*sucaka*), provided with one or more high arched gateways (*toraṇa*), of a structure suggesting development from a wooden prototype. Similar railings were sometimes erected around other objects of Buddhist veneration, such as sacred trees, &c. It appears to have been a practice of pious Buddhists in ancient times to enlarge an existing *stūpa* by erecting another on the same site, enveloping and covering the old one.

Dimensions.

As now seen, the great *stūpa* at Sānchi is a solid dome of brick and stone rising from a circular plinth, the diameter

[1] *Buddhist Art in India*, translation by Gibson and Burgess, p. 20.

2. Chaddanta Jātaka. Sculptures on the Southern Gateway of the Tope at Sanchi.

of the plinth being 121½ ft., and that of the base of the dome 110 ft.

Forming a circle round the *stūpa* there is a massive stone railing, 11 ft. in height, which stands on a stone pavement and has four gateways facing the cardinal points. These gateways are 34 ft. high with triple architraves, and are profusely adorned with sculptures in relief illustrating the Buddhist scriptures. The railing is otherwise plain. On the *stūpa's* summit there is another smaller stone railing, in a square, surrounding a stone umbrella. The height of the plinth is 14 ft., and that of the whole structure, excluding the railing and umbrella on the top, 53½ ft. **Railing and gates.**

The inscribed pillar stood near the south gateway of the great ground railing.

The successive stages of the building, as traced from existing indications, are thus described by Sir John Marshall:[1] **Stages of construction.**

The earliest structure, which was erected, apparently, by Aśoka, at the same time as the lion-crowned pillar near the south gateway, was of brick, crowned by a stone umbrella, and of not more than half the present dimensions. At that time, the floor laid around the *stūpa* and column by the workmen of Aśoka was several feet below its present level. As years passed by, however, much débris collected above this floor, and, over the débris, another floor was laid, and then a third one still higher up, and, last of all—at least a century after the erection of the column—a stone pavement covering the whole hill-top . . . simultaneously with the laying of this final pavement, the *stūpa* itself was also enlarged to its existing size by the addition of a stone casing faced with concrete; on its summit was set a larger umbrella with a plain stone rail in a square around it, and, encircling its base, another rail, equally plain, but of more massive proportions.'

These works, Sir John Marshall estimates, must have taken many decades to accomplish.

'Then came the construction of smaller decorated rails round the berm of the *stūpa*, and flanking the steps by which it was ascended, and, finally, and to crown all, the four gateways at the entrances between the quadrants of the

[1] *Cambridge History of India*, vol. i, ch. xxvi, p. 627.

ground rail, which can hardly be relegated to an earlier date than the last half-century before the Christian Era.'

In the above computation it is assumed that the pillar near the south gateway was set up by Aśoka, apparently, because it bears one of his inscriptions ; there does not seem, however, to be any evidence that its erection did not take place before his time. For the reasons given above, we are justified in assigning it, less precisely, to the period covered by the reigns of Candragupta, Bindusāra, and Aśoka. Again, Sir John Marshall places the laying of the final stone pavement and enlargement of the *stūpa* to its present size, at least a century later than the erection of the pillar, allowing that time for the gradual accumulation of debris on the site, but, having regard to the Buddhist practice of enlarging *stūpas*, it seems possible that the edifice may have grown to its present dimensions in a shorter time. Close by, on the same hill-top, there is a fifth sculptured gateway, which evidently belonged to the railing of another *stūpa*, and, on a lower spur of the hill, there is a third *stūpa* of similar design surrounded by a stone railing, which has no gates, but is itself elaborately decorated with sculptured panels.

Other reliefs at Sānchi.

The Bharhut *stūpa*.

Other works of art, for which we have indications of date, are the sculptures in relief, chiefly representing scenes from the *jātakas* (edifying stories from the successive 'births' or lives of Buddha), on the railing and east gateway of the Bharhut *stūpa*, and the railing round the temple at Buddh Gaya, which are similar in general style to those of the Sānchi gates. Those of the Bharhut reliefs, which represent *jātaka* episodes, bear inscriptions in Brahmī character, giving their titles. Bharhut is a village in the small native state of Nagaudh, in Baghelkhand, about 95 miles south-west from Allahabad, where remains of a brick *stūpa*, about 68 ft. in diameter, and the railing around it, were discovered in 1873. The portions of the railing recovered, including its eastern gateway, are now preserved in the Indian Museum, Calcutta.

Inscriptions on railings.

Like other Buddhist structures of the same class, this railing bears a number of inscriptions recording that different parts of it—pillars or uprights (*stambha*), rails (*suci*), coping stones, &c.—were given by pious Buddhists. On one of the pillars of the east gateway there is an inscription in Prakrit recording that the gate was built by one Vatsiputra Dhanabhuti, *suganam raje* (Sanskrit, *suṅgānām rājye*), i.e. in the kingdom, or in the reign, of the Suṅgas, and from this it has been inferred that the gateway in question was erected in the days of the Suṅga kings, who succeeded the Mauryas on the throne of Magadha. Sir John Marshall assigns the whole *stūpa* to that period.[1]

The Suṅgas.

We know, however, actually, very little about the Suṅgas. According to Purāṇas, the first Suṅga king of Magadha was Puṣyamitra, who served as commander-in-chief under Bṛhadratha, the last Maurya king, and, having assassinated his master, usurped the throne. According to Buddhist accounts, Puṣyamitra was a persecutor of Buddhism. Purāṇas give the succession of ten kings of the Suṅga dynasty after Puṣyamitra, and the total duration of the dynasty as 112 years. As we have seen, it is probable that, under the empire of the Mauryas, there were subordinate or feudatory rājas in different parts of their dominions, and it seems quite possible that the Suṅgas may have been, in their origin, a dynasty of vassal chiefs, whose territory included Bharhut. So that the expression *suganam raje* occurring in the inscription on one pillar of a gateway of the Bharhut *stūpa* does not establish that the gateway, still less that the whole railing, or the *stūpa*, was erected after the Suṅgas had replaced the Mauryas on the Magadha throne. Two of the pillars of the Buddh Gaya railing bear inscriptions showing that they were donations of the queens of kings Indramitra and Brahmamitra respectively, and from the script of the legends of coins struck by rulers bearing these names it has been inferred that they flourished not earlier than the year 100 B.C. These are weak grounds for assigning the whole of the Buddh Gaya railing to the period of the Suṅga dynasty.

The Buddh Gaya railing inscriptions.

Pillars represented in reliefs.

There are other indications which connect the railing sculptures of Buddh Gaya, Bharhut, and Sānchi, and also

[1] *Cambridge History of India*, vol. i, ch. xxvi, p. 626.

those found on twelve stone railing posts at Sārnāth, with the edict pillars. In these reliefs, representations of pillars with pedestals and capitals of various designs are a common decorative feature, serving sometimes to adorn the uprights, sometimes to divide the sculptured panels of the cross-pieces. Some of the pillars so represented have bell-shaped capitals surmounted by groups of seated lions bearing wheels exactly similar to the lion-capitals of Sārnāth and Sānchī. This would indicate that, at the date of the railing sculptures, pillars of the type of the edict pillars were well known and generally admired, if not venerated, by Buddhists in Northern India, and, consequently, that the date in question must be placed not earlier than that of the edict pillars.

The Maurya art period. On the whole, it seems that we shall be justified in holding the opinion, with great deference to eminent authorities, by whom certain monuments have been assigned to the Maurya and others to the Suṅga period, that there is not at present evidence enabling us to fix the date of any of them confidently within a century. In any case, there is nothing to make it likely that the Suṅga period was marked by any special development in art, or produced anything that could be called a new school. In the present state of our knowledge, it seems that it will be safest to assign all the monuments in question to one art period, embracing roughly the last three centuries before Christ, which may conveniently be called the Maurya period, although it may have included that of the Suṅgas as well. The pillars bearing Aśoka's inscriptions may, for reasons given, be assigned roughly to the first century of the period, beginning with the reign of Candragupta, and ending with that of Aśoka, about the year 230 B.C.

Lack of Maurya remains at Patna. It may seem strange that, for examples of the art of the Maurya period, we have to go so far afield as Sānchi and Bharhut, while at Patna, the site of the Maurya capital, very little has been found which can with certainty be assigned to that period. This may be variously explained. At Patna, a town of greater or less importance has probably

3. Railing Pillars found at Sārnāth.

4. Corner Posts of Buddhist Railings found at Sārnāth.

existed continuously during all the centuries which have elapsed since the Maurya period. In India successive generations have not shown themselves very scrupulous in respect for the monuments left by their predecessors, and at Patna there must have been a constant temptation to dilapidate ancient buildings for the purpose of obtaining materials for new ones. Again, on a site thus continuously inhabited, the material evidences of Maurya civilization would be likely, in the course of ages, to become buried out of view through the gradual accumulation of debris. Remoteness has saved the monuments of Sānchi and Bharhut from complete obliteration, but, even at Bharhut, the dilapidations of neighbouring villagers have completely destroyed the *stūpa*, and greatly damaged the railing. Then there was the instability of the site of *Pāṭaliputra*, owing to which, as already mentioned, the buildings of the Maurya city were constructed chiefly of wood, and the stone portions of them are likely to have become buried, through diluviation or sinkage at unknown depths. The excavations carried out hitherto in and around Patna have been on a small scale; on inhabited sites they must, in any case, be strictly limited, and they are impossible on sites occupied by religious buildings and graveyards.

In the course of the excavations referred to there have been discovered, besides the fragments of a pillar of dimensions similar to those of the pillars bearing Aśoka's inscriptions, fragments of smaller pillars, distributed at regular intervals, and indicating a great pillared hall, as well as parts of three stone railings. Dr. Spooner has advanced reasons for surmising that the pillared hall in question formed part of a royal palace designed on the model of the Achaemenian palaces, but this surmise has not, so far, been definitely confirmed, and, apart from it, there is really nothing to connect the hall with the Mauryas.

Colossal statues.

Three colossal statues, rude and primitive in style, of which two were found in the neighbourhood of Patna, and the third at Parkham, between Agra and Mathura, were formerly attributed to the Maurya period, but of late a theory has been put forward that they are of earlier date—that the Parkham statue represents King Ajātasatru, and the two Patna ones other kings of the Saisunāga dynasty.[1] This question remains unsettled.

Stages of development in art.

The works above referred to represent various forms and stages of development in the sculptor's art; the colossal figures of Parkham and Patna being almost barbarous in their execution, while the lion-capitals of Sārnāth and Sānchī, conventional and decorative, display an exquisite finish and highly developed technique, and the reliefs of Sānchī, Buddh Gaya, and Bharhut, somewhat primitive in technique, are yet graceful and vigorous compositions, full of life and feeling. Sir John Marshall, who attributes the lion-capitals of Sārnāth and Sānchi to the reign of Aśoka, holds it 'incredible that any Indian hand at this period should either have modelled in clay or chiselled from the stone such perfected forms as those of the Sārnāth capital,' [2] and considers, apparently, that the artist must have been a Greek or Hellenized Asiatic, who drew his inspiration from Bactria, formerly an Achaemenian satrapy, which, about this time, under the leadership of Diodotos, had revolted against the Seleukid Antiochos Theos, and become an independent kingdom. 'Every argument, indeed,' Sir John Marshall says, 'whether (1) based on geographical considerations, or (2) on the political and commercial relations, which are known to have been maintained between India and Western Asia, or (3) on the happy fusion of Hellenistic and Iranian art visible in this monument indicates Bactria as the probable source from which the artist who created it drew his inspiration.' [3]

Sir John Marshall's view.

The same eminent authority places the sculptures of the Buddh Gaya railing in the early part of the second century B.C., those of the Bharhut railing and east gate in the middle of the same century, and those of the Sānchī railings and gates in the last half-century before Christ, and regards these monuments as marking a rapid development in the national art of India with the rise of the Suṅga power in Hindustan

[1] Cf. *J. B. O. R. S.*, vol. v, Pt. IV, Dec. 1919.

[2] *Cambridge History of India*, vol. i, ch. xxvi, p. 622.

[3] Ibid.

during the second century B.C., and the simultaneous extension of the Bactrian dominion to the Panjab. Generally, the view put forward by Sir John Marshall is that the sculptures of the Maurya and Suṅga periods, which show an advanced and superior technique, are probably the work of foreign artists, and that it was only in the jewellers' and lapidaries' arts, as exemplified in certain relic caskets found in the Sānchī *stūpas*, that the Maurya craftsmen attained any real proficiency. This theory may be correct, but in view of the scanty evidence available, the argument by which it is supported cannot be regarded as very strong. It is needless to enlarge on the errors which similar reasoning from evidence of foreign influence on different European schools of art might involve.

Bactrian influence.

The facts with regard to the extension of Bactrian dominion over the Panjab simultaneously with the rise of the Suṅga power in Magadha are not clearly established. We have the evidence of Strabo and Justin, showing that, about the year 190 B.C., Demetrios, King of Bactria, son of Euthydemos, made conquests in Northern India, probably including the Panjab and Sind, from which he was later ousted by Eukratides, another Bactrian, and that later still, perhaps about 155 B.C., further conquests in India were made by a ruler named Menander, who probably belonged to the family of Eukratides. Then it is established by numerous coins which have been found that for about two centuries and a half, from the time of Demetrios to about the year A.D. 50, a succession of Bactrian Greek kings reigned over different parts of the Panjab. Again, we find in Indian literature—Pātanjali's grammar, probably of about 150 B.C., the Gārgī Saṁhita, a work on astrology of uncertain date, and Kalidāsa's drama, Mālavikāgnimitra, probably of the fifth century A.D.—allusions to an invasion or incursions of Hellenes (*yavanas*), in the time of Puṣyamitra, the first Suṅga ruler of Magadha, which swept over Oudh (*Saketa*), the Ganges-Jumna Doab (*Pancāla*), Mathura, and parts of what are now Rājputāna and the Gwalior State, and even penetrated to Pāṭaliputra. It is evident that, during the long period of Bactrian rule in the Panjab, there must have been ample opportunity for Hellene influence on the plastic arts in Northern India. Greek sculptors may have been employed in the Suṅga dominions, and Indian sculptors may have adopted Greek methods of technique.

Earlier Hellene influence probable. It is equally probable that such Hellene influence on Indian art may have been in operation from a much earlier date, the Mauryan empire having been, from its very foundation, in contact with Hellene powers on its north-western frontier. In Aśoka's thirteenth Major Rock Edict, among the peoples of his empire, Yonas, that is to say, Hellenes, are mentioned, apparently distinct from the subjects of the Yona King Aṁtiyoka. And long before the Maurya period, India may have been affected by Hellenism through contact with the Persian empire, where Hellene influences had been at work from a time centuries earlier than Alexander's conquest.

Indian character of reliefs. Whether any of the sculptures of the Maurya art period are the work of foreign artists or not, it is at least certain that the sculptors who produced the reliefs representing scenes from the life of Buddha and the jātakas had lived long in India, and were familiar with Indian scenes. Much of the charm and interest of these reliefs lies in their delineation of the everyday life of the Indians of that time—their dress, their cottages, ploughs, carts, and boats; cities, palaces, temples, *stūpas*, and caityas—and the numerous representations of elephants—a subject not often successfully treated by modern European artists—are specially lifelike and characteristic.

Unknown artists. These works are anonymous like many masterpieces of sculpture adorning European cathedrals.

In the *Arthaśāstra* we find no mention of sculptors as a class distinct from masons. Kauṭilya's work, indeed, is severely utilitarian, and says little about the fine arts. In the rules for the construction of the palace, we find mention (according to Shamasastry's rendering) of 'carvings of images' (*sthūṇāvabandha*)[1] and 'ornamental arches' (*toraṇaśira*).[1] Skilled artisans (*Kāru, Kāruka, Kāruśilpi*)

[1] *K. A.*, Bk. I, ch. iii, p. 57.

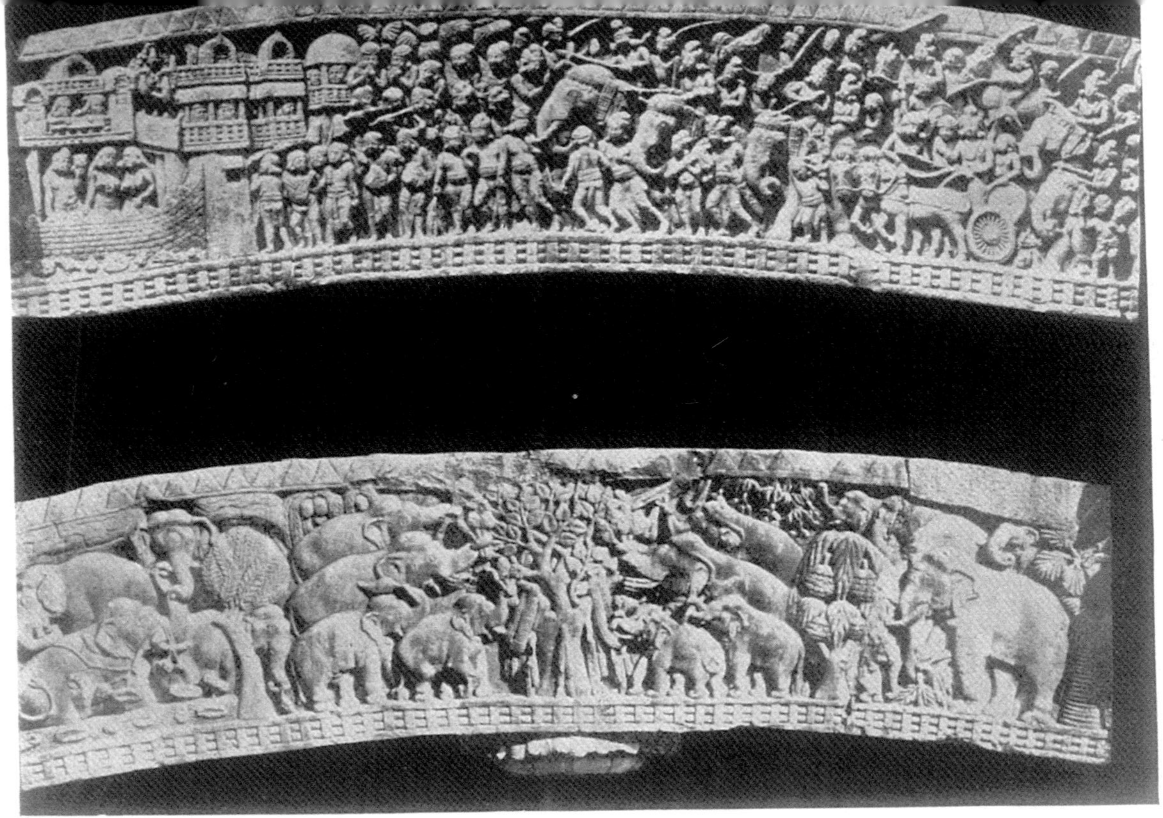

5. Chaddanta Jātaka. Sculptures on the Western Gateway of the Tope at Sanchi.

are often mentioned—we have *pradhāna-kāravaḥ* (master craftsmen), and according to one reading *svacitta kāravaḥ*, meaning 'artisans working according to their own designs.' [1] Perhaps in India of the Maurya period, as in mediaeval Europe, the class of sculptors was not sharply distinguished from that of stone-masons.

The paucity of surviving monuments of the Maurya age has been referred to. It is partly accounted for by a climate very destructive of man's handiwork, of the rapid effects of which countless examples may be found in India. One has only to think of the ruins of Gaur, or Lakhnauti, which as late as the seventeenth century was capital of Bengal, with a population, probably, of over a million, or of the present state of the town of Murshidabad, which, in Clive's time, rivalled London in magnificence. Other destructive agencies have been the ravages of war, and sectarian iconoclasm, but both of these have operated in Europe, perhaps on as great a scale and with as much fury as in India. When all allowances are made, the fact that so little remains of the artistic productions of the Maurya period is remarkable. Perhaps the explanation is that they were never very rich or numerous in comparison with the extent and power to which the Maurya empire attained. Probably, then as now, India was poor according to European standards. The sculptured reliefs of the period suggest that, then as now, the peasantry lived in thatched cottages with earthen or mat walls, wore scanty clothing, used little furniture, and practised a primitive agriculture. The *Arthaśāstra* affords evidence that famines were frequent. There were rich men—princes and high officials, as well as wealthy traders, and other private individuals, who dressed sumptuously and lived in palaces, but such were few and far between. In the few great cities, and at sites of special sanctity, there were magnificent temples, *vihāras*, and *stūpas*, with great stone railings and gateways, but probably the village shrines, like the village dwellings, were small and simple structures, with roofs of wood or bamboo, and thatch, or earthen *stūpas* or caityas with plain wooden or bamboo rails.

Paucity of Maurya remains.

Poverty of India.

[1] Ibid., Bk. IV, ch. i, p. 253.

In such material conditions, masterpieces of art might be produced; a profuse and widely distributed artistic out-turn could not be looked for.

Greek visitors to India, three centuries before Christ, found the country backward, on the whole, in respect of material civilization—at the same time found much to admire in the moral character of the Indians, and in their social institutions. It is worthy of note that the verdict of Chinese pilgrims in the seventh century of our era was substantially the same.

Conclusion. In concluding this volume, it is important once more to emphasize the historic fact that in the India of the Maurya period the chief centre of political power and civilization was at Pāṭaliputra in the Lower Ganges Valley, and the legitimate inference that the evidence which we possess for the period, bearing on the institutions, arts, manners, and civilization of India relates especially to that region, embracing the territories now known as Bihar and Bengal. We have the general picture, dim, it may be, in outline, and faint in colours, of a population poor and simple in their habits, yet neither barbarous nor degraded, capable of organization and co-operative effort, and of producing work, in architecture and decorative sculpture, of imposing proportions and high artistic merit: already capable of 'building like titans and finishing like jewellers'. As the system of government portrayed in the *Arthaśāstra* is not democratic, so we may be sure that, in the social organization and general outlook of the people, there was nothing democratic in the modern European sense. Then, as now, the feature which arrested the attention of foreign observers was the caste system, so radically opposed to the idea of democracy. Neither can it be said that the social system of ancient India was aristocratic, as that epithet is understood in Europe. In India, the sentiments of regard for family and ancestry and inherited standards of conduct have never been the monopoly of a limited wealthy or powerful class, but pervade every class of society, and every caste, high, middle, and low.

INDEX

Printed in England at the Oxford University Press